PRAISE FOR
BECOMING AMAZED

"In a time when everything is a version of something else, how wonderful and exciting to read a book that subverts convention to create fresh experiences that evoke the positivity of risk, challenge and change. In *Becoming Amazed* author Brenda Smith continues to reveal the spark and fire that burned when she shattered her privileged shell and took to a grand adventure in Africa, a blaze of a trip that lit her to possibilities, validation, and new identity. Now she continues to explore, both physically and spiritually, the later journeys that added colors, emotions, layers, and insight. This narrative is an inspiring love song to the transformational power of adventure, an instruction manual on how to discover hidden strengths and joys by venturing well beyond the comfort zone. Brenda is a trailblazing boundary-breaker with an oversized plume, sketching real-life stories that shine with her particular mix of intelligence, wit and newly minted courage. Lucid, luminous, daring, and spirited, *Becoming Amazed* is all a memoir should be, and more."

-RICHARD BANGS, ONE OF EXPLORERWEB'S
100 GREATEST EXPLORERS OF THE LAST 100 YEARS

In *Becoming Amazed* Brenda Smith demonstrates in vivid detail the power of travel to transform our personal worlds. Smith takes readers along on her amazing journeys to discover people and places in some of the most remote places on earth inspiring us to seek out adventures outside our comfort zone, and to explore and appreciate our diverse world. Her compelling accounts of each journey captivated me and reminded me of the importance of travel. A great read!

-JUDI WINELAND, CO-OWNER OF ADVENTURE WOMEN,
CO-FOUNDER OF THOMSON SAFARIS AND
FOUNDER OF OVERSEAS ADVENTURE TRAVEL

Adventurer Brenda Smith's account of descending the Omo River in Ethiopia is both intriguing and harrowing. I was moved by her description of a young Mursi boy who created beautiful music by using Smith's tent pole as a flute, and later, captivated as she described her stint as crocodile bait while being among the first rafters to shoot the rapids of the lower Omo. Smith's retelling of these first encounters with remote rivers and the people and wildlife met along the way are the makings of river running history.

- BRIDGET CROCKER, RIVER EXPLORER
AND AUTHOR OF *THE RIVER'S DAUGHTER*

BECOMING AMAZED

DISCOVERING THE WORLD WITH EYES WIDE OPEN

BRENDA E SMITH

"There is no end to the adventures we can have if only we seek them with our eyes open."

—Jawaharlal Nehru, First Prime Minister of India

THE EVOLUTION OF AN ADVENTURER

September 1, 2024

MAGICAL WORLDS CAME ALIVE in my imagination every night of my young childhood, as Mom sat beside me on my bed, reading stories to me. My favorite book followed the adventures of an eccentric young girl named Pippi Longstocking, an orphaned nine-year-old who lived on her own in a ramshackle house with a horse, monkey, and a trunk of gold coins. Pippi *never* did anything the "normal" way. She didn't climb up trees; she climbed inside them. Pippi could turn any activity into an adventure. I adored Pippi and dreamed of going on hair-raising pursuits with her.

When I entered grade school, homework and school reading assignments replaced my mother's bedtime stories. My yearning for Pippi-style escapades gradually diminished, although not entirely, quietly hibernating in my soul. Being a shy girl raised in a prim and proper New England family, my parents expected me to conform to and live by the societal norms of those times. Their blueprint for my life involved getting an education, finding a husband, raising two children, avoiding dangerous situations, and blending in with the crowd.

The first signs of my divergence from their plan appeared when I begged my parents to buy me a chemistry set rather than a useless Barbie doll. Then, in junior high school, I insisted on learning to play the trumpet rather than a flute or clarinet, the instruments normally favored by girls. Math and science classes fascinated me, while I found English boring, and I sweated through nightmares about studying French, a language I never expected to use since I had no intention of ever stepping beyond the US borders.

In college, I majored in accounting and found myself the only woman in a class of 100 male students. Though not thrilled with my chosen major, my parents surely expected I'd find a suitable mate among my peers. After graduating with highest honors, the prestigious CPA firm Arthur Andersen & Co offered me an auditor position in their Boston office. As one of only five women on a staff of 200 auditors, it gave my parents renewed hope that I'd find at least one of my colleagues worthy of marrying.

Instead, I found that one of my female colleagues shared my eagerness to take a 13-day whitewater rafting vacation through the Grand Canyon. Excited, but apprehensive about the potential perils of the journey, we booked a late summer departure in 1978. Empowered by my experience on the Colorado River, I sent my mother into hysterics when I announced I wanted to leave my job as a CPA. Thanks to the glowing recommendation of the head guide on our trip, the owner of the California-based rafting company that had guided us through the Grand Canyon offered me a position as his Controller. He sweetened the deal by promising to train and certify me as a whitewater guide.

I could feel the mischievous spirit of Pippi Longstocking awakening within me. The concept of fear didn't exist for Pippi, as she boldly navigated through life. However, 25 years of leading a sheltered life left me grappling with unfounded anxieties about encountering strangers, exploring new territories, and encountering unfamiliar objects. I wondered if I could ever be as brave as Pippi. My first scary step was leaving home to move 3,000 miles away.

Once in California, I discovered I'd be managing the finances for a second fledgling company called Sobek Expeditions that pioneered whitewater rafting in exotic locales around the globe. After a year, my thrill-seeking Sobek boss decided I needed to go on a "real" adventure. He assigned me to go with him as crew members on the first commercial trip down a Tanzanian river system that traversed Africa's largest uninhabited game reserve, home to millions of wild beasts. The idea of sharing a river teeming with hippos and crocodiles in inflatable rafts for 12 days terrified me, let alone tromping through the domain of wild lions, elephants, and cape buffalo.

I racked my brain for a valid excuse *not* to go to such a dangerous place. I honestly feared I'd be risking my life. The dread of being branded a coward made it impossible for me to confess my reluctance to my boss. So, with grave doubts about the sanity of this adventure, I went to Africa.

Surviving this trip marked a pivotal turning point that forever changed the course of my life. In *Becoming Fearless: Finding Courage in the African Wilderness*, I recounted in vivid, heart-pounding detail our frequent encounters with wildlife, including a hippo biting one of our rafts. I detailed the arduous journey of carrying heavy loads through dense, untouched jungle, as we navigated around a waterfall rivaling the size of Niagara Falls. The uncertainty of navigating our course using inaccurate maps heightened the suspense of whether we'd be successful in locating the end point of our journey. Once safely off the river, we even took on the challenge of climbing Mount Kilimanjaro, the highest peak in Africa, following a rarely used trail.

The Brenda who had arrived in Africa, fearful and reluctant, had undergone a remarkable transformation. Tanzania had worked its magic on me. I'd gained a deep admiration for the untouched beauty, tranquility, and inherent peril of wilderness unspoiled by human intervention. Nature had instilled in me the wisdom that as long as we didn't provoke the wild animals (intentionally or accidentally), though curious, they willingly shared their territorial spaces with us. This wilderness filled my heart with joy as no other place I'd been on Earth had. I finally understood why my boss wanted me to experience this "real" adventure, while extraordinary places like this one still existed.

The enchanting spell of wanderlust had taken hold of me, and I couldn't help but feel regret as I prepared to leave Africa. This trip had opened my eyes to a world I never knew existed. Now, inspired by dreams of being as fearless as Pippi, I felt compelled to travel to distant lands where amazing wonders lay waiting to be discovered.

Over the next decade, I worked relentlessly to realize those dreams. I crewed on several Sobek Expeditions before deciding I wanted more than traveling to fascinating destinations for just a few weeks or months. I craved becoming fully immersed in the daily life of cultures so varied from my own. Karma kissed me when I discovered a job advertisement for overseas financial managers with the United States Department of State. I impressed the recruiters enough to be hired. For eight years, I lived overseas, and at every opportunity I went off the beaten path in search of adventure.

The following chapters reveal eight unexpected discoveries that amazed me. I hope that they'll amaze you too.

MAP OF ETHIOPIA

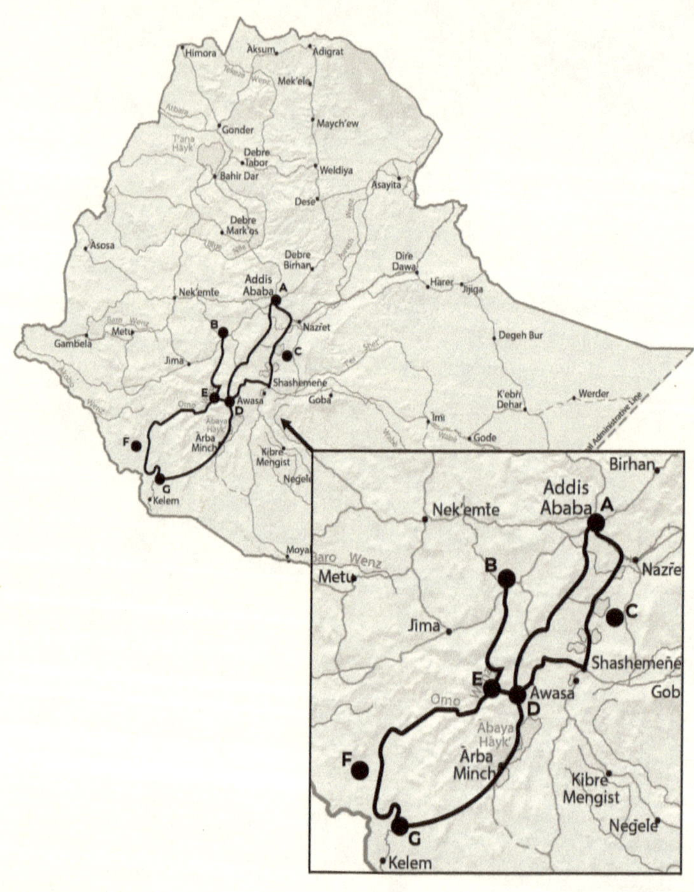

A : Addis Ababa - Capital City

B : Abelti - River Trip Launches

C: Lake Langano - My First Night

D: Soddu - Near Makeshift Bridge

E: Bale Bridge - I Join River Trip

F: Omo National Park - Guests Leave on DC-3

G: Karo Tribal Land - End of Trip

1

EXPECTING THE UNEXPECTED

ETHIOPIA – NOVEMBER 1981

WANDERLUST is a powerful addiction.

Eight months had passed since I had my first hit of exotic travel while rafting in the unfamiliar wilderness of Africa's largest uninhabited game reserve, crewing for my company, Sobek Expeditions. Thankfully, I survived the ordeal. Since then, I'd been busy managing our finances for the hectic summer season of whitewater rafting in California. I occasionally escaped from the office to guide day trips on nearby rivers, but I'd been impatient to set off on another mind-bending adventure. The chance arose sooner than I expected.

"Hey, Brenda, we're one guide short on the Omo River trip that's coming up in November. You wanna go?" Richard Bangs, the charismatic daredevil CEO of Sobek, stood in my office doorway, eyebrows raised, grinning. "The trip departs in six weeks."

"Are you kidding?" I studied his exuberant expression, trying to gauge if he seriously meant it. The last time he informed me we were going to Africa, he'd left me speechless and terrified. But our trip to Tanzania earlier in the year had opened my eyes to a new world. He'd witnessed how wanderlust had kindled my passion for the exhilaration that comes with discovering remarkable, unexplored corners of the world.

"Really? Can I? I'd love to go to Ethiopia." The prospect of embarking on another Sobek expedition filled me with delight. In contrast to the first commercial exploration of unknown territory during the Tanzanian trip, Sobek had been offering expeditions along the Omo River since their initial descent in 1973. It had become a client favorite with two or three departure dates every year. The more experienced guides knew every twist and bend in this river.

"We're short-staffed for this Omo trip because most of our regular Omo guides are going to work our first descent of the Zambezi at the same time. Conrad will lead your Omo trip, along with George, Peter, and Val. We'll need to get you a visa, but you've had all the vaccinations you need. Oh, and Conrad is planning to add a seven-day extension so the crew can explore the stretch of river below our normal 21-day trip take out." He winked, spun around and left me to ponder the fact I'd be rowing for 28 days straight.

Conrad, our head guide in Africa, and I had gotten to know each other well while working together on Sobek's Tanzania trip earlier that year. Several years ago, he'd grown disillusioned with life in the United States. A graduate of Stanford University, with a brilliant mind, he taught college-level mathematics in Texas, but felt smothered by academia's inflexible rules for advancement. Shortly after an acrimonious divorce, he sold everything he owned and moved to Ethiopia, where he'd previously served as a Peace Corps volunteer from 1964 to 1966.

Upon his return to Ethiopia, the math department of Haile Selassie University in Addis Ababa hired him. While he still occasionally taught at the university, he'd settled into a more relaxed expat life, completely free of other people's expectations, preferring to spend most of his time exploring vast parcels of East African wilderness. One of his friends described him as a literate, perceptive, witty, but often cranky adventurer, a math nerd with the soul of an artist.

Richard met George, a small freckled man with thick glasses, while preparing to do a first descent of Ethiopia's Awash River in 1973. Hired by Haile Selassie University as a field researcher, George studied an organism that transmitted a disease related to malaria and sleeping sickness. A hobby rafter with additional credentials of anthropologist, artist, and medical doctor with a specialty in tropical medicine, he perfectly fit the qualifications to become Sobek's trip doctor.

Over dinner one night, Richard knew he'd found the right guy when George told him, "They pay my expenses to go to places nobody else will go, which is fine with me, because I love those places. I love hot and humid. What most people call miserable, I love." Ever since that first expedition on the Awash, George had carved out time to do a Sobek expedition or two in Ethiopia every year.

The head guides in California had recommended Peter for the final guide position on the trip. He'd joined our company, and we'd trained to be guides at the same time. I'd only worked a few trips with him, but technically, he had superb river skills and passengers loved his friendly, outgoing personality. His lovely wife, Valerie, who also worked as a guide, often teamed up on one-day and overnight trips with him.

When Sobek chose him as a guide for the Omo trip, he immediately negotiated with Richard to bring Valerie with him at no additional cost to the company, in exchange for an additional pair of hands on the crew. When Richard approved Peter's plan, the two celebrated as if they'd hit the jackpot by getting the assignment. The prospect of embarking on their first rafting expedition beyond the borders of the US thrilled them. I welcomed the idea of another female joining our crew.

WHEN THE GATE ATTENDANT at the San Francisco airport announced there would be a one-hour delay for my flight to London, I worried it might be a bad omen. An hour later, a second announcement informed us the airline had extended the delay, with no mention of how long it might be. I had a six-hour layover in London, so as long as the delay didn't exceed five hours, I'd make my connecting flight to Ethiopia's capital city, Addis Ababa. But nearly five hours after our scheduled departure time, with no sign we'd be leaving soon, I hunted for a pay phone in the terminal to let Richard know about my predicament.

"Hey, I'm still in San Francisco. My flight's delayed. I don't think I'll make the connecting flight in London. What should I do?"

"Hold on. Let me check with our travel agent to see when the next flight leaves London for Addis." While I waited on hold, the gate attendant finally announced to the infuriated passengers that the airline had ordered a part to fix a mechanical issue with our plane. She explained they had put the replacement part on another plane that would land within an hour. Then, the repair would require an additional hour. Crap! This wasn't supposed to happen. Exasperated, I let out a loud sigh. For sure, I wouldn't make the connection.

When Richard came back on the phone with the flight schedule, I broke the bad news to him. "I'm not going to make it. We've got at least another two-hour delay here."

"Well, the next direct connecting flight out of London is in three days. Other flights will leave sooner, but have extended layovers in places I don't think you'd be happy spending time in. You could go and spend the three days waiting in London, but that will cost a fortune. I think you should come back here, and we'll get you rebooked on that next flight in three days."

"What about the trip? Are we going to delay it?" I asked. Not only would I be late, but so would the two Sobek duffel bags I carried with me, packed full of essential supplies for the trip.

"Just come back and we'll figure out what to do," said Richard.

I slammed down the phone with more force than I intended. When I explained my hopeless situation to the gate attendant and requested my luggage back, her answer only frustrated me more.

"I'm very sorry, Ms. Smith. We've already securely stowed all the luggage on the plane so we're unable to access it. But I can put in an order to have your bags sent back to San Francisco if you'd like."

I doubted that my luggage could fly all the way to Africa and back, before the next flight leaving in three days. I decided just to let it go, hoping I'd find it waiting in Addis Ababa when I eventually arrived.

THE TEAM IN AFRICA opted to launch on the scheduled date without me, because delaying the trip would have involved the nightmarish task of changing everyone's departure flights at the end of the trip. Conrad and George, seasoned veterans of many Omo runs, and Peter would each captain a raft. Now, with my delay, Val eagerly agreed to man my raft until I arrived. Conrad had arranged for a driver from the Ethiopian National Tour Operators (NTO) to meet me at the airport and drive me to a remote access point on the river four days into the trip.

Three days later, I retraced my route back to the airport. This time I had only my carryon backpack with me. If I didn't find the luggage that I'd checked on the first delayed flight, I'd be living with just two changes of clothes for 30 days in the wilderness. Richard, the globetrotting expert, confidently assured me my luggage *would* be waiting for me in Addis. But just before I left for the second time, we got a message from Conrad that the luggage of one of our passengers had gotten lost. He asked me to check for the guy's missing duffel in London and in Addis. His request left me with a bad feeling about being reunited with his or my missing bags.

As soon as I entered the Heathrow terminal, I inquired where I might find lost luggage. I followed the security officer's directions, which brought me to a counter in front of the entrance to a massive warehouse filled with hundreds of rows of ceiling-to-floor shelves. Every imaginable type of luggage crowded the racks. I estimated the room easily accommodated 50,000 bags. I gave the attendant the luggage check numbers and descriptions of our baggage. After searching the shelves for about 15 minutes, he returned, claiming he didn't find our bags. My scowl prompted him to say, "Don't worry. There's a good chance you'll find them at your final destination."

When our eight-hour flight arrived in Addis Ababa, I exited the plane and inquired of the flight attendant stationed on the tarmac at the bottom of the stairway about how I might locate my lost luggage. She beckoned toward one of the baggage handlers, signaling him to join us. After conversing with him in their native Amharic, she translated for me, "He says as soon as all the bags are unloaded, he'll help you. Just wait right here."

I paced back and forth on the tarmac between the parked jet and the terminal. This entire airport could have fit inside the Heathrow lost baggage area. My mind raced with questions about what I'd do if the baggage handler couldn't find our bags. Just the thought of trying to replace equipment, clothes and gear in a strange city made my head ache. When they finished emptying the baggage hold, the handler approached me.

I doubted he'd understand my English, but I said, "Sir, I'm looking to retrieve some bags that should have arrived three days ago." I handed him my baggage claim stubs, expecting to follow him into the terminal building. Instead, he led me to an outdoor concrete structure the size of a garden shed off to one side of the terminal building. He tugged a bulky key ring from his pocket, fumbling to find the key which would unlock the padlocked door. Time stalled. I held my breath, gripped by the same intense anticipation I'd felt when clutching the envelope from the college I desperately hoped would accept me. Would it reveal good or bad news? Finally, the padlock released, and he swung the door open.

Less than 10 bags formed a small mound inside the shed. Immediately, I saw all three of the duffels I'd checked in San Francisco heaped on top. I did a little happy dance while the handler pulled my bags out of the shed. Then I provided him with the name of the passenger whose bag never arrived. He pawed through a few bags before extracting one that matched the description. The baggage tag confirmed it belonged to him. "Woo-hoo!" I shouted. So far, so good. Now I just needed to get to the river and meet up with the Sobek crew.

As promised, an NTO representative waited for me in the airport lobby holding a cardboard sign with my name on it. I hurried toward him, steering a pushcart loaded with my luggage.

"Welcome to beautiful Ethiopia, Miss Brenda. I am Kebede. I hope *this* time you had a pleasant flight?" Conrad had obviously briefed him on the reason for my late arrival.

I shook his extended hand. "Thank you, Kebede. I did. I'm so relieved that my bags made it safely here ahead of me. Can you believe I even found our client's missing bag, too?"

"Ah ha, that will make him soooo happy." He glanced at the three overloaded duffle bags piled on the cart next to me. "You wait here. Let me bring the Jeep around so we can load your bags."

While Kebede retrieved his vehicle, I rested on top of the duffel bags. I thought of Richard's prediction about our bags and grinned, knowing that *once again* he'd been right. Maybe the rest of this trip would be easy and go as planned.

When the white Jeep stenciled with NTO in giant green letters pulled up, Kebede jumped out and quickly loaded my gear in the back while I climbed into the front passenger seat.

"I, with two other drivers, took your group to Abelti, near the start of your trip. Now I'll take *you* to a place farther down the river where you can join them. It's a long trip, I'm afraid, and the road will be very rough in places." He shrugged his shoulders apologetically. "But it's the only way to get there."

"So, are we leaving right now?"

"Yes, but it will take us two days of travel, since it's too dangerous to travel after dark. I've booked a room for you in a comfortable hotel on the shores of Lake Langano. Then tomorrow we'll complete the journey."

The first day of the drive on a level, well-traveled road passed enjoyably, while Kebede pointed out sites of interest and briefed me on many aspects of his culture. Though a native Amharic speaker, Kebede seemed equally comfortable conversing in English. We drove past small farms growing *teff*, a type of tufted grass high in vitamin C, whose edible seeds, when ground into flour, then slightly fermented, make a spongy sour-tasting flatbread called *injera*, a staple part of every Ethiopian meal.

After three hours on the road, Kebede stopped at a hole-in-the-wall restaurant he knew and trusted would prepare food safely. He encouraged me to sample the *injera* along with a fragrant, spicy stew of cooked orange lentils. Instead of drinking water of dubious quality, he recommended their national beverage called *tej*, a slightly alcoholic honey mead whose sweetness perfectly complemented the spicy stew and sour *injera*. The melding of unfamiliar tastes in this meal left me with a desire to try it again, given the chance.

A few more hours of driving brought us to scenic Lake Langano, where we checked into a rustic hotel. Except for cat naps on the flights, it had been two days since I'd slept. The nerve-wracking uncertainty about finding our bags, followed by the excitement of being in a strange new land, had kept me going until we reached our overnight accommodations. I felt my brain powering off, and I couldn't resist the heaviness of my eyelids. I needed some dream time.

As soon as Kebede handed me my room key, I told him, "I'm exhausted. I don't think I can stay awake for another minute. I'm going to get some sleep so you won't see me again until morning."

"It will be good for you to rest. I'll keep your luggage safe tonight." He pointed at a hallway that led to my room. "Sleep well."

I grabbed my backpack and hurried off. After entering my room, my mind went blank. I didn't even remember climbing into bed.

I WOKE 12 HOURS LATER at 6 a.m., feeling refreshed and ready to face the new day. Because the rising sun outside already promised a spectacular show, I quickly threw on my clothes, and with camera in hand, I dashed outside. Brilliant golden rays peeked through a gap between two layers of violet-and-sapphire-colored clouds, reflecting on fine mist rising from the water's surface, creating an illusion of the lake's center ablaze. Like a slowly revolving kaleidoscope, the brightening sky held me spellbound.

While appreciating nature's beauty, suddenly, my stomach rumbled, reminding me I'd skipped dinner. Upon reentering the hotel, I noticed Kebede sitting in the small lounge next to the reception area, sipping a cup of rich, nutty-scented coffee.

"You're already awake. How did you sleep, Miss Brenda?"

"I conked out and slept like a corpse. I only woke up when the sun drifted above the horizon." Lifting my camera, I said, "I think I got some gorgeous photos."

"I bet you're hungry now," said Kebede with a knowing wink.

Moments later, a server entered the lounge carrying a platter of cheese, buttered slices of toast, and an assortment of jams. I asked for a cup of black tea. Kebede filled me in on the plans for the day while we devoured our breakfast. "From here," he said, "the road will progressively worsen in condition. By getting an early start, we'll buy some extra time if we have to alter our route." Hmm? I wondered what he meant, considering he'd already told me only one route to the river existed.

He hadn't exaggerated when describing the road beyond Lake Langano. Driving became a game of avoiding washouts and potholes in the road. Our route seemed more appropriate for off-road all-terrain vehicles than our Jeep, but Kebede kept his focus and even appeared to be enjoying the challenge of navigating the obstacles. Late in the morning, we entered a small village where Kebede spotted an outdoor market just off the road. Figuring it would be a good place to stretch our legs and visit with the vendors in open thatched stalls, he pulled off the road and parked at the top of a downward-sloping grassy field.

Exiting the Jeep, we meandered down the hill. I greeted the vendors with a smile, inspecting their bins of tear-inducing, fiery red chili peppers, sacks of brown and orange lentils, softball-sized onions, and foot-long carrots. The curious vendors stared at me with wrinkled brows when I didn't answer their questions in Amharic. Or maybe they felt offended that I didn't buy any of their produce. I'd almost reached the last stall when something hit the back of my arm. Spinning around, I saw an orange rolling away from me on the ground. As I searched to see who had thrown it, a potato whizzed by, nearly hitting my head.

The vendors' heckling grew louder as they hurled more projectiles in my direction. A group of them left their stalls to surround me. Why were they so mad at me? I gasped in panic, suddenly afraid of their intentions. Kebede yelled at them, motioning them away with his arms. I saw a look of alarm spread across his face. "Miss Brenda, we have to leave right now." He broke into a run toward the parked Jeep. I tried to follow, but got pelted with more fruit.

The circle closed in on me. Someone shoved me from behind.

Terrified now, I realized they *wanted* to hurt me. I extended my arms in front of me to fend off the incensed crowd that had me trapped. Their angry gestures conveyed spite, as they shouted nasty insults that needed no translation. A sudden deafening staccato honking filled the air as Kebede steered our Jeep down the hill, aiming at the crowd. Startled and realizing the danger they faced, the crowd leaped out of the path of the approaching Jeep. Kebede skillfully maneuvered the vehicle to a standstill, aligning the passenger door directly in front of me.

"Jump in! Quick!" he shouted, as I lunged into my seat and slammed the door shut.

Two seconds later, Kebede sharply swung the steering wheel to make a tight 180-degree turn and sped up the hill away from danger.

"Wow! *That* was a close call. Why were they so angry?" I asked.

"These people didn't approve of the way you dressed. They rarely ever see tourists here. They felt you showed disrespect for them by revealing bare skin on your arms and legs."

I had on a mid-calf-length pair of capri pants and a Sobek T-shirt. Though I knew enough not to wear shorts and a tank top, apparently, *any* exposed skin other than hands, feet, and head constituted lewdness to them. I chalked it up as a "live and learn" experience.

SODDU, ANOTHER RURAL VILLAGE, marked the halfway point on our journey that day to the Omo River. We stopped for lunch just beyond its center. Kebede parked on the side of the road, where a view of the scenic high plains panned out in front of us. He surprised me by offering me one of the cheese-and-tomato sandwiches he'd requested the hotel make for us earlier that morning. He'd stashed them along with two bottled soft drinks in a small cooler with a bag of ice.

As soon as we'd gobbled down the sandwiches, we resumed our drive. The road worsened into a barely passable muddy, rutted track, as my hopes for reaching the river faded. After another hour on the road, we came to a scary obstacle blocking our path. The road crossed over a deep, 15-foot-wide ditch. A group of men from the area labored to complete constructing a makeshift bridge.

Kebede got out of the Jeep to talk with the workers about the bridge's weight capacity and the best strategy for crossing it. He learned that during the late summer flood season, the creek, barely a trickle now, had transformed into a raging torrent that overflowed its banks, sweeping away the previous bridge. When Kebede climbed back into the Jeep, he said, "If we're going to get you to your group, we'll have to cross that bridge. Are you ready for a little excitement?"

I stared at the improvised bridge, which reminded me of two narrow Huck Finn-style rafts made of tree trunks lashed together, their ends overlapping the land on both sides of the creek, with a three-foot gap between them. It had to be the scariest structure *I'd* ever seen labeled a bridge. I figured that crossing this bridge safely would require the same precision as an Olympic gymnast traversing the length of a balance beam. "Do you think you can do it?" I asked Kebede.

"The only tricky part will be to get the front wheels up over the 18-inch rise onto the bridge. We have four-wheel drive, so we'll give it a try."

I turned away from him and rolled my eyes in doubt. When he stepped on the gas, I clenched the roll bar for dear life and shut my eyes tight. When the front wheels first hit the ends of the tree trunks, all four wheels spun uselessly, but then caught traction, and I felt the front end of the Jeep lifting. With a little more gas, the front tires found the level top of the bridge, dug in, and helped to haul the rear tires up onto the bridge. I exhaled the breath I'd been holding and opened my eyes as our Jeep slid off the far side of the bridge. I burst out laughing with relief, grateful for at least one bridge I'd never have to cross again.

We slogged on for another hour through unpopulated plains and forests until we approached the Bale bridge, the only rickety structure that spanned the Omo for hundreds of miles. Rot had eaten away at the wooden plank surface, giving it a dilapidated appearance. I wondered how often this bridge actually got used. We'd seen nothing but wilderness since leaving Soddu. I knew from looking at a map back in Sobek's office that the other side of the river led into the remotest heart of the Omo Valley wilderness.

I certainly appreciated the existence of this track through the middle of nowhere to the Omo because, without it, I would have had to forfeit this trip, but who else on Earth would have any reason to drive out here? Kebede parked the mud-splattered Jeep well back from the start of the bridge, where he had enough space to reverse his direction. "From here we go on foot down to the river."

I couldn't see any trail. "How are we going to get down to river level?" I asked, already dreading lugging the heavy duffel bags in the humid afternoon heat.

"It looks like we'll have to do a little bushwhacking."

His pause before answering and the vagueness of his reply reminded me he'd never been to this spot either. We divided up the gear, then followed the path of least resistance through the strip of lush forest thriving along the border of the river. Half-buried rocks cluttered the steeply descending slope, forcing me to focus on my foot placement, while high overhead, raucous black-and-white colobus monkeys swung nimbly from branch to branch, screeching at our invasion. This had to be the wildest, in every sense of the word, *rendezvous* I'd ever been part of.

The stars needed to align perfectly for this to work. The Sobek crew had been out of communication with the world since launching this plan five days ago. They hadn't a clue if I'd made it to Ethiopia and would arrive at this middle-of-nowhere destination as scheduled, while I had no way of knowing if an unforeseen obstacle, like a hippo attack, or someone getting sick or hurt, had delayed their progress. Nothing could go wrong for this to work.

The last 25 yards down to the riverbank became a near vertical slope. As we searched for the safest way to descend, I glimpsed a patch of bright orange below that looked out of place in the natural environment of greens, browns, and grays.

"Kebede, look down there. Do you see that patch of orange? Could it be a life preserver? A brightly colored T-shirt?"

"Helloooo! Anybody down there?" Kebede's bellow echoed across the canyon.

Suddenly, the orange patch and everything surrounding it sprang into action.

"Helloooo!" came the instant reply. "Brenda, is that you?" Conrad's voice had never sounded so sweet. I pumped my fist in victory.

"Yes, it's me! I've got good news. I found our client's lost duffel bag."

A gleeful whoop of gratitude echoed through the air. Pleased that I'd brightened that man's day, I asked for help to lower our gear down over the last pitch. The Sobek guides and a few of the passengers scrambled up the slope, spacing out to form a brigade to pass our bags down to the riverbank.

"Miss Brenda, do you need anything else from me?" Crossing back over that rickety matchstick bridge before dark surely weighed on Kebede's mind.

"No. You pulled off a minor miracle here, and I'm *so* grateful." Though I doubted a hug would be proper, I threw my arms around his neck anyway, and thanked him again. I watched him scurry back up the hill while Conrad, deeply tanned with a head of unruly black curls, helped me traverse the last stretch down onto the sandy beach where the rafts snugged up against the shore. At last, I inhaled a deep breath of fresh air and gazed out over the mighty Omo River drifting placidly southwestward.

THAT NIGHT, THE CREW and our clients filled me in on the four days I'd missed. They'd already covered 80 miles of the estimated total 330-mile journey, arriving at the bridge ahead of us by just an hour. Most of the river upstream cut through a deep canyon with a few spirited rapids. Though the canyon walls still rose steeply, dense forest carpeted the land, providing a playground for the frisky monkeys and baboons that dwelled within it. The early days of the trip provided sightings of plenty of hippos and crocodiles and an abundance of other birds and wildlife, but no signs of humans.

The river stretched wider and flowed deeper than the African river I'd rafted earlier in the year. On that river, restrained to a smaller space, hippos and crocs inhabited the river waters from bank to bank. Here on the Omo, the wildlife didn't stray into the deeper currents mid-river, but stayed closer to or on the river banks. I almost felt relaxed on this river, though I knew it would be a mistake to let my guard down for even a minute.

MY THIRD DAY ON THE RIVER as the canyon walls gave way to rolling plains, we rowed into an enormous swarm of tsetse flies, considered one of the peskiest vermin on the planet. Many of them carried the trypanosome parasite capable of infecting both humans and livestock with African sleeping sickness, which, when left untreated, could be fatal. Conrad hollered for us to cover our bodies with neutral-colored clothing, leaving as little of our skin exposed as possible, and to cover our heads with the head nets Sobek recommended we purchase for this trip. The half-inch long tsetses buzzed relentlessly around us in never-ending circles for hours while we swatted at them in vain.

As long as we kept our body parts moving, we could ward off the flies. George, with his encyclopedic knowledge about tropical diseases, explained that not all the flies carried the parasite. Since we weren't in close proximity to any humans or livestock on this section of the Omo, even if the flies bit us, it wasn't likely they would infect us with the parasite. Still, the tsetses resembled stealth bombers, looking for just the right opportunity to dive onto a bare patch of exposed ankle or hand, driving their hypodermic-like snouts into our flesh for a sip of warm sweet blood. While the rest of us wore our bug nets over baseball-style caps, George, savvy to the tsetse's ways, sported a straw hat with an extra wide brim that kept his bug net well away from his face and neck.

Their pricking bites, like a bee sting, led to irate cursing as, one by one, despite a generous application of DEET, we all suffered from their attacks. During the midday heat, the swarm grew dense, but once the cooler dusk arrived, they disappeared, at least until the sun rose the following morning. Fending off the tsetses with constant swatting and fanning reminded me of an all-day aerobics class. It left us exhausted. Thankfully, their pursuit lasted only two-and-a-half days. If we'd had to contend with them for much longer, I think I would have gone mad from their whirling-dervish circling and constant buzzing.

A FEW DAYS LATER, much to my delight, we spotted our first tribal people. Five barefooted males met us as we pulled up to where they stood on a wide patch of rocky shoreline. Since the sight of Sobek raft caravans once or twice every year for the last seven years had become predictable, they knew we meant no harm. The local men welcomed us, intrigued by our fair-skinned group and our unusual bloated boats loaded with gear.

This tribe, the Bodi, plied the waters of the Omo, standing in narrow wooden dugout canoes, propelling themselves forward with sturdy poles. They dressed in loose-fitting woven cloth either wrapped around the core of their bodies or draped around their body and knotted on top of one shoulder. Around their necks hung bone and clay bead necklaces, and a few of them wore pierced ear ornaments made of hollowed bone or decorated metal.

They shaved their heads, but collected colorful feathers out of which they fashioned simple adornments secured in a bun of clay that dried solid, trapping the feather quills securely in place on top of their heads. Each carried a wood walking stick equal to his height, and a barbell-shaped wooden stool about six inches high with a six-inch-wide slightly concave top. The solid flat base allowed it to serve as both a seat and a solid pillow to raise his head off the ground while sleeping.

Farther downstream, Bodi women of the tribe tended their gardens of sorghum, maize, and squash. With no shared common language, we used gestures to communicate. During the first descent of the river in 1973, the terrified Bodi women and children ran to escape the approaching rafts. There had been no previous recorded encounters with the tribes in this section of the river. Now comfortable with our annual visits, the women led us away from the river toward their settlement.

On solid high ground, they'd built eight domed huts that, in shape and size, resembled igloos. Long sticks about two inches in diameter, slightly bent, met at the top of the dome, while other sticks wove horizontally around the circumference to form the foundation of each hut. A dense layer of dried tall grasses completely covered the domed shell, except for a three-foot-high entrance, next to which rested a hatch door made of the same materials. The interior floor space equaled that of a four-man tent. Outside, clay cooking vessels sat next to a communal fire pit. Even now, the children shied away from us, hiding behind their mothers.

The bare-breasted women also wore strings of beads around their necks and metallic bangles wrapped around their forearms. They practiced the ritual of scarification, cutting their skin to create distinctive designs around their breasts and along the front of their stomachs. By packing the open wounds with ash, they created a more pronounced scar. The denser the pattern of scars, the more desirable the woman would be as a wife. Having endured the pain of scarification proved the woman could survive the pain of childbirth. Animal hides wrapped around their waists concealed their private parts.

For these pastoral tribes, cut off from the rest of Ethiopia, survival became their prime goal. The women cultivated crops, while the men tended small herds of cows, goats, and chickens. Most importantly, they procreated, raising children to ensure the continuity of their tribe. Though it appeared to be a simple life, the work of the Bodi, always at the mercy of weather, injuries, wild animals, and raids by neighboring tribes, presented constant challenges, and anything but a certain future.

I figured I could live the Bodi lifestyle for a few weeks, maybe even a few months, but not for my whole life. It suddenly struck me just how privileged my life truly was. What would a Bodi woman think if she entered a supermarket with 20 aisles of shelves stocked with food? Or if she entered a home, humongous by her standards, with heating and air conditioning to keep the temperature inside always comfortable? Would it astonish her that by simply turning a metal handle, a plentiful stream of crystal-clear water would gush out? The passage of several millennia separated our two lifestyles on the timeline of human existence.

THE FOLLOWING DAY, as we drifted downstream, now and then navigating a rapid, I noticed a trend. Pulling alongside Conrad's raft, I asked, "How come where tribes live along the shoreline, we hardly see a hippo, but there are tons of crocodiles? Big ones too!"

He answered, "Over time, the tribes have killed the hippos for food. With fewer hippos to keep the crocodile population in check, they now rule these parts of the river. You missed the first days of the trip, where we passed through the gorge where people don't live. There, we saw lots of hippos and not so many crocs. It's a perfect example of how human intervention can upset the delicate balance of nature."

At midday, Conrad noticed a level sandy clearing on river right, a perfect place to stop for lunch. Beyond the clearing, the land abruptly ascended 20 feet to a plateau where a dense thicket of towering trees stood. Their shadows cast just enough shade on the beach below so we could eat out of the direct rays of the scorching sun. We spread out a vibrant red-and-white plaid vinyl tablecloth directly on the sand and arranged the lunch offerings in the center. Then we cozied up around the edges.

The yeasty smell of Conrad's homemade crusty bread, baked overnight in a Dutch oven sandwiched between glowing coals buried in the ground, made my mouth water. For fillings, we had canned sardines, deviled ham, and peanut butter and jelly. While our clients dug into the meat items, I opened the peanut butter container and smeared a glob of the nutty paste across one piece of bread, then opened the jar of grape jelly and spooned out an ample helping of the sweet-smelling jelly, smoothing it over the top of the peanut butter. I'd barely had time to place the second piece of bread on top of the sandwich when I heard bees buzzing nearby.

As I took the first bite of my sandwich, the buzzing grew louder. I felt something tickling my inner ear. I swatted at it, but it wiggled deeper. A fraction of a second later, I felt a fiery hot stab inside my right ear. I screamed, "Ow! Help! The bees are attacking!" From out of nowhere, a swarm of a hundred bees instantly surrounded our group.

A second person screamed, "Me too. I just got stung!"

My survival instinct kicked in. I dropped my sandwich and bolted toward where the bees couldn't find me—the river. Just before I flung myself into the water, my brain screamed *NO!* flashing images of savage man-eating crocodiles through my mind. I veered to the left and jumped inside my raft, curling into a fetal position on the bottom of the middle section. I heard Conrad trying to calm the chaos.

"Just grab the four corners of the cloth and run for the rafts. We're outta here."

Moments later, bodies hurtled into the rafts. Even though the entire side of my face felt swollen and ached like I'd been branded, I sat up and clutched my oars just as Conrad shoved my boat into the current. He followed suit, and we all rowed to the center of the river. We hadn't entirely escaped the menace. A few angry bees trailed us, but most had stayed back at the beach.

"How many of you got stung?" Conrad asked as he and George surveyed the group, looking for any signs of anaphylactic shock. About half the group had fallen victim to the frenzied swarm. They revealed small welts on their arms or hands, but otherwise seemed fine. My bite appeared to be the worst, turning my outer ear red and puffing up the side of my face. It hurt like hell.

Only as we headed downstream did I finally notice the bunch of Bodi men that had assembled on the plateau above the beach. No doubt the sight of our panicked flight caused them to roar with laughter. To them, our mishap must have been comical to watch, but it irked me to think that our suffering gave them that much enjoyment. My ear and face continued to throb as we rowed downstream while the river curved, reversing its direction around a horseshoe turn.

We'd only been back on the river for 15 minutes when we saw the same group of Bodi standing on the shore, wildly waving for us to pull over. They'd made the short walk across the spit of land around which the river wound to wait for us. Conrad directed us to head for shore, though I doubted we'd covered enough ground to be out of the bees' range.

On shore, two older women approached me. I held one hand over the ear that still pulsated with intense pain. Judging from their gestures, they wanted to examine my ear. I nodded and followed them to a nearby rock, where I took a seat. Imitating a buzzing sound, I gestured how the bee had circled around my head, then dove into my ear. One woman tugged on my earlobe as she peered inside, while the other scurried away. The woman who stayed with me murmured softly, conveying her deep empathy for my pain.

When the second woman returned, she brought a white paste and a thin twig split at one end. Though they couldn't explain their actions to me, they seemed confident in their skills to deal with bee stings. I nodded my permission to proceed. I figured out that they used the twig first as makeshift tweezers to wiggle out the stinger still embedded in the soft flesh of my inner ear, then as a tool with which to spread a generous coating of the white paste over the inflamed surface around where the stinger had lodged. The paste had an immediate cooling effect.

Other women of the tribe checked the rest of our group and dotted raised red welts with the same curative paste my healers had used on me. Meanwhile, Conrad and George learned from the Bodi men that the spot we picked for lunch lay directly below the tribe's carefully protected beehives, high in the branches of the trees that had provided shade for us. Our frantic screams brought them running, but by that time, it was too late for them to help us. Their eagerness to mend our wounds when we reached their settlement proved a welcome apology for their bees' misbehavior, and we thanked them for their kindness.

Back on the river, George shared some tidbits he'd learned about honeybees in Africa. "Honey is gold to these remote tribes. Since they don't use currency, they pay for other products with honey. So, they are very protective of their hives. A honeybee's sense of smell is 100 times more sensitive than ours, so they can sense pollen up to 500 feet away. I bet the sweet smell of the jelly excited those bees into a frenzy."

A FEW DAYS LATER, we floated out of the Bodi tribal lands and entered the homeland of the Mursi tribe. One afternoon, we encountered a dozen men who waved at us to stop. They stood on a narrow rocky shore backed by dense vegetation, a difficult spot to land the rafts. But on the opposite side of the river, a wide-open sandy beach beckoned.

"Hey, guys, let's pull over here," Conrad shouted. "This beach looks like an excellent camp for tonight. And we can spend some time with these guys."

The sculptured muscular physiques of these completely naked fierce warriors thoroughly intimidated me and surely must have left their enemies with second thoughts about engaging in battle. I wondered what had made Conrad think it was a wise decision to camp in their backyard.

When they saw us landing our rafts across from them, they waded into the river watching for crocodiles, bravely crossing the chest-deep, silty water to our side. We'd already begun to unload gear when a few of them offered to help. Conrad pointed to three of the men, passing the chosen ones our propane cook stove, lanterns, canned food, grills, and the tabletop with its detached screw-in-legs. They'd seen none of these things before. They curiously rotated each object, inspecting it from all angles before carrying it away from the river's edge to the level spot we'd chosen for our kitchen. The men not selected as helpers sat and bounced on the tubes of the beached rafts, entertained by the sight of our portable kitchen and tent village sprouting up right in front of them.

"Hey, everybody, keep an eye on these guys, and keep your personal gear close to you," Conrad warned as he watched our helpers shuttle items back and forth from the rafts to the kitchen. "Our gear fascinates them, and I don't want them helping themselves to any of our stuff."

"But, Conrad, if they don't know what these objects are or how they work, why would they even want to take our stuff?" I asked.

"They probably won't. But these guys can be pretty resourceful about finding uses for unusual objects."

As if to prove Conrad's point, a boy of about 10 years old sitting among the men on the rafts lifted a hollowed-out, 18 inch-long stick an inch in diameter to his lips and blew into it. To my surprise, a melodic tune floated out of this crude instrument. The music sounded similar to an oboe, but had none of an oboe's openings used to create distinct tones. By varying the pressure of air flowing through the stick, he could play an octave or more of notes. His melody reminded me of music played by Native American flutists, haunting, ethereal, and calming.

All work on setting up camp paused while the boy played his music. Lovely notes floated in the air, captivating our attention for several minutes. He played with his eyes closed and swayed with the rhythm as if the earth's song was flowing from the ground into the soles of his feet and out into the world on his breath. Upon finishing his performance, everyone clapped wildly in appreciation. George, with the inquisitive mind of a scholarly researcher, approached the boy and gestured that he'd like to inspect the musical stick.

The boy proudly handed it over to him. George examined the instrument. "This is nothing more than a section of a tree branch with its center whittled out. It's incredible he can get any sound from it."

The boy pretended to lift an imaginary stick to his lips to encourage George to blow some notes on his stick. George brought one end to his lips and blew air into the hole. Only the rushing sound of his exhalation came out. The Mursi men laughed at his failed attempt. He tried again without success, prompting our entire group to join in the laughter. Cheeks flushed pink from failing at the impossible task, George handed the stick back to the boy.

Once we'd finished the kitchen set up, we searched the beach for level spots on the sand to pitch our tents. When I unrolled my nylon tent wrapped around the aluminum poles that formed the frame, the boy jumped up and hurried over to watch. He pointed at one of my poles. I noticed his longing expression, so when he waved his cupped fingers, asking to hold it, I handed him the pole. He put it to his lips, blowing gently to form a perfectly clear note. He smiled and nodded his approval of my musical instrument.

Again, he put it to his lips and produced a series of distinct notes. How could he be making such beautiful music come from an aluminum tent pole? I stared dumfounded at his astonishing feat. "Come see what this kid is doing now!" I yelled to the others. My colleagues and the Mursi men crowded around as I encouraged the boy to proceed with his unique performance. As he created a melody, jaws dropped. Heads shook in disbelief. Val voiced the question we all had. "How is he doing that?"

When he finished the song, we again applauded his efforts. The boy, now uncomfortable with the attention directed at him, returned my tent pole and joined his elders. I wanted to give this boy his very own tent pole as a gift, so he could continue with his musical exploration, but if I did, my tent wouldn't function properly. Besides, Sobek's policy of leaving no trace behind prohibited us from giving or taking any object from the natives. Only by doing so would their culture remain pure.

A short while later, the Mursi men crossed back over the river. From that day forth, whenever I pitched my tent, I found it impossible to think of those hollow aluminum tubes as just tent poles. They would be a poignant reminder of a unique concert by a young maestro in the African wilderness.

FOR THE NEXT SEVERAL DAYS, we floated past tribal groups on both sides of the river. We'd wave, and they would wave back. One afternoon, we stopped at a settlement where a group of women tended leafy green crops. They'd planted their seeds in the soil after the seasonal floods earlier in the year deposited a fresh layer of nutrient-rich silt. These Mursi women followed a tradition that differentiated them from all other tribes in the Omo Valley.

Though the veteran guides had forewarned us, it shocked me to see the gruesome facial contortion caused by the disc-shaped wood plates stretched into a cut made just below the edge of their bottom lip. I shuddered at the thought of how much pain these girls had to endure. With nothing to numb the surrounding flesh, no medical tools or medicine to fight off an infection, it seemed terribly dangerous to me. I'd probably faint just *watching* the procedure. I wondered if they ever died while having a lip plate inserted.

George had done research on the practice and told us, "When a girl reaches puberty, she asks her mother to cut her lip. I suspect they cauterize the wound with wood embers to staunch the bleeding. A small wooden plug holds the wound open until it heals in 3 months, unless it becomes infected. Over time, the girls stretch the opening by inserting larger plugs ranging from 2.5 inches to 5 inches wide. The larger the lip plate worn by a woman, the more beautiful the tribe finds her."

I stared at the women's faces, noticing they followed the same practice with their earlobes, cutting and inserting silver dollar-sized wooden ear plugs in them. Not all the women sported lip plates. Some had a shriveled loop of lip dangling in front of their chins, which reminded me of a flabby, elongated turkey waddle. While I struggled to see the beauty in their self-mutilations, for all I knew, to these women, I might be the epitome of ugliness, given my complete absence of a lip plate and ear plugs. It clearly proved the adage that beauty *is* in the eye of the beholder.

I fought to keep a smile on my face while the women led us up a path to their cluster of dried grass huts. Our hosts showed us mounds of freshly ground grains and spices spread out on the soil. Their domed huts had a similar design to those of the Bodis. Naked children scampered around in a spirited game of what looked like tag, dashing in and out of the huts, hoping not to be seen. The women wore only short skirts of woven grasses or animal skins strung around their waists. The breasts of those who had born several babies sagged like empty socks against their chest walls, while those of the adolescent single girls remained firm and pointed. While visiting with them, I recalled offending the crowd at the farmer's market by revealing too much skin. I almost laughed out loud thinking of how shocked that crowd would be if they ever visited this village!

THE NEXT DAY, George suffered a relapse of the malaria parasite that still lived in his body from a previous bout years earlier. He displayed the classic symptoms of chills, sweating and tiredness. As a doctor, he carried a personal stash of the treatment he needed to quell the flare. To help George's body fight his infection, Conrad allowed us to slack off on rowing, opting to let our rafts glide effortlessly downstream with the current. I'd started taking chloroquine two weeks before I left the US and would continue taking it for four weeks after my return to prevent becoming infected. This protocol had worked for me during my trip to Tanzania, so I expected I'd stay safe.

Other than a quick noontime lunch break on shore, we spent a long lazy day on the river. When the height of the sun had fallen halfway from its apex to the horizon, we rounded a bend in the river to find a spacious, level, sandy beach perfect for a campsite. Not until we'd secured our rafts by pulling them partway onto land and began to unload did we realize we weren't alone. Several tribal members had staked out their own territory on a bluff just above the sandy beach. Five men and two women came down to investigate our unexpected arrival on their turf.

Conrad approached them and, with the use of lively charade-like moves, convinced them to let us stay on the riverbank overnight. They stayed out of our way, watching from a distance as we set up our camp. Once I'd pitched my tent and stashed my belongings inside, two women approached me. They chattered in their language, words that meant nothing to me, but their intense eyes pleaded with me to come with them. Timidly, one woman put her hand on my arm and gently tugged, while the other woman took a few steps away from the river and motioned me to follow.

I stalled for a minute, weighing how wise it would be to leave camp with them. I didn't feel threatened by them, rather more curious to know what they wanted me to see. But I wanted the crew to know where I was going. "Hey, Conrad, is it okay if I go with these women? I think they want to show me something."

"Yeah, go ahead, but I need you back here to help prep dinner in 20 minutes."

Along the base of the slope leading to the top of the bluff grew a dense thicket of green leafy bushes. With no obvious path through, the women forced aside the branches, clearing an opening barely wide enough for us to fit through the 15-foot-wide ribbon of foliage. Then we climbed the slope to reach the forested hilltop where they lived. I saw no huts, only woven mats on the ground in the shade under a few of the larger trees. Even with the river in full flood, I couldn't imagine it would rise to this level. The trees, rooted in solid ground, shored up the land on which they lived.

The women led me to a young mother, who sat on a worn mat rocking her wailing infant baby. Her mat snugged against the sturdy trunk of a tree, with a sprawling umbrella-like canopy overhead to provide a generous circle of shade. My guides plopped down on either side of the mother, cooing and stroking the baby's skinny arms. Still the baby screamed. A distinct rattle accompanied his fits of coughing.

The mother's pained expression reflected fear for her baby. Disgusting thick yellow mucus crusted the opening of the baby's nostrils, and salty tears deposited crystalized tracks as they flowed down his cheeks. She had no medicine to cure her sick baby. With tears in her own eyes, she held out her baby to me.

My heart broke knowing *I* couldn't help this child. The two other women urgently motioned for me to take the baby. I figured the vaccinations I'd gotten prior to coming to Africa gave me protection against all the common killer diseases, so I sat down on the edge of the mat and accepted the emaciated naked baby in my arms. His hot clammy skin confirmed the fever raging in his tiny body. Compassion in the face of misery was the only thing I could offer. I clutched the sobbing baby and rocked him back and forth, hoping in some small way he felt comforted.

We sat quietly together for some minutes, listening to the baby's uncontrolled coughing and labored breathing. When I gestured I needed to return to camp, the mother nodded and waved that I should go. I held her baby out toward her, but she refused him, shaking her head and waving for me to go. Her intention suddenly hit me. She wanted to *give* me her baby! She must have known *she* couldn't save her child and that, if I took him, perhaps *I* could save his life. Panic overwhelmed me as I let out a gasp and vigorously shook my head in disbelief. Instead, I motioned for her and the other two women to follow me. At the edge of the slope down to the beach, I handed her back the baby, and we all pushed our way through the dense thicket, finally emerging onto the sandy beach.

"Hey, George, I need your help. I have a sick baby here."

He came over, took one look at the baby, shrugged his shoulders, and said, "There's nothing I can do for him."

"What do you mean? Don't we have some antibiotics we could give him?"

"Brenda, this child needs more help than I can offer. I don't know what disease he has, or whether the antibiotics I have would even work. These drugs could kill this baby if the mother doesn't know how to administer the treatment. I'm sorry, but I can't help this baby."

"So, we're just going to let him die? There must be *something* we can do. What about your oath about not doing harm?" In that moment of anger and hopelessness, I crossed a line of civility with George, but I didn't care. My accusing stare must have unnerved him.

I wasn't about to back down. He threw his arms in the air and muttered, "I can give them some Tylenol that might temper the fever. But that's it." As he stormed off to get pills from the first aid kit, Val, curious about what had caused the commotion, came over.

"What's going on?" she asked. Then, spying the sickly baby, she said, "Poor little thing."

George looked back over his shoulder and yelled, "For God's sake, don't any of the rest of you go near that baby!"

Quickly, Val backed away. George used his buck knife to cut the tablets into quarters and handed them to the mom. Using the position of the sun as an improvised timer, he explained when she should give them to her child. She bowed to him in appreciation, and he to her. After the tribal entourage returned to the top of the bluff, George lit into me.

"Please don't tell me you handled that baby," he said in a tone as if addressing a dolt.

"I held him and rocked him to make him feel better."

"Jesus, Brenda! My best guess is this child has tuberculosis, which happens to be quite contagious. You are going to have to get a TB screening when you get home. Understand?"

Like a chastised child, I nodded and hung my head, only now regretting the consequences of my actions. Sensing that his reprimand had landed a punishing blow, his voice softened.

"This world we live in is anything but fair, Brenda. *Many* children die in these remote areas, mothers die in childbirth, and animals sometimes kill the men hunting them. This is their reality. Out here, nature's law rules. Only the fittest survive."

Just then, we heard shouts from the kitchen area. Conrad held a six-foot-long driftwood club. Peter and Val, both strict vegans, begged, "Don't kill it! Please don't kill it!"

George and I sprinted in that direction, only to stop dead in our tracks when we saw the bright neon green snake that had slithered out of the bushes heading toward our fire pit.

"Are you nuts?" Conrad glared at Peter and Val in disbelief. "That snake is a green mamba, one of the deadliest snakes in the world. If it bites you, you're dead."

"Can't we just try to steer it out of our camp back into the bushes?" said Peter.

"At least let us try?" pleaded Valerie.

Both hurried off in search of long sticks to serve as snake prods. Our clients raised concerns about allowing the snake to remain so near our campsite. I shivered when I realized the snake had emerged from the ridge of bushes at the base of the banking that I'd just tromped through wearing nothing but open-toed Teva sandals. Twice! What were Peter and Val thinking?

They returned with two sturdy 10-foot-long prods they'd found just upstream from our beach. Immediately, they went to work poking at the wriggling snake, talking to it as if it would pay attention to their directions. The rest of us stayed a safe distance away. After a few minutes, the snake, probably tired of being poked, reversed direction and slithered back toward the thicket, disappearing inside it. The tense muscles in my body relaxed a bit after the snake's departure.

The Sobek crew began preparing dinner, while our clients found "snake sticks" to protect themselves as they went to collect firewood. I finished chopping three onions for our vegetable stir-fry and prepared to peel some carrots when I looked up and saw the green snake headed back towards us.

"Conrad, it's back! It's over there." I pointed to the snake. Conrad grabbed his club and closed in on it as the venomous creature slithered on a beeline toward the closest tent.

"With all due respect to your vegan values," Conrad glanced at Peter and Val, "this snake is too dangerous to be slinking around this campsite."

Before Peter or Valerie could protest, Conrad raised his club over his head and slammed it with full force down on the snake's head. It stopped wriggling. Conrad pummeled it a few extra times to be sure the creature was dead. Using one of the long poles, he scooped up the limp body, walked down to the river, and, like an angler fly-casting, flung it into the center of the current.

MY ENCOUNTER WITH A DYING BABY and a deadly green mamba heightened my vigilance. The next day we easily navigated a few rapids, passed more tribal people and once again made camp on a smooth sandy beach. All afternoon long, huge, pure white, puffy clouds hovered above us. Only in Africa had I seen such dense cotton-ball clouds floating in a sky of pure sapphire blue, untainted by human pollution. As we prepared and ate dinner, we witnessed the vibrant, ever-changing colors of a magnificent sunset. The disappearing sun cast shadows of rich gold, rusty orange, and finally dusky mauve across the sky behind the silhouettes of umbrella thorn acacias on the far side of the river.

As I prepared for a restful sleep, reflecting on our uneventful day, I felt grateful for the absence of any new chaos and psyched that I'd completed my 14th day on the river, making this the longest raft trip

I'd been on. I had a few sore back muscles, but I'd avoided developing blisters on my hands. No one had gotten sick on the trip except George, but he managed his mild flare easily. No hippos or crocs had chomped on our rafts. Just two days remained until the end of the commercial trip. Lying by the side of the river that night, listening to the gentle sounds of flowing water, my mind filled with serenity as I drifted off to dreamland.

Hours later, a sudden brilliant flash of light and the distant rumble of thunder jolted me awake. I sat upright in the center of my tent, waiting for the next lightning bolt so I could count the seconds between its flash and ensuing thunder. My dad, a master electrician, had told me that if I counted the seconds between, then divided by five, I would know how close the lightning had struck. Five seconds equated to one mile. The mounting wind speed rattled branches of the trees just beyond the beach. I could feel the sheer force of it as it pushed against the side of my tent, making one wall curve inward, pressing firmly against my shoulder.

What a dilemma! I remembered the saying they taught us in elementary school; when thunder roars, go indoors! Out here, no indoors existed. Another bolt illuminated the sky. I counted 15 seconds until I heard thunder. Shit! Our campsite now fell within striking distance. I cowered, curling myself up as tightly as I could, beneath the metal-framed cage that surrounded me, remembering that Dad had taught me that lightning needs at least a three-foot wide ground connection to create the arc needed to electrocute a person.

Another flash. Eight seconds. Kaboom. Headed straight for us. The wind howled ferociously, as if the devil himself wanted to drive the storm toward us. Suddenly, a heavenly spigot opened wide. Torrents of rain pelted the earth. A maelstrom raged outside. Sheets of rain, blown horizontally, pounded viciously against the side of my tent. The air crackled, immediately exploding with a moment of brilliant daylight as the ground trembled from the deafening crash. I cringed, holding my breath, frozen with fear. The howling sound of wind and rain would drown any shouts for help.

A terrifyingly powerful gust of wind forced two of my tent poles to bend. The protective canopy of my tent collapsed on me. Water soaked through the nylon material draped around me, drenching my hair and clothes. A mix of rainwater and tears washed my face. Amid the raw fury of the gale, I cowered alone and profoundly humble. Another flash of lightning illuminated the sky. I counted 10 seconds. The worst of the storm had passed. Tears of fear turned to tears of joy. My thoughts veered to figuring out how to extricate myself from the battered ruins of my tent. Where would I sleep for the rest of the night?

In total darkness, I felt for the zipper of the door but found only folds of wet nylon. Perhaps it would be easier if I could locate my head-lamp, which I'd carefully positioned beside my head before the storm, but it, too, remained elusive in the mangled mess. Five minutes later, the wind quieted, and the rain stopped almost as quickly as it began.

Outside, I heard Conrad's voice. "Is anyone hurt?"

"I need some help over here," a client called out.

I yelled, "My tent collapsed and I'm not sure I can get out, but I'm okay."

I heard Peter and Valerie outside evaluating the damage to my tent. "We've got you, Brenda. Just have to figure out where your door flap is. Ah, here we go," said Peter.

I heard unzipping and felt the top of the tent rising off me. When I saw the beam of light from his headlamp, I dove forward, escaping my confines, leaving behind only a flattened heap on the waterlogged ground. Surprisingly, a quick visual survey of the rest of the camp revealed that all the other tents survived undamaged, despite complaints about water seeping inside.

After making rounds to check on our clients, Conrad joined Peter, Val, and me. He winced at the sight of my crumpled tent and said, "We're not going to fix that tonight. Come on. You can sleep in my tent." Inside his tent, he handed me one of his dry T-shirts and his sleeping pad to stretch out on. At least I had shelter over my head for the rest of the night.

EARLY THE NEXT MORNING, Conrad and I worked on salvaging my damaged tent. We pulled my sleeping bag and pad, gear bag, ammo can, and camera case out into the sunny, fresh air. The last three items, all waterproof, had protected my belongings inside. We threw my unzipped sleeping bag and pad over some low bushes to dry.

After extracting the aluminum tent poles from their sleeves, we spread my tent out to dry on the sand. We found no tears in the nylon material, but two of the poles had curved into a 40-degree angle. Conrad found a pounding stone and banged away at the bends until they looked nearly straight.

"If we need to, we'll make more adjustments tonight."

The talk at breakfast centered on how my tent bore the most damage from the storm.

"You're lucky you didn't end up in Oz," said Val.

"Believe me, I worried that those hurricane-force winds would roll my tent over with me in it."

That day, we maneuvered through a couple of feisty rapids that disrupted the otherwise languid current. The gradient of the river lessened as we approached the region of the Omo National Park, the departure point for all but two of our commercial passengers. However, the crocodiles remained plentiful, requiring constant vigilance.

At our camp that night, I reassembled my tent. I felt confident, absent another bout of foul weather, the tent would function well until the end of the trip. While Peter and Val prepared a tasty onion, carrot, sweet potato, and rice casserole flavored with French onion soup mix for dinner, Conrad kneaded a fresh loaf of bread dough which we'd eat for breakfast and lunch the next day. After dinner, we relaxed around our last communal campfire, recounting our most fun and most stressing moments of the trip. In 24 hours, more than half of our expedition members would gratefully fall asleep wrapped in clean white cotton sheets on a soft springy mattress in a luxury Addis Ababa hotel.

THE LAST DAY OF THE COMMERCIAL TRIP, we spent just four hours on the river, before meeting three safari vehicles waiting for us on a bluff above the river. They would transport our group to the rustic, lone building that served as the Omo Park headquarters and its adjacent grass airstrip, about six miles inland. We left our rafts secured well above river level, but took all our personal gear with us. The local rangers drove their vehicles north across the trackless plain of tall grasses. We caught views of distant herds of zebra and antelope chomping on grass in the shade of scattered tree groves. One driver told Conrad we had to watch behind us for any sign of a fire igniting from the dry grass passing under the vehicles' hot engines. They carried jugs of water and hoes to extinguish immediately any flame a vehicle might spark. A wildfire raging across these vast plains would be unstoppable and devastating.

Conrad had booked a DC-3 charter flight for that afternoon. The American military used the DC-3 as an integral part of their air fleet during WWII. Later in the 1940s, commercial airlines put it to work carrying up to 28 passengers. Because of its durable construction, it still found service flying into remote landing strips around the world. Though Conrad had contracted with Ethiopian Air for the flight back to

Addis to depart at 3 p.m., the Omo National Park ranger told Conrad that scheduled flights rarely arrived on time, if at all.

We'd brought enough food to the headquarters to put out a nice spread of Conrad's fresh baked bread, canned meats, peanut butter, jams, and condiments. Once we'd finished lunch, those departing double-checked they'd stored all their gear for the expected midafternoon getaway. With little air circulation this far inland from the river, the sun's rays seared everything they touched. The intense heat made everyone feel sluggish. We sought shade in the shadow cast by the building and along the nonexposed sides of the safari vehicles. Beads of sweat escaped, trickling down my cheeks, soaking my T-shirt.

At first, we waited patiently, hopeful to hear the distant hum of airplane engines, but while we waited and waited and waited, the sun dipped toward the horizon, tanking any possibility of a plane arrival.

Conrad confirmed our fears when he called us together. "Listen up, people. The ranger says our flight won't come today. It's impossible to land on an unlit grass runway, and we've only got about an hour until the sun sets. Peter and I will go with a driver back to the river to get some more food, water, and kitchen gear, so we can cook dinner and breakfast here. While we're gone, set your tents up and get settled in before it's dark."

The air temperature dropped significantly, as the sky deepened to ebony, bringing welcome relief from the heat. During dinner, Conrad tried to calm our anxious passengers, who had flights booked out of Addis the following day. "Ethiopian Air knows you have connecting flights, so they'll probably send the DC-3 here early tomorrow so they can get you back to Addis in plenty of time."

George, who'd planned to leave with our clients, rolled his eyes, and muttered, "Yeah, right," as if he'd played this waiting game before. With no campfire to socialize around, and everyone eager to be ready when the plane arrived early the next morning, bedtime came soon after dinner. The park ranger and the drivers kept rifles handy, promising to keep watch over us that night.

WE ATE BREAKFAST under a cloudless blue sky, watching distant herds of wildlife forage during the cooler morning hours. The perfect weather made us believe the plane had to be on its way that morning. But by noon, as the temperature again soared, feeding the formation of puffy cumulus clouds above us, no plane had arrived.

As we ate our 10th lunch of canned tuna on crackers, Conrad told us, "Hey, guys, this is all part of your adventure. Out here, we're on bush time. There's no use getting upset about something that's completely out of our control. The pilot knows we're waiting. At some point, a plane's gonna get here. In the meantime, the ranger has agreed to take us out into the valley to look for wildlife when it cools down if the plane isn't here by then."

A few minutes later, Conrad summoned the crew and told us we needed to go for a short hike. His furrowed brow and an edge to his voice indicated he had something important we needed to know. We walked through the shoulder-high grass to a solitary clump of trees well out of earshot of our clients. Just beyond the trees, a narrow, shallow stream of clear running water wound its way across the plain. We sat on its bank as Conrad spilled out his concerns.

"There's nothing we can do to get the damn plane to show up any sooner. The rangers say they *are* sure it will come. They're expecting a resupply for themselves too. But here's the thing. We packed food for the entire group for 21 days and extra food for six of us for the extra seven days. By tomorrow, we'll have dipped far enough into our food supplies to keep everyone here fed for two days. I'm not sure we'll have enough for us to continue for those seven extra days. I'm considering calling off the extension. Remember that we don't know what waits for us in that stretch of river, either."

"Have we got enough iodine to purify water to drink for that long?" I asked.

"Yes, we do. I never skimp on iodine. I guess what I'm asking is are you up for some roughing it if we run low or out of food? Any of you want to fly out with George and the clients?"

"I bet we could trade with the tribes for extra food," said Peter. Conrad cocked his head to one side, acknowledging the possibility.

"If Peter's in, then so am I," said Val.

Already we'd encountered so many unexpected challenges on this trip, but we'd been able to find solutions by being creative with what we had. I believed, with our skills and abilities, we'd finish our journey. "Since I missed the first five days, as long as we have plenty of water, I don't want to miss the last seven. We can stretch out what food we have left, as long as the airlines don't maroon us here for a week! But what about the two clients that paid extra for the extension?" I asked.

"If the three of you are up for going on, then I'll talk to them and tell them we'll be facing some hardships and give them the option of staying or leaving."

With our discussion finished, the cool stream of water proved irresistible. "Now, who wants to take a dip with me?" asked Conrad.

George waggled his finger, signaling that it was not a wise choice. Nearly shouting, he begged, "Please don't! This is the perfect habitat for the snails that carry schistosomiasis. If you go into that water, the microscopic parasites that the snails release in their feces can penetrate your skin, maturing into parasitic worms that will live in your blood vessels. Do you really want that?"

I trusted George's knowledge of tropical diseases. This one sounded especially gross, but that clear running water just inches away promised immense relief from the blistering heat.

Conrad shrugged off George's warning. "I'm just going to dip in to cool off for a minute. This heat is unbearable. If I use my T-shirt to towel off briskly after I get out, there's little chance of infection." Removing his shirt, he waded into the stream and squatted, then sat in the waist-deep water. His expression instantly turned from irritated to tranquil, as if he'd dosed on morphine. I wanted to feel that chilled out, too. I couldn't resist joining Conrad in the refreshing, silt-free water.

Though I would have enjoyed sitting in the stream's luxurious waters for the rest of the afternoon, the sight of an uninvited visitor—an 18-inch-long baby crocodile swimming upstream—alarmed us. It shied away when we moved, but where there's a cute baby, there's usually a mama lurking nearby. We quickly returned to land. I used the bandana I wore around my neck to rub dry my exposed skin.

"Now you've got to get tested for tuberculosis *and* schisto," George chided, his waggling index finger now pointed directly at me. "Get your boss to put you in touch with the tropical disease doc we use in San Francisco." I smirked, looking away from my colleague, as his overly dramatic scolding continued. "I'm not joking, Brenda! You've got to do that as soon as you get home. Do you understand?"

For the second time, I hung my head like a reprimanded child and mumbled, "Yes, sir."

THE PLANE DIDN'T ARRIVE. Instead, Conrad made a second trip back to the river to check on our rafts and collect more food while the rest of us had a wild ride bouncing across the plains, chasing glimpses of zebra, gazelle, and wildebeest. We even saw a couple of lions stalking antelope, but from a distance, far enough away that they wouldn't decide to change their dinner menu to something more exotic.

At least this diversion broke the monotony of waiting. Even though *this* flight wasn't my ticket home, I empathized with our client's hopelessness about being abandoned in the African wilderness. While floating on the river, every bend or curve brought new wonders: a distant mountain range, a frolicking rapid, colobus monkeys leaping from tree to tree, and fascinating native tribes. But hunkered on this vast unchanging plain in the relentless heat, how could we not be bored to tears? Maybe tomorrow our luck would change and the DC-3 would finally appear.

BOUND TO STAY OPTIMISTIC, everyone woke early and had their bags packed less than an hour after sunrise. But after a second breakfast in the Omo National Park with no sign of an arriving plane, our clients became irritated and grumpy. Late in the morning, one man seated on the ground leaning against his bulging duffle bag made a sarcastic suggestion. "I think we need to place bets on when this frigging plane will arrive. Everyone gets to guess a day and time, for say… $5 for the pot. Then when the plane touches down, whoever's guess is closest wins the pot!"

"Oh, splendid idea," replied one woman client. I couldn't tell if she really meant it, but then she added, "I've got some paper and a pen so we can record our guesses."

While she rummaged through her backpack, Val tilted her head, then spun around to the north. "Hey, guys, listen up. I think I hear something." Everyone went silent, straining to pick up a noise out of place with the natural sounds around us. "There it is again. Anyone else hear it?" she asked.

A few seconds later, a chorus of "I dos" erupted. Everyone clapped and whooped. Even though we couldn't see the white-and-silver-winged DC-3 for another two minutes, I knew the rescue we'd been hoping for would happen soon. The ranger warned us to stay close to his hut as the metallic bird swooped down toward the ground. The aircraft passed directly over our heads, kicking up a cloud of dust as it touched the earth 100 yards beyond us, then taxied to a stop.

George and the departing clients grabbed their luggage and hustled toward the plane. Within 20 minutes, the headquarter's resupplies had been offloaded and the departing individuals had swiftly loaded their baggage and securely buckled themselves in place. The plane taxied further down the valley, then turned 180 degrees, revved its engines, and headed back along the ground, gaining speed and lifting off the ground just in enough time to climb above the headquarters building.

Mostly, I felt relief watching them disappear from view. I wouldn't have to listen anymore to their whines about how we'd screwed up their schedules to get home. Now the six of us could resume exploring the river. A driver shuttled us back to the river, where Val took over rowing George's boat. Peter and I continued on in our rafts, while our intrepid paying couple climbed aboard Conrad's raft. I couldn't wait to see what waited for us ahead, where no Sobek guide had ever gone. It even excited me to be back in crocodile territory and to match wits with the river's current as it pulled and pushed us along its route.

LATER THAT AFTERNOON, we stopped and visited a village a short walk inland, led by a few men of the tribe. Conrad had stashed some fishhooks in his gear to be used as a bribe if we encountered any hostility from the tribes living beside the river. The upstream tribes had seen us pass by their homeland for seven years. They'd gotten to know our groups as friendly, curious strangers. Below the Omo National Park, the tribes had never laid eyes on us.

Conrad, using only gestures, attempted to explain to the tribal leader that we wanted to exchange fishhooks for food. The leader finally seemed to understand Conrad's plea and directed the women to bring a few offerings. We scored some dried beans and four fresh chicken eggs from that village. Our food replacement strategy involved a stop at one village each day to replenish the food stock we'd exhausted during the two-day delay.

The only real challenge on this lower section of river came on our third morning when we approached a nasty-looking rapid where a small rocky island split the river's current. We stopped 100 yards above the rapid's initial drop. Leaving our clients behind with the rafts, we walked along the bank to scout what lay ahead. I grew more worried the closer we approached the head of the rapid.

Conrad analyzed the scenario we faced. "Most of the current flows down to the right of the island. There's a bunch of boulders scattered throughout the rapid with vicious pour-overs leading directly into tall standing waves. It would take absolute precision to weave through that obstacle field."

"Yeah, but on this side there's like a 10-foot drop through a channel barely wide enough for our boats," said Peter. "Not to mention the current crashes into another boulder at the bottom of the falls that could easily roll a boat and dump us into the pool at the bottom."

"Look over there!" Val and I yelled in unison. We'd seen the croc's enormous head slowly lift out of the water. Silently, it glided toward us, then 20 feet away stopped and glared.

"Holy shit," said Peter. "It's enormous. The head alone looks three feet long, which means a total length of 20 feet!"

I pointed with one of my sweaty palms toward a second monster's location. "Guys, I hate to say this, but off to the right, there's another one."

"Son of a bitch. Both these routes could be suicidal." Conrad heaved both arms up in exasperation.

A surge of panic mounted within me. Had we come this far to be stymied just days before the end of the trip? What odds did we have of finding a workable solution? I listened like my life depended on it as Conrad described our options.

"We know there are huge crocodiles in this part of the river. If we go for the far side of the rapid, the first boat down would *have* to make it through unscathed. Without a rescue boat at the bottom, a flip means we're going to be in deep shit. No one has run this rapid before, and you can see how gnarly it is. Any of you feel up to running the gauntlet first?" No one volunteered. "I thought so. Here, on this side, if we didn't have man-eater size crocs to deal with, it might be worth a try. But I don't think any of us want to be croc bait."

The normal practice followed when a rapid is deemed too dangerous to run is to do a portage. The rafts and everything in them are removed from the water, the rafts deflated, and everything is lugged along the shore around the obstacle(s). Once downstream, the rafts are reinflated and re-rigged. Or the rafts can be lined around an obstacle in the river's current using multiple guide ropes attached to the raft which the guides control like a puppet by pulling on the free ends. With this technique, the raft doesn't need to be unloaded, but the guides manning the ropes must be very strong. If they let go of the ropes, they risk that the current will drag the 800-pound boat away from safety. If the downstream tug on the ropes is too great, they risk being pulled into the water behind the runaway raft.

Peter suggested, "What if we try to line the boats through? I think we can control it through the narrow channel and over the falls."

Conrad looked doubtful. "We'll need two ropes on each side of the rafts. I'm a little concerned because the boulder field on this side will make for awkward footing, and if a raft flips at the bottom, we'll have a hell of a time getting it flipped back over, especially with those crocs hovering so close," he said.

Every one of our options involved high risk. We had to choose one, and my brain calculated the lining route would be least difficult (maybe) and least time-consuming (maybe).

"Let's try lining with one boat and see how it goes," I said. "If that doesn't work, we could always portage the other rafts."

With all four guides in agreement, we brought the boats and our clients downstream to just above where the narrow channel began. Now that we had a plan, determination replaced anxiety as we worked as a team, attaching the guide ropes and tightening up the strapping securing everything inside the raft. Conrad and Peter held the two front ropes; Val and I controlled the rear two ropes.

"Let's go," shouted Conrad as we let up enough slack to push the raft into the current. As it floated down into the channel, we moved along with it on shore, holding it back from picking up speed. Just above the falls, the raft rotated 45 degrees sideways, wedging itself between the boulders on either side of the channel. Despite strenuous tugging on the rear end ropes, the raft didn't budge. Conrad decided one of us had to get into the boat and push against the far-side boulder while we tugged on the rear ropes.

It made sense for the lightest-weight guide to do the honors. For once in my life, I appreciated every one of the extra 10 pounds I had over Val.

"You can do this, Val!" Peter cheered her on and gave her a kiss. She hesitated, took a deep breath, and then courageously leaped onto the boulder that bound the front end of the raft. From there, she hopped down into the raft and pushed with all her might against the boulder, while we pulled with all our might on the rear ropes from shore. The back end slid off the boulder and straightened in the channel. The plan had been for Val to scramble back onto the shore before the raft took the 10-foot plunge, but the raft had already slid past the boulder she used to climb on board.

"What should I do?" Val hollered hysterically.

She wasn't the only one terrified about what the next few seconds held in store for her. I pulled with every ounce of strength I had to slow the raft's progress, as did Conrad and Peter. Even the client couple grabbed Val's unmanned guide rope and tugged.

"Sorry, Val, we can't slow the raft down. Get in the middle of the boat and hunker down. Hold on—you're going for a ride," said Conrad. Val curled into a ball, gripping onto the strapping with both hands. Seconds later, the front end of the raft tipped forward and plunged over the falls. Val screamed. The boat bounced off the surge of water, cushioning the boulder at the bottom. Seconds later, we safely pulled the raft snug to the shore of the crocodile pool, and a triumphant Val climbed out of the raft. She whooped and danced around us like she'd just won an Olympic medal.

It surprised us that the raft had landed so nicely at the bottom of the falls. Conrad ordered the next raft to be prepared. He winked at Val and asked, "Are you ready to be the boat rider again?"

While we expected she'd swear at Conrad for even teasing her with that suggestion, she shocked us by saying, "Heck yes! That was a blast!"

The second time, she easily climbed into the raft from the edge of the riverbank above the channel. As we pulled the raft through the channel, she shifted her weight back and forth to keep it straight on course, only crouching down as the raft went over the falls. We celebrated a perfect landing once again. It took us 30 minutes to line the first raft into the lower pool. The second raft took only 12 minutes. The third raft, with Val still aboard, took just 10 minutes.

As we readied the final raft-mine, Val said, "I think I'll sit this one out. Brenda, why don't you take your own boat through? You'll never get this chance again."

I moaned. I hated roller coasters, and this short ride reminded me of the stomach-lurching free-falling I'd experienced only once in my life. Never again had I gone back on that thrill ride. I'd just watched Val make the raft-lining maneuver look easy, but just because she'd mastered it didn't mean that I would. If she wouldn't do it again, then I'd have to.

"Come on, Brenda, quit stalling. Get in the boat so we can get this job done," said Conrad.

All my instincts argued I shouldn't go. Now that they knew how to line the raft through, why not send an unmanned boat down? But being part of this team, I had a responsibility to carry my share of the work. They needed me to climb into the raft and do what Val had already done. So, putting aside my heap of misgivings, I climbed into my raft.

I felt the current pulling me forward. *Please, dear God, help me keep this raft right side up!* Entering the channel, I rocked back and forth, keeping the raft from chafing against the channel's sides. *Here it comes, God. Pleeeeease keep me safe!* I crouched down and held on for dear life. I squeezed my eyes shut just before reaching the pour-over. *One, two, three, four, five.* The landing jolted me to one side, but the raft remained upright and level. It happened so fast, yet the adrenaline rushed through my body, making me feel like a superwoman for those few seconds. As we pulled away from the crocodile pool, we saw no trace of the giants. Maybe they'd hid from the crazy humans dropping boats into their pool?

THE LAST TWO DAYS on the river passed uneventfully as it gradually widened and its current slowed. On the last day, Conrad told us to keep our eyes open for the two vehicles he'd hired to retrieve us from near a settlement called Kara Dus. For the crew and our equipment, he'd hired a five-ton transport truck for the two-day drive back to Addis Ababa. But for our two paying clients, he'd arranged for a four-wheel-drive Jeep from National Tour Operators so they could ride in comparative comfort along the infrequently traveled dirt track that led back to the capital. Conrad made George promise to inform both NTO and the truck company in Addis of our revised pickup date because of the delayed departure of our clients from the Omo National Park.

I'd had an amazing adventure on this journey meeting the people who called the river valley home, but I longed to be clean and sleep in a bed again, so I had no qualms about saying goodbye to the Omo River. Finally, just after midday, we saw a man on the open left bank waving his hands above his head. We rowed over to where he stood. Conrad spoke to him in Amharic. He identified himself as the Jeep driver and pointed behind him to a Jeep parked back from the river in the shade of a grove of trees.

Conrad asked if the Jeep driver had seen our truck, but he just shrugged his shoulders. He'd seen no sign of a truck on his way to the river. He informed Conrad that *only* this one track led to the river for countless miles in both directions. Dismayed at finding our truck had failed to show, I realized the other crew members and I had no means of returning to Addis. After more discussion with the Jeep driver, Conrad called us together to explain his plan.

"The Jeep driver is eager to get started back. He's agreed to let me hitch a ride with him to see if I can figure out what happened to our truck. Obviously, you three will have to stay here with our gear."

Shocked by what Conrad said, I asked, "For how long?" *I couldn't believe he would leave three white kids, all in this country for the first time, unable to communicate with anyone, unarmed and running dangerously short on food, by ourselves in this vast wilderness!*

"I don't know. It depends on how far I have to go and how long it'll take me to get this straightened out. Might be a day, might be a week. But you'll be okay. There's no other option. Don't worry. I *will* come back."

Logically, I knew Conrad had to leave in the Jeep. But what made him think we would be okay? Peter and Val looked as shellshocked as I felt. We helped to pack the Jeep, then watched helplessly as it drove down the track away from us, our only lifeline floating away out of reach.

Peter, Val and I settled on making camp where the Jeep had parked on a level clearing shaded by the canopy of several tall trees. The process of unloading the rafts and carrying all the gear up to our camp required multiple trips that left us tired and thirsty. But we still had to secure our rafts. By flinging bailing buckets full of water from the edge of the river, we rinsed out the insides of the rafts, one at a time, before hefting them onto our shoulders to carry them to our camp.

While we occupied ourselves with arranging coolers and gear boxes, six men wearing nothing but skimpy loincloths trotted into our area, halting opposite us with only an overturned raft separating us. For an uncomfortable moment, laden with uncertainty, we stood motionless, staring at each other. Their exposed muscular physiques and serious facial expressions made them look fierce.

"We're outnumbered. Somehow, we've got to convey we mean them no harm." I spoke in a low voice to Peter and Val. With no verbal way to communicate, I resorted to charades. I gave them a little wave. Peter and Val followed suit. They showed no reaction. Did they expect us to leave this area? My stomach knotted as I recalled this tribe had never interacted with previous Sobek trips. Had these men ever even seen white people before? Were we in danger? How would Conrad ever find us (or our bodies) if these men abducted us?

I racked my brain for a way to show the tribal men that we wanted to be friends with them. Looking at the raft, I got an idea. I stepped closer to the raft, sat on the inflated tube, and bounced up and down. Then I pointed at them and gestured an invitation for them to try bouncing on the tubes. They exchanged curious looks before one man stepped forward and gingerly sat on the side of the raft. I watched as his body sank two inches into the neoprene material, his eyes opening wide with surprise, then rose again as the pressure in the tube rebounded, pushing him back up.

His tribe mates broke into laughter and chattered with excitement. A few moments later, the rest of them joined their leader, bouncing with carefree abandon on the side tubes of the raft. One even lost his balance and tumbled backward onto the upside-down floor, sagging in the middle of the raft. Their laughter and playfulness amused us.

"Great icebreaker, Brenda." Val grinned as we got back to organizing.

The men enjoyed bouncing for a while before returning their focus to our activity. All six lounged across the surface of the overturned raft as if nestling into a comfortable sofa to watch a football game. Because locals now knew our camp was close by, we needed to figure out how to protect our rafts and gear. By standing two rafts on their sides in an inverted "V" shape and lashing the top edges together, we covered the mound of gear and remaining food. We sealed off our stash by staking our tents up against the ends of the rafts.

The other two rafts remained overturned on the ground close by. We could use their smooth, though slightly sagging, surface to sit, eat, read, or relax on. For the rest of the afternoon, our visitors hung out with us, entertained by the construction of our mini-fortress. Just before dusk, they stood up and marched off on a narrow trail through the brush that grew along the border of our clearing.

"I'm glad they left before dinner," said Peter. "I think it would be rude to eat our meal in front of them without offering them some, but I don't think we have enough food left to cook a banquet."

We opted to cook a lentil-and-rice stew for our dinner, carefully rationing the food we still had left. The space around us faded to ebony as we ate. As soon as we cleaned up, I had planned to crawl into my tent for a long, restful sleep. So, it took us by surprise, giving us a fright, when the men we'd met that afternoon tromped back into our clearing carrying armloads of firewood.

A safe distance away from our tents and rafts, they dug a shallow hole in the ground and lit a fire. Waving, they invited us to join them as they squatted in a circle around the dancing flames. We brought our bailing buckets and turned them upside down for seats, to keep us off the ground. To preserve my headlamp's batteries, I carried instead a powerful small flashlight I'd brought as a backup. I noticed the tribal group had grown by four more men. Once the fire roared with fury, the men stood and launched into a sing-song chant to which they stomped their feet, leisurely shuffling around the fire.

I swayed from side to side with the rhythm of the chanting and the drumming of their feet on the ground. Listening to the repetitious chant of meaningless words and gazing at the circular motion of the men's dance led my mind into a dreamlike trance. The flames stretched higher, creating an illusion that the men on the far side of the circle were dancing through the flames rather than behind them. I found myself so absorbed in their performance that I had no sense of whether it had lasted for three or 30 minutes.

When they finished, Peter, Val, and I clapped and offered English words of praise, hoping it would convey our appreciation of their performance. After a brief rest, they resumed chanting and dancing, though with altered movements and a gentler-sounding mantra. Their performance that evening offered a variety of dances to entertain us. In between dances, the men added more wood to the fire to keep it blazing. The fire cast so much heat that I moved my seat away from the blaze into the shadows. I kept waiting for them to encourage us to dance with them, but thankfully, they never did.

During a pause in their performance, one man wandered over and squatted in a sitting position next to me. He gestured toward the fire, drawing a circle with his arm while he waggled his head. I assumed he was asking my impression of the show I'd been watching. I clapped my hands together and nodded to convey their dances fascinated me. He smiled back at me. Suddenly, he reached over and snatched the flashlight resting on my lap. His quick motion startled me. Was he brazenly stealing it in front of so many witnesses?

"No!" I tried to grab back my flashlight, but he pushed his arms out toward me with splayed palms bent up to convey I should stay still. He fumbled with the flashlight, then handed it back to me for help. After I turned it on, he took it from me, shining it on the ground between us. The flashlight's beam illuminated a huge black scorpion. I recoiled in fright, seeing only 12 inches separated it from the section of exposed skin on my foot not covered by the straps of my Teva sandals. I estimated the creature's length to be two-and-a-half inches, not counting its tail that curved up over its body.

"Oh, my God! There's an enormous scorpion right here!" I yelled to Peter and Val, who raced over to get a glimpse. The man holding my flashlight impressed us by deftly pinching hard from behind on the middle of the curved tail to immobilize its stinger, then lifted it off the ground. He handed me back my flashlight, then separated the stinger end of the tail from the rest of the scorpion's body. He threw the stinger into the fire and heaved the rest of the body away from our group.

After that scare, I only wanted to go back to my tent and zip myself into its protective cocoon for the rest of the night. I bowed in gratitude to my protector, feeling ashamed that I'd ever considered he wanted to steal my flashlight. As the three of us walked back to our camp, I kept my eyes peeled on the ground, scanning for the army of scorpions I imagined waiting in the dark to attack. None appeared.

With a hefty dose of adrenaline still circulating in my body, I lay awake trying to figure out how the tribal man could have known how close that the scorpion came to us. It almost seemed as if he'd heard it. It occurred to me that to survive in this environment, these tribal people's senses must have developed in ways different from ours.

THE NEXT MORNING, our tribal visitors plus a few friends returned and settled in to spend the day with us. After we ate breakfast, we had no plans for the rest of our day. We had no chores to do, no place to go, nothing to worry about (except that Conrad would leave us here forever). Peter and Val shared one of the overturned rafts with five of the locals, while I sprawled out on our other raft with four of our self-invited guests.

Rising at least 20 feet high, the flat-topped canopies of the grove of trees surrounding us provided enough shade to keep us from sweltering. Most of our visitors, all men, seemed to be in their 20s, though a few looked younger. One boy seemed fascinated by Peter's unruly mess of thick brown curls. In contrast, one side of the crown of the boy's head was clean-shaven, while on the other side a thick one-inch mat of black hair, the consistency of lamb's wool, grew from his scalp. Because of his distinctive hairstyle, Peter bestowed upon the kid the name Yin Yang.

The man sitting closest to me had a youthful look, but as he chatted with his tribe mates, his demeanor suggested a confidence and wisdom that only comes with age. He wore two strands of gray beads the size of pearls around his neck and a silver arm bracelet tightly coiled 10 times around his right upper arm. I wondered if I could discover his name. I turned to look directly at him to catch his attention.

Pointing at my chest, I said, "Brenda." Again, I pointed at myself and spoke my name. Then I pointed to his chest, turned my palms up, and waited for a response. He looked puzzled and cocked his head to the side. I repeated my charade a third time, leaning toward him to show I expected him to respond. At last, it dawned on him that I had asked his name. Proudly puffing out his chest, he answered, "Ademi."

When I sounded out, "Ademi," he nodded and broke into a smile, revealing his perfectly formed white teeth. As Ademi practiced saying my name, I applauded his effort. Next, I pointed at each of the men sharing my raft to learn all of their names. Since everyone seemed to enjoy this exchange, I continued the game by pointing at objects: my hand, my foot, my eyes. I would say the name of the object in English. Then they would say its name in their language.

I got some paper and a pen from my tent so I could make a vocabulary list of the English words and their tribal equivalents. We spent a couple of hours exchanging and practicing words. Though I suspected I'd never have a use for them once we left this camp, my list grew to about 60 words before we ran out of physical objects to name. The exercise left us mentally tired, so we just kicked back and sat silently together. My thoughts wandered in a daydream about what it would be like to live with a tribe here in the Omo Valley. It would be a simple life, devoid of all the gadgets and technology that complicated a life in America.

This tribe depended solely on the resources that nature provided them: their food, water, shelter, and clothing. They needed nothing more than what they could gather right from their immediate surroundings. The men sitting with me seemed relaxed, carefree, and genuinely happy. Most Americans I knew felt stressed, pressured by obligations to family, jobs, friends, and other responsibilities, leaving little time for feeling genuine joy and happiness.

I pondered what appeared to be a philosophical contradiction. Is it better for the wellbeing of our human spirit to live a joyful, simple life, dependent on natural resources, than to live in a fast-paced, stressful, achievement-oriented, technology-dependent environment? I feared I belonged to the latter group, not by any personal choice but through conditioning to conform to American standards and expectations. Pretty deep thinking for being in such a remote wilderness.

Peter and Val asked me what I thought about sharing our last bag of peanuts with our new friends. They needed a snack but didn't want to eat food without sharing. I felt the same about eating in front of them without offering them a taste. "I hope none of them are allergic to peanuts." I grimaced at the thought of unintentionally poisoning half the tribe. "If Conrad bought the nuts here in Ethiopia, I guess it would be fine."

We savored every peanut, eating slowly to make them last. Our guests recognized the nuts we offered them and accepted our generosity. Toward midafternoon, the men headed back to their village, leaving Peter, Val, and me to have some quiet time for ourselves. We still had a handful of uncooked spaghetti left and a partial tube of condensed tomato paste. Combined with water and a few dried herbs and spices, it filled our stomachs.

Just before dusk, our tribal friends returned. They chattered excitedly among themselves. One older man, completely naked except for a hollow gourd tied around his waist with a vine, held a foot-long piece of dried wood, four inches wide at one end, that pulsed with glowing red-hot embers. The log tapered down to two inches wide at the opposite end, where he gripped it with one hand. Were they going to perform some sort of ceremony? I hoped it didn't involve any sort of branding, thinking of how cattle breeders used red-hot branding irons to mark their cattle. Ademi must have noticed my concerned look as he approached me, smiling, and pointed up toward the sky. I looked up but saw only the treetops. What on earth did they have planned?

Just then the naked man started to shinny up the trunk of one tree in our grove. He defied gravity by clinging to the trunk with just his bare feet and one arm, the other holding the smoking log out away from his body. He climbed easily, as if on a ladder rather than a branchless tree covered with smooth bark. For his sake, the smooth bark must have been a godsend!

Near the top of the tree, he stopped and used the embers at the end of his log to poke at something. Several minutes passed. When he called down to his colleagues, Ademi pulled me farther away from the base of the tree. The log plummeted down, landing on the ground with a thud. The tribesmen cheered and hooted. Nearly as quickly, the naked man descended. He strutted over to where Peter, Val, and I stood.

We watched in amazement as he scooped his hand into the gourd and pulled out a clump of amber-colored liquid still mostly encased in its honeycomb for each of us. He placed a gooey clump of fresh African bee honey in my hand. Despite the less-than-sanitary conditions of the collection process, I knew that honey had antibacterial properties, so I figured eating the honey would be safe. I took a bite of the honeycomb. A divine wave of sweetness washed over my taste buds as the comb's crushed chambers released the warm, thick liquid. Such a delicious treat!

Not until I swallowed the honey did I feel the unexpected tingly burning sensation as the honey coated my throat. To me, the sweetness of the honey symbolized the gracious hospitality of this tribe in sharing their precious honey with us, while its afterburn reminded me it came from potentially dangerous wild African bees.

"This is sooo delicious." Valerie licked the last bit of honey from her fingers.

"Best thing I've tasted in Ethiopia," I replied. "At least these bees have behaved while we've been here. Let's not tempt them with any jelly."

Peter, still in awe of what we'd witnessed, said, "I think he used smoke from the burning log to paralyze the bees temporarily so they wouldn't attack him while he collected the honey, and that's why he wasn't wearing anything. That way, the bees wouldn't get trapped under skins and sting him while trying to escape."

Peter flinched as he asked Val and me, "Do you have any idea how painful a bee sting in a man's private parts would be, especially while dangling 20 feet in the air, clutching burning embers? I just don't know how he could do that. *I* couldn't shinny up that tree, even clothed and without a torch," he laughed.

The heavens darkened while we ate our sweet treat. We found the honey man and bowed our thanks to him for his dangerous effort. He dipped his head in response and offered to dig out more honey from his gourd for us, but we declined since our first helping had been more than generous. The men of the tribe gathered and headed back to their village while we settled in our tents. I expected to have 'sweet' dreams that night.

THE LOCAL MEN shuffled into our camp the next morning as we gobbled the last few spoonfuls of our oatmeal breakfast. As we'd done the previous day, we spread out and lounged on the rafts. While my Sobek mates and I speculated on when Conrad might return, the men from the village occasionally chattered in their own language. I wondered if they considered it their responsibility to protect us, or if they just enjoyed hanging out with friendly white-skinned strangers.

That morning, relaxing on the raft, it felt like the rest of the world no longer existed. I had no interest in the dramas unfolding in the bustle of American life. My world had shrunk to a 900-square-foot clearing within a grove of trees in the wilds of Africa. I had no inkling of what the next second or hour or day would bring. This feeling of being completely carefree filled my body with peace. My brain had only to deal with *this… present… moment*. My senses focused acutely on the tiny actions happening around me.

I listened to the breeze fluttering through the tree leaves above me. One man on my raft crunched on the end of a small twig. A page ruffled in Valerie's journal as she turned it and continued to scribble her thoughts. I listened to the sound of my breathing, and I could feel every beat of my heart. I had a sensation of floating, relaxed and inexplicably overflowing with joy. How could I preserve this moment? I wanted to remember it forever. I could think so clearly here, but once I got back home, I knew useless distractions would flood my brain, and constant disruptions from every angle would dull my senses.

A while later, the grinding gears of a truck in the distance interrupted our reverie. Could it be Conrad coming to our rescue? The whining of the engine grew louder as we waited. At last, the five-ton truck arrived at the edge of our clearing. We cheered to see Conrad jump down from the cab of the truck.

"We're outta here! Let's get this stuff packed up," he said, prancing about triumphantly. We engaged some of our tribal friends to help deflate the rafts by lying on the tubes to expel the air. Peter, Val, and I quickly broke down our tents and packed up our personal gear. Then all four of us folded and rolled the rafts into 100-pound round bales secured with bowlines wrapped around their centers. We heaved them into the back of the open truck bed, where Conrad supervised the loading. He called out the order in which he wanted to load the rowing frames, decks, oars, coolers, and other equipment. Our tribal friends willingly pitched in to help carry items to the truck.

"Any food left in the food boxes you can give to these guys." To carry out Conrad's thoughtful suggestion, we put aside what remained of the staples we'd been rationing: flour, pasta, rice, lentils, and oatmeal.

"Hey, guys," said Conrad, "I'm gonna ride shotgun with the driver in the cab, so you're gonna have to make yourselves comfortable back here. The trip will take us two days to get back to Addis, so we'll load your personal bags and the life jackets last."

With the truck fully loaded, I found the man named Ademi, my partner in learning their language. I led him to the small mound of surplus food where I gestured I wanted him to take it. Puzzled at first by what lay in the pile, after I pointed toward my mouth, he realized the clear plastic bags contained food. He nodded his acceptance.

Peter, Val, and I climbed to the top of the gear pile on the roofless truck bed. We rearranged our bags and life jackets to form what we thought would be a comfortable nest for the long ride. From where we sat, we could see over the side panels. The driver revved the engine, causing the truck to lurch forward. We waved farewell to our tribal friends. As they waved back, I reflected on the impact of our brief visit with them and hoped it had enriched their lives as much as it had mine.

IT DIDN'T TAKE LONG, just five minutes into our return journey, for me to realize that any hope of being comfortable was merely wishful thinking. For the first hour, we bounced, rattled and tilted precariously as the driver navigated an overland course, absent any clearly marked track I could see. The equipment below us shifted and resettled, lowering our perch by a foot. My neck became sore as I turned into a human bobblehead, unable to absorb the constant jarring of the obstacle-filled route. Eventually, we connected to a rutted dirt track, equally jarring. The oversized truck tires churned up a billowing cloud of thick dust that trailed behind us until the driver hit the brakes. Then the dust would swirl backwards, trapping us inside the choking cloud.

Toward midafternoon, the driver slowed to avoid a pack of 10 spotted hyenas bunched on both sides of the track. They growled ferociously as we approached, but when the driver stopped so we could have a closer look, they pounced on the sides of the truck, making a yipping noise that could be mistaken for a wicked laugh. Baring teeth, they snarled, but posed no threat to us in the truck.

However, I would have been terrified of being shredded to pieces had I encountered them on foot. I wondered if the creator made them so bizarre-looking by constructing them from spare parts of other animals. Each wore a coat of spotted fur like a leopard, stretched around the up-sloping frame of a giraffe, though similar in size to a coyote.

Their face, ears, and snout bore a resemblance to that of a small bear. Once the driver resumed our journey, they yelped and chased us until we could no longer see them in our dense trailing dust cloud.

By late afternoon, we arrived at the first settlement we'd seen since leaving our riverside camp. Only a dozen people lived in four buildings constructed of handmade bricks, and a few other less-sturdy dwellings framed by sticks and insulated with dried grasses. Conrad and the driver went to negotiate shelter for us for the night.

Returning to the three of us waiting in the truck, he explained, "A few residents have agreed we can rent space from them. It ain't luxury digs—I can tell you that. But it's just for a night."

Conrad paid the women to prepare a pot of spicy steaming lentil stew for us. We devoured it, hoping it wouldn't upset our stomachs later. With full bellies, Conrad and I followed a local man to a windowless six-foot by six-foot brick structure, topped by a tin roof, with a wood door and a dirt floor. All the shed contained was a filthy, cloth-covered, two-inch thick single mattress spread over a wood-framed cot, no table, chair or lamp. The air inside smelled of stale urine and old wood smoke. I wrinkled my nose and backed away.

"This is really gross, Conrad!"

"The rooms that we have are just about the same. Just make the best of it and get some sleep."

"Can't we just camp in our tents?" Already I missed our camp in the grove.

"You saw the hyenas. The men told our driver other types of wildlife roam through here at night, so no, you don't want to be in a tent tonight."

What a choice. Risk being eaten alive by a leopard or torn to pieces by a pack of hungry hyena or sleep in a filthy shed lacking air circulation with a stench that turned my stomach.

"Since you're a woman sleeping in here alone, this guy is going to put a padlock on the door to keep you safe, so no one can enter your space."

My jaw dropped. "What? He's locking me in here? What if I need to get out? What if I have to pee… or vomit? This is worse than a prison, Conrad."

"If you feel the need, just do what others have done based on the smell. Pee on the floor in the corner. Don't worry about it." He slapped my shoulder blade in a suck-it-up-way and wished me a good night. The door closed, and the lock clicked shut. I never dreamed I'd be a prisoner, locked in a windowless cell in solitary confinement. I spread my sleeping bag out on the cot but didn't climb inside. With no way for the air to circulate once he'd closed the door, residual heat from the sun absorbed by the tin roof and bricks radiated heat into the room like a sauna. Soon sweat soaked my clothes and dripped from my head. I tried so hard to fall asleep, but the heat and stench, my salty sweat, and the lumpy mattress conspired to keep me awake.

After about an hour, I heard scratching come from the other side of the room. Something had breached the armor of my cell. Listening carefully, I figured it had to be an animal digging for grubs or some other treat, probably a rat. I wasn't going anywhere, and neither apparently was it.

"You stay on your side over there and don't come near me, and we'll be just fine." Startled by my spoken words, the frightened critter abruptly stopped scratching, and silence filled the air once again. My eyelids slowly drooped shut.

I WOKE ONLY WHEN I HEARD the padlock rattling. The inside of the shed remained dark, but as soon as the door swung open, cooler fresh air rushed in, and the brightness outside momentarily blinded me.

"Time to get the hell out of here," said Conrad. "Grab your stuff and meet us at the truck. We're skipping breakfast, but we'll stop for an early lunch in a few hours."

It took me less than a minute to gather my things and escape to freedom. I climbed up to the top of the gear pile and took my place next to Peter and Val, who looked as relieved as me to be leaving this way station. The ride that morning offered some fantastic views out over the plains to the mountains in the distance. But the nonstop bouncing over the rutted track tempered my enjoyment of the countryside's beauty. I felt I might have to glue my head back onto my body when we finally reached the city. My neck and shoulders muscles ached from the strain of trying to keep my head upright in place. I could swear I felt my brain sloshing inside my skull.

Prior to noon, we stopped at a tiny quaint café in a sleepy village of a dozen newer-looking buildings. Three unoccupied weathered wooden tables and stools crowded the interior. Conrad spoke in Amharic to the man who greeted us as we entered. My mouth watered in anticipation when I heard him order *injera* and *wat*, the appealing food I'd enjoyed on my way to the river.

Turning back to us, Conrad said, "I wanted to get some *dorowat* with chicken and hard-boiled eggs for me and Brenda, but the owner reminded me that today is one of their meatless days, so we're all having vegetable *wat*. He also doesn't serve alcohol on fasting days. I don't trust the water here, so I asked him to boil some water for at least 15 minutes to make us tea."

He must have prepared the *wats* earlier that morning because he quickly delivered a large platter lined with the sour, spongy, pancake-like pieces of *injera* topped with four mounds of different vegetable *wats*. The selection included collard greens simmered in spiced butter, mushy yellow split peas cooked with onions, garlic and spices, a mixture of turmeric and coriander-spiced cabbage, potatoes and onions, and green beans and carrots cooked in a piquant green sauce.

The pungent scents invited us to dig in. Conrad started with a taste of the green beans and carrots. He coughed and sputtered before swallowing his first bite.

"Unless you want to try eating fire, I'd advise you to stay away from this one."

Tearing pieces from the *injera* with our fingers, we scooped up morsels of the other three *wats*. Each had a bearable level of heat. I favored the collard greens. Peter and Val liked all three. Each time Conrad dipped back into the green bean *wat* between bites of the others, beads of sweat formed on his forehead. He exhaled through his mouth as if that would lessen the burn left after he swallowed.

Watching Conrad consume the green bean *wat*, Peter said, "Man, you're eating it, so it can't be that hot. I use hot sauce on everything I cook at home."

"Go ahead. Try it then, but don't say I didn't warn you."

"Don't do it…" Val begged.

Peter tore off a piece of *injera*, scooped up a section of carrot and some of the sauce, and tossed it into his mouth. The full blast of fiery hot chili sauce exploded as he chomped on the carrot. "Holy shit, that's hot!" he mumbled with his mouth still full, while his arms flailed, waving in front of his mouth. Finally, he swallowed the bite he'd taken.

"The rest is yours," he said to Conrad, who chuckled at Peter's misfortune.

Unable to resist testing the heat level of this sauce, I decided to experiment. I barely touched a tiny part of a hefty piece of *injera* to the sauce. The others waited, watching for my reaction. At first, I only tasted the sourness of the *injera*. After a few chews, despite the miniscule amount of sauce I'd ingested, I felt the blaze on my tongue and inner surfaces of my mouth. It expanded into my nasal passages and made my eyes water. After I swallowed, I said, "That sauce could kill someone." The others laughed in empathy.

We finished all the *wats* and were chowing down the last pieces of *injera* when suddenly Val screamed, "Help!" She spat the *injera* in her mouth into her hand. "Help, I can't breathe! I need water! Quick!" Tears streamed down her face, and her wide-open eyes bulged in fear. Conrad shouted for the man to bring us tea.

"I see what happened," said Conrad. "The hot sauce from the beans soaked through the *injera*, and the excess liquid spread underneath, soaking the pieces next to it. She got a piece under the collards soaked with dynamite."

Val continued to cry and wince in agony. Peter held her hand. "Please help! I can't feel my mouth. Everything's burning."

Conrad shouted to the man again. He hurried over with a bowl of raw sugar crystals and a tray with our four cups of tea. Conrad ordered him to remove the lethal platter from our table. Then he mounded a spoon with sugar.

"Val, suck on this now. It'll help. I promise."

Valerie took the sugar and put it in her mouth. We waited. After a minute, she swallowed the sugar and asked for more. "I think it's helping," she said.

The shock to her system left Val looking like a limp rag doll. Conrad offered to let her sit up front in the cab, where the ride for the next few hours back to Addis would be more comfortable. That afternoon, the road showed continuous improvement the closer we got to the capital. Small farms scattered across the landscape also signaled our approach. The outskirts of the city sprawled with newer businesses, including a storage unit that Conrad directed the truck driver to stop at. There we unloaded the Sobek gear, safe behind a locked door until the next Omo trip departed.

Conrad accompanied us to our tourist-grade hotel in the center of the city, before returning to his own home in Addis. We met up later that night for laughs, drinks, dinner, and a last farewell, before the three of us would return to the United States the next day.

I'd spent nearly a month in a part of the world I hadn't known existed, with people who'd remained untouched by the accelerating speed of human invention. Tomorrow, I would board an aircraft that would carry me through time and space thousands of years ahead. I'd be returning to a world where people had largely lost touch with how to use nature's gifts to survive without permanently scarring the earth, or consuming natural resources at a rate faster than nature could replenish them. How *does* one prioritize the competing demands to continue creating gadgets, gizmos, and technologies that purport to improve the quality of human lives with the need to protect the natural world and its resources that have successfully supported human life since its origins? What an enigma!

Bodi tribe

UPDATE:

Since my journey down the Omo River, the Ethiopian government has authorized the building of a series of five massive dam projects along the length of the Omo that have or will drive tribes from their homelands and bury the river under massive lakes.

The Gibe I hydroelectric dam, located upstream from where Sobek's Omo River run began, went into service in 2004. The Gibe II hydroelectric dam south of Gibe 1 became operational in 2010.

The massive Gibe III 800-foot-tall hydroelectric dam, located 16 miles downstream from where I joined the trip, is Africa's tallest dam and has the third-largest power plant operating since 2015. This dam prevents the natural flooding on which 100,000 indigenous people depend for crop cultivation. Tribal people are suffering from hunger and continue to suffer abuse and harassment if they speak out about the situation. Many communities are under pressure to relocate to government villages, a policy that most oppose.

Construction on Gibe IV (known as Kyosha) began further downstream in 2016. It is expected to be completed in 2025. The Ethiopian government has already authorized Gibe V but has not yet funded the project.

In one of the most audacious land grabs that Africa has yet seen, since 2012, the eight tribes of Ethiopia's Lower Omo Valley are being evicted from their ancestral homes, and their grazing and farming lands are being transformed into vast industrial sugarcane, cotton, and biofuel plantations using water siphoned from the river.

Current estimates of the Mursi population are 7,500. The semi-nomadic Bodi tribe has an estimated population of 10,000. The chief visible distinguishing characteristic of the Mursi women, their lip plates, have made them a prime attraction for tribal tourism. Today, more than a dozen tour operators regularly offer quick, in-and-out photo-op trips to their villages. But now, many of the natives dress in recycled secondhand Western clothes and expect to get paid for the photos tourists take of them. Being aware that most visitors have no interest in getting to know them and their way of life, and only want an exotic souvenir, leaves the Mursi frustrated and feeling exploited.

Bodi man with feathers

MAP OF PAKISTAN

A : Islamabad - Capital City, My Home

2

ALMOST A KIDNAPPER

PAKISTAN - 1983 TO 1986

I CAME OF AGE during the flower child era of the late 1960s and early 1970s, at the height of America's cultural revolution when idealistic, freethinking youth protested to gain equal rights for all and argued for sexual liberation. The free-love phenomenon of Woodstock took place during the summer between my sophomore and junior years in high school. The live reports on television fascinated me as half a million "hippies" gathered in blissful harmony for the three-day music festival. On the fields of a rural Bethel, New York dairy farm 20 miles north of Woodstock, they transformed it into a community that symbolized peace and love.

Against the backdrop of the unpopular Vietnam war, the mantra of the event was "make love, not war." And the concert-goers openly made love with whoever they were with, shredding to pieces the taboo of being intimate with a partner before marriage. This changing norm confused me.

On the one hand, as a Congregationalist, churchgoing, prim and proper New England teen, the religious and societal norms of my parents had instilled in me the belief that having sex before marriage constituted a sin. But as a young woman filled with raging hormones, Woodstock's message sounded enticing: that having sex with a consenting partner illuminated the path to peace, love, and nirvana. Ultimately, peer pressure won out as my friends and I secretly experimented with Woodstock's new norms.

During the next decade of my life, I partnered up with several men. Some ended in heartbreak. Some fizzled from boredom. But the prospect of finding a new love always excited me. Still, I wondered if I would ever find my perfect soulmate, a person who could bring me a lifetime of happiness and fulfillment.

Gradually, the idea of spending the rest of my life with just one partner felt increasingly unrealistic, though I never gave up my belief that somewhere out there my prince might exist. With that mindset firmly established, I accepted an overseas position with the Department of State working for the United States Agency for International Development (USAID) in November 1983.

My first four-year posting landed me halfway around the globe in Islamabad, Pakistan, an Islamic country ruled by men who went to great lengths to protect the chastity of their female relatives. Most women only left their homes after dressing in clothing that covered every bit of their skin and *never* without a male relative to escort them.

I'd been briefed that the clothing appropriate for an American female in Pakistan excluded miniskirts, shorts, and tank tops, all clothes I'd been very comfortable wearing at home in the States. It seemed insane to have to wear long-sleeved shirts and pants when I'd been told the summer temperatures in Islamabad would soar to 100 degrees Fahrenheit, with some days topping out at over 120 degrees.

Far worse than my concerns about what clothing I'd be allowed to wear, I discovered women had *no* say in whom they would marry. An elder male relative, usually the bride's father, would negotiate the terms of a dowry, an exorbitant amount in gold jewelry, cash, or livestock to be offered to the patriarchs of other families looking for wives for their sons. Nearly half the time, the most desirous matches happened between first cousins, to keep wealth within the extended family and to strengthen the two families' reputations in their communities. This shocked me since the United States strongly discouraged marrying a first cousin. Many states prohibited the practice, while in other states, this form of inbreeding constituted a criminal offense.

That a father could "sell" his daughter, as a piece of property for the best price, to a groom's family for the purpose of enhancing a familial alliance disgusted me. How could marriage in Pakistan be nothing more than a business transaction? Where was the passion? What about love? It seemed inhumane. *Nobody* would ever tell *me* who I had to marry. I, alone, would make that decision. How would I ever make sense of this barbaric culture where women had no freedom and lived practically as prisoners in their homes?

When I arrived in Islamabad, I discovered I would live outside the walled American embassy compound, in a newly constructed sector of the capital city. Diplomats who had homes in the city employed local men as cooks, cleaners and gardeners because women, except in rare instances, did not work. I hired a dour-faced elderly man, at least twice my age, recommended by another diplomat. But I felt uncomfortable as a single woman, with him lurking around in my house. After two weeks, I discovered money missing from my wallet. I fired him on the spot. No way would I have a strange man, who barely spoke English, living in my house. I could take care of myself.

I soon learned how difficult it could be to buy fresh vegetables from vendors at the outdoor markets when I couldn't speak their language. The same went for fresh meat, slaughtered on demand at the blood-spattered butcher's shop. Whenever I went shopping, men stopped to gawk or hurl insults at me, an unescorted woman with an exposed head and parts of my arms and legs showing bare skin. My vulnerability in these uncertain situations left me fearful.

A few weeks after dismissing the man who stole from me, I heard a knock on my door. Through the peephole, I saw an attractive young Pakistani woman waiting outside. She appeared to be alone, which surprised me. Where was *her* escort?

The woman wore a traditional blue cotton flowered dress draped over solid blue matching baggy pants. A matching thin gauzy scarf covered her jet-black hair twisted in a bun. She smiled when I opened the door. Her brown eyes twinkled with anticipation, whether from relief that I had opened the door, or with anxiety about the proposal she had come to make.

"Hello, Madam, I am Laila." She struggled with the English words as if she had practiced to perfect them. "I can work for you."

I couldn't tell if she was making a statement or asking a question. She handed me a handwritten note written in English. It explained that she sought employment working for a foreign diplomatic family as a housekeeper, cook, or nanny. The note did not include any references from previous employers, nor was it signed.

She watched me read her note. When I looked up, her eyes eagerly searched mine for a reaction. She'd been brave to present herself at my door without another diplomat's formal introduction. Gutsy, I thought. My sixth sense urged me to take a chance on this woman. She might be the answer to my prayers for finding a trustworthy housekeeper.

Impulsively, I grabbed a pen from my desk and scribbled the amount in rupees I could offer her as pay. Her eyes opened wide with surprise as she nodded enthusiastically. She pantomimed she needed to retrieve her possessions from Lahore. "*Juma, teek hai?*"

Though I'd just started taking daily Urdu lessons at USAID, I'd learned that *Juma* was the name for Friday, the Islamic holy day and *teek hai* meant OK. She'd be back in two days. I responded "*Teek hai, Juma.*"

"*Shukriya, Madam, shukriya,*" said Laila, expressing her gratitude for the new job before scurrying down my driveway to meet a man who waited for her in the street just beyond my gate.

When Laila returned on Friday, I asked about the man traveling with her and discovered she was married, but her husband needed to return to a job he had in another city. Though an unconventional arrangement, her husband felt confident his wife would be safe with me until he could find employment in Islamabad.

That afternoon, we visited the huge outdoor market where I pointed out to her which vegetables I liked. She surprised me by fearlessly bargaining for fair prices with the much older leather-skinned male vendors with dirty white turbans twirled atop their heads. That evening, the vegetable curry, aromatic cooked rice, and homemade chapatis she prepared for dinner far outshone those of the male housekeeper I'd fired.

Laila managed all the household chores with ease and possessed a work ethic I admired. She'd point to household objects asking me to pronounce their name in English. One day, she pointed at a bottle in the refrigerator. Before I could tell her its name, she said to me, "Ketchup."

Her declaration amazed me. I wondered who had taught her that word. "Yes, Laila! It's ketchup." She beamed with pride.

She persisted in her efforts to learn my language, often surprising me with yet another new word she'd learned. When she'd finished cleaning up the kitchen after dinner, I often invited her to watch TV with me. Though Pakistani television rarely aired programs in English, except the BBC news, they broadcasted intriguing primetime dramas.

My Pakistani office colleagues encouraged me to watch these shows to bolster my understanding of Urdu. It not only allowed Laila the treat of watching these dramas, but she could help explain the parts I didn't quite follow. While shows on American TV increasingly leaned toward more sexually *risqué* content—bare body parts and explicit displays of affection—the fully clothed actors on Pakistani programs conveyed plenty of sexual tension but through subtle body movements and facial expressions. It seemed the popularity of these Pakistani dramas tapped into the unmet sexual desires of their viewers.

During my first four months in Pakistan, I dressed in the typical business attire I'd worn to my jobs in America, as did most of my American colleagues. But I'd noticed a few of my American female colleagues had adopted wearing the native women's *shalwar-kameez* and *dupatta*. One of them explained, "The local staff I work with love that I wear their style of clothing. By wearing their clothing, as a way of showing respect for them, I've been able to earn their respect in return. You should try it."

"Where did you get yours from?" I asked.

"There's a bunch of tailor shops in the center of the city. I happen to like this one guy whose prices are fair, and he offers a larger choice of more fashionable fabrics." She wrote his name and address on a scrap of paper and handed it to me.

That night, I told Laila that I'd like to visit the tailor to purchase a couple of outfits and asked her to come with me. My announcement took her by surprise, but she eagerly agreed to accompany me.

Normally when a Pakistani woman wanted a new outfit, she gave her husband a list of her body measurements and either a picture from a magazine showing the color and design she'd like, or her own hand-sketched design of the neckline, sleeve cuffs, or the band above her ankles. Her husband would deliver her information to a tailor, all of whom were men. The following day, her husband would return to retrieve her custom made *shalwar-kameez* and matching *dupatta*.

The address my colleague gave me led us to a row of eight tailor stalls, packed tightly together. Dozens of bolts of cotton and silk fabrics crowded the tables in front of each stall. The designs varied from pastel florals, bold stripes, paisley prints, and just plain solids, in every color of the rainbow. Several of the turban-wearing, white-bearded tailors, with bright orange-stained teeth from chewing betel nuts, called to us in an attempt to persuade us to stop at *their* stall. Laila located the recommended tailor and explained I wanted to buy two *shalwar-kameezes* from him.

I searched through the bolts of material and, with Laila's advice, selected four cotton bolts that would make two coordinated outfits. Unfortunately, I didn't have a list of my body measurements to give him, so he got out a tape measure and left his seat behind the table to come into the street where I stood.

The other tailors stared and goaded him on as he wrapped his tape around my bust, an awkward motion I suspected he'd never attempted on a Pakistani woman. I wanted to swat his hands away from my chest, but he obviously couldn't make my outfit without getting my measurements. When he tugged the tape measure taut across my breasts, Laila immediately scolded him for his touchy-feely liberties. The male onlookers sneered at the reprimand. I sorely yearned for the Jordan Marsh store back home.

Two days later, we retrieved the finished outfits. I tried them on at home and found that they fit well and felt delightfully comfortable. Still, it felt strange to wear clothes that reminded me of pajamas. The first day I got the courage to dress for work in *shalwar-kameez*, the locals in my office praised me with compliments. "*Memsahib*, you look like one of us now," the male supervisor of the accounting office told me.

Anadia, one of the female project accountants, who always wore the latest in vogue styles of *shalwar-kameezes*, admired my new outfit. "That looks so pretty on you," she remarked, while Muzhirah, our department's administrative assistant, clapped with delight to see her boss dressed like a native. "Now, you must buy some gold jewelry to wear with it."

Honestly, I had no intention of dressing like the Pakistani women, but I loved how comfy my new clothes felt. Even more, I enjoyed seeing how thrilled it made my staff that I would willingly wear their style of clothing. Also, despite having blue eyes and light brown hair, a conspicuous rarity in Pakistan, I attracted less attention outside the USAID mission building when dressed in Pakistani garb.

Encouraged by the success of my wardrobe change, I wanted to buy more *shalwar-kameezes*, but I dreaded the thought of returning to the original tailor. Laila sensed my hesitancy.

"Madam, I bring you to Aminah," she said. The young female seamstress she knew accepted private sewing orders. Laila praised Aminah's innovative designs and told me they exceeded the quality of the male tailors in the stalls where I'd bought my first outfits.

A FEW DAYS LATER, after buying six more two-yard pieces of cotton material at the market, we knocked on the door of a mud-plastered dwelling in a poor section of Islamabad. A petite girl dressed in a fashionable *shalwar-kameez* cordially greeted us and invited us inside. Draped over her neatly coiled bun of shiny dark hair, she wore a shimmery embroidered gossamer *dupatta*. She led us into a small room where her treadle-powered sewing machine rested on a table next to neatly piled bundles of colorful cottons.

Laila translated as we drank the obligatory cup of chai she had prepared. Fourteen-year-old Aminah lived in this three-room home with her parents and three younger siblings. Word of her creative designs had spread throughout her neighborhood, with satisfied clients recommending her to their friends.

Aminah's growing list of clients brought their materials to her house, selected their designs and returned a few *weeks*, not *days* later, to retrieve their completed orders. To keep up with the constant backlog of orders, she began sewing right after school, stopping only when exhausted, to climb into bed.

She opened a folder containing dozens of pencil-sketched designs. The inspiration for her *shalwar-kameez* drawings came from *avant-garde* dress styles in European fashion magazines. She got the glossy publications from wealthier clients looking for innovative chic. No tailor shop in the city would have anything like her exclusive designs, she stressed, proudly displaying her drawings for me to see.

It surprised me that Aminah had such an entrepreneurial spirit at her young age. Despite her proven talent, she confessed I made her nervous, being the first diplomat that she'd ever met, let alone designed clothes for. I selected one sketch with an intricate braided design around the neckline of the *kameez*, one with a Nehru-style standup neckline, and a third with a stylish eight-inch pintucked placket on the front. She skillfully recorded my measurements on a piece of paper, then attached it to the folded materials I handed her. She and Laila decided on a date when we'd return to retrieve my new clothes.

Three weeks later, Aminah welcomed us inside her home once again. I couldn't wait to see the creations she had fashioned with my materials. She retrieved my *shalwar-kameezes* from a pile of folded clothes on a shelf behind her sewing machine. Shyly, she unfolded each piece, watching my face for signs of approval.

Laila watched for my reaction, too. "You like, Madam?" she asked.

"*Bahot, Bahot pasand hai!*" At my expression of delight with her workmanship, Aminah relaxed and giggled with relief. I paid her an amount greater than what she told Laila I owed, and I promised we'd return soon. I said nothing to build up her hopes, but after I started wearing her designs, I felt sure she'd be adding more female diplomats as customers.

My beautiful new outfits fit perfectly, garnering me more compliments. Aminah became my "go to" seamstress. I grew fond of our monthly visits to her house with new fabrics to be transformed into wearable fashion. At each visit, she revealed exciting new designs for me to choose from. I never had to repeat a style.

During one visit, she dared to share her secret dream with us. Nearly all Pakistani girls fantasize about marrying and producing sons for their husband's family. Aminah, however, envisioned a completely different future for herself: studying fashion design abroad and creating her own clothing brand.

It seemed an impossible goal given the financial resources required, let alone how much Pakistani society frowned on an unmarried woman leaving her home unchaperoned. A single Pakistani woman traveling abroad on her own was unthinkable.

To keep her plan secret from her family, she'd discreetly begun to hold back a portion of her earnings before contributing the rest to assist with the family's expenses. I feared she might be setting herself up for disappointment, though she'd already created a small but viable moneymaking business for herself. Sheer determination drove her forward. I wanted her to succeed and readily offered words of encouragement.

OFTEN, I ATE LUNCH in our mission's cafeteria with the three highly educated Pakistani women in my department, all married to men who valued their wives' lucrative US government jobs. Through our casual conversations, they enlightened me about women's roles in their culture. I'd gained their trust enough to question them about their arranged marriages. That tradition continued to gnaw at my belief that women should be treated as equals with men and take part in decisions that affected them.

Genuinely curious, I asked, "Isn't it scary to marry a man you don't even know?"

"It is," said Ayesha, a younger project accountant, who had wed two years earlier. "But we trust our parents to find us a good husband. A man with a good job, a supportive family and wealth."

My mother's cynical critiques of past boyfriends and *my* father's advice to look for a husband at local bars made me cringe at the thought of who *they* would pick for me. "But what if your parents pick someone who you don't like or who doesn't like you?"

"It doesn't work like that," said Anadia. "After my husband and I married, it took time to get to know each other, but we agreed to work together to do our best to create a successful marriage."

"But do you love him *now*?" I asked, hoping that between them they had kindled a spark of true love.

"Oh, Brenda, what is love?" She stared at me as if I'd spoken a foreign word that didn't apply to her.

"Here, marriage is our duty. It's an obligation we fulfill for our families. They expect us to produce offspring, preferably sons. Our marriages are more like a partnership. We grow to respect and support each other. We don't expect to have the *romantic* type of love you Americans chase after. Besides, I'm told it doesn't last."

Ayesha interrupted to drive home that point. "Look, compare our two countries. When our parents choose spouses for us, a divorce is rare. But when *you* choose who *you* want to marry, how many marriages end in divorce in the United States? 50 percent?"

Touché! Her estimate sounded embarrassingly true. "But I'm not sure I could ever marry someone I didn't love," I replied, "I'd want to spend time with a person to see if we shared common interests and values before making such a lifelong commitment. How in the world do they expect you to be intimate with a stranger?"

Muzhirah, ten years older than me, giggled. "I didn't know my husband at all. On our wedding night, I told him to stay away from me over in the far corner of the room. For several days, I made him sleep on the floor."

A comical image arose in my mind of strong-willed Muzhirah fending off her bewildered new husband on their wedding night, but the scene lacked humor. I couldn't understand how being forced to be intimate with a man you didn't know could be anything but rape, and that thought sickened me.

Even Ayesha looked startled before saying, "You did?"

Muzhirah retorted, "I certainly did! But now, after a decade together, we have a strong bond and three amazing kids. Things *do* get better with time."

"Would any of you say you love your husbands?" I asked timidly.

Muzhirah quickly answered. "My husband treats me well. He's dependable and kind. If anything happened to him, I would be sad."

Ayesha added, "Of course we have differences of opinions, but my husband *will* listen to me. We have fun doing things together, like taking picnics high in the foothills. I think he's a good match for me."

Anadia, more reserved in her response, said, "Sometimes I worry. Even after five years of marriage, we still don't have children, despite trying. My husband and his family are extremely eager to have a child." The heads of her two Pakistani colleagues swayed from side to side in empathy, acknowledging the burden she bore from being unable yet to deliver a baby.

Our illuminating conversation left me with much to consider, but didn't alter my belief that I could pick a better husband for myself than anyone else.

PAKISTANI FAMILIES EXPECTED to spend a small fortune on a lavish wedding to honor and celebrate the groom bringing a new member into his family. The wealthier the couple's families, the more extravagant the wedding events and the larger the number of invited guests. For her special day, the bride's tailor meticulously adorned her maroon wedding *shalwar-kameez* and *dupatta* with intricate gold thread embroidery that dazzled in the light. The size of the dowry the bride's family offered could be measured by the number of 22-karat gold earrings, bangles, and intricately designed necklaces embellished with rubies, diamonds, and garnets that garlanded her bosom.

But such celebrations weren't always possible, I had learned, when first introduced to one of my older staff members shortly after I arrived in Islamabad. The first time we conversed, he immediately lamented, "Ah, *memsahib*, I am the unluckiest man in the world."

"Why do you say that?" I asked. A look of unmistakable misery saddened his face.

"*Memsahib*, I have 11 daughters and not one son. Even if I work until I die, I will not earn enough to save for a dowry for every daughter. How does a father choose which of his daughters he will provide a husband for?" His voice trembled with anguish as he shook his arms in the air. "I have failed as a father. It is a father's highest priority to arrange marriages for all his daughters, and I have betrayed some of mine the opportunity for a husband and their own babies. It is a terrible thing!"

I didn't have words to console him, but empathized with the quandary he faced. It underscored for me the significance of marriage in this male-dominated culture. At least a single woman like me in the United States could work and support herself if she chose, an opportunity denied to an unwed Pakistani woman.

DURING MY POSTING in Islamabad, I received an invitation to attend the wedding of the sister of a member of my staff. Being curious about the marriage ceremony, I accepted. It took me aback to learn that the bride would marry her first cousin. I urgently attempted to warn my staff member of the genetic risks of the proposed liaison, but my words fell on deaf ears as his family clung to their traditional practice.

The bride's family organized the first event of the three-day long celebration. Along with the bride's female friends and relatives, I attended her *mehndi* ceremony, during which a skilled artist applied a red-orange paste of henna to stain the bride's hands and lower arms with a delicate, intricate, lacy pattern.

It took hours to complete the design, during which the gathered women sang, danced, and ate delicious treats. They took turns feeding the bride sweets soaked in rose syrup, since she couldn't use her hands to touch anything once the artist applied the wet paste. Also, during the ceremony, the women taunted the bride with descriptions of her future husband.

"Your groom is bald and looks hideous!" said one friend.

"And he's only got one good eye and walks with a limp!" another exclaimed.

The cruel taunts became worse as time passed. An older female relative mocked the bride, "You'll have to watch out for his fierce temper if you don't want a beating. And his nauseating body odor surely will make you sick."

Confused and upset by the brutal mocking of the groom as the bride sat silently helpless, I turned to Muzhirah, sitting next to me. "Why are they being so mean to the bride? Isn't it horrible enough that tomorrow she'll be leaving the only home she's ever known to go off to live with a stranger and his family?"

She explained this women's tradition played a useful role in lowering the bride's expectations. "They aren't really being mean. They do this because if they can plant an image of a hideous ogre in the bride's mind, when she gets her first glimpse of her new husband, whatever he looks like, she'll be relieved by the pleasant surprise."

As I watched the ongoing barrage of insults, I noticed the bride put on a show of being upset, but she timidly embraced her role, playing it to perfection. When the artist completed the design, which included concealing the couple's initials within it, she wrapped the bride's hands in towels to protect her artistry until the henna fully dried by the following morning.

"The purpose for concealing the initials within the pattern," Muzhirah explained, "is to spark a conversation between the couple once they are alone. It allows the husband to approach his wife tenderly. Together, they search for their initials, giving him the chance to caress her hands."

THE FOLLOWING DAY, my staff member's family rented two large outdoor tents to be set up in the field across from their house, one for the men and another for the women. I entered the women's tent to witness the "ceremony." Even though the couple had yet to meet, the bride, surrounded and encouraged by her female entourage, took her place inside the tent and waited.

Meanwhile, in the men's tent, the groom, attended by his father and the male elders of both families, signed the marriage contract in the presence of two witnesses. The signed contract then went to the bride, who also signed it in the presence of two witnesses. Once the mullah had reviewed and blessed the document, they became legally married. Sight unseen! It reminded me of the stories I'd read of mail-order brides shipped to pioneers in the 1800s American west.

Once news of the mullah's blessing reached the assembled guests, everyone dug into a feast of epic proportions, including roasted legs of lamb and goat and a variety of meat and vegetable curries, rice, and naan bread. Male guests filed through the buffet serving area outside the tents first, then ate together in their tent. The women needn't have worried about there being slim pickings after the men filled their plates because the caterers hustled to keep the serving platters topped off with fresh steaming delicacies.

I spotted one of my favorites, biryani, a rice dish cooked with pieces of chicken, raisins, cashews, and cardamom pods, seasoned with saffron, turmeric, ginger, and garlic. I scooped a mound of the aromatic combination on to my plate, then topped it with a few spoonfuls of mouthwatering sweet-and-sour tamarind chutney. Inside the women's tent, my female work colleagues had saved me a seat.

While we enjoyed our meal, skilled musicians played traditional songs, inspiring some women to dance, swaying and twirling gracefully among the guests in the tent. The bride sat alone on one of two chairs placed on a raised platform. Her female relatives took turns offering her food and showering her with congratulations. I noticed she barely ate anything. Although she looked fine to me, I'd heard that often mothers gave their newly married daughters heavy doses of tranquilizers to calm their anxieties about starting their new lives with an unfamiliar family.

By midafternoon, the solemn part of the wedding arrived when the groom's closest relatives led him to meet and claim his wife. The bride's mother, upon hearing the procession approach, stationed herself beside her daughter.

Muzhirah whispered to me, "Watch what happens now." The mother draped her daughter's sparkling *dupatta* over the entire upper portion of her body, fully concealing her face. "Here he comes now," she said. The men's tent emptied as they marched to the opening of the women's tent. Inside, the women formed a pathway extending from the tent's entrance to where the bride sat waiting patiently. Only the groom and one attendant entered as a hush fell over the crowd. Muzhirah explained the process. "He'll go sit beside the bride now."

I watched in curiosity as the groom approached and stepped up onto the platform. Was he as nervous as his wife at that moment?

"Now, the bride's mother will cover him, too, with the other end of the *dupatta*, so that no one can see either of their faces."

When properly veiled, the bride's mother accepted an eight-inch square mirror from another woman. Leaning in close, she whispered to her daughter through the *dupatta*, before reaching under the cloth to find a hand from each of them. She slid the handle of the mirror into their hands and stepped away.

Muzhirah grinned, perhaps remembering *her* first glimpse of her husband. "They are now seeing each other for the first time, not directly, but as their reflections in the mirror."

I had a tough time reconciling the contrast of how in America, before we ever went on a first date, we usually would have seen and spoken with each other, whereas a Pakistani woman wouldn't even see her husband until *after* she had married him. It seemed absurd and somehow ethically wrong, but there it was, unfolding in front of my eyes. I could never imagine myself in this bride's place.

Silence ensued while the guests eagerly waited for the couple to reveal themselves. Muzhirah whispered, "This is a very private, intimate moment for the couple, preparing to face the world as man and wife. When they are ready, together, they will lift the *dupatta*."

When I saw the bride's shy smile, I could tell that their concealed introductions had gone well. I joined the women, clapping for their happiness, hoping this shared moment would ignite a deeper connection between them that would ultimately strengthen their marriage. The most challenging part of the marriage for the bride came next: parting from her family, the only ones who had ever held a special place in her heart. The time had come for her kin, who had taught, protected, sheltered, fed, and loved her to let her go. She now belonged to her husband's family.

The couple stood together, hand in hand. Her husband helped his wife down from the platform and led her through the cheering crowd in the tent to the colorfully decorated vehicle waiting outside to bring them to her new home. Her female relatives behind in the women's tent hugged and shed tears. I couldn't tell if the tears flowed with sorrow or happiness—probably both.

With the events of the day over, the guests thanked the bride's family and headed back to their homes. My staff member, brother of the bride, found me. "What did you think of the wedding?" he asked, grinning with pride.

I assumed he expected superlatives to flow from my mouth, but all I could muster was, "It was… different. Elaborate. Lots of gold. Fantastic food. I hope your sister will be happy."

THAT NIGHT, I felt spent as I changed out of my clothes and flopped onto my bed. I could only imagine the busy night ahead for the new bride. Although not as common in larger cities like Islamabad, many families still followed the custom of displaying a bloodied bedsheet the morning after the wedding as proof the marriage had been consummated and the bride's virginity taken. To me, the vulgar practice bordered on obscene and humiliating.

Not only that tradition bothered me, but I'd felt shocked when I read a newspaper story one morning during breakfast about a married couple living in a remote village. Their baby had been born only eight months after their wedding. Convicted of having sex out of wedlock, the local officials condemned them to death by stoning! The villagers buried the parents in the ground with only their heads exposed, then heaved heavy stones at them to fracture their skulls. I felt like vomiting. What if the baby had been a preemie? With no educated doctor to intervene, they'd committed this horrific act.

I skipped the new couple's celebratory feast hosted by the groom's family the following day, knowing I'd get a full report of the event from my staff who attended.

THROUGHOUT THE THIRD YEAR of my assignment, I continued to receive compliments on my unique *shalwar-kameez* designs from friends and staff. On one of our trips to Aminah's house, I noticed, when she greeted us, an alarming difference in her normally energetic demeanor. Her eyes no longer twinkled, but appeared red and swollen, as if she'd been crying. As usual, she politely invited us to come in.

She'd made a pot of tea. After serving me, she turned to serve Laila. Behind her back, I caught Laila's attention. Silently, I pointed at Aminah and then to my eyes, shrugging my shoulders in question. Laila noticed too and inquired what had happened. Aminah burst into tears, inconsolable as Laila hugged and rocked her like a baby. I sat helplessly waiting for Laila to reveal what tragedy had beset our distraught seamstress. Had one of her parents died? Had a doctor diagnosed her with a serious medical condition?

Finally, in a serious voice, Laila spoke to me. "Madam, her parents have arranged Aminah's marriage."

"What! She's barely more than a child. She's only 16! What were they thinking?"

Laila stared at me sternly as if to say, "It's done. There's nothing *you* can do about it."

Obviously, Laila could see how much this decision had upset Aminah, but *she* failed to understand the tragedy *I* saw unfolding. "This can't happen!" I said, waving my hands in front of me, like a magic wand that could erase the past.

With a steady voice, as she continued to comfort the sobbing young seamstress, Laila said, "Madam, this *is* the time, when daughters turn

16, that families start their search for mates for their daughters. They want to give her the chance to have her own family."

"No, it's not right." I vigorously shook my head. "She hasn't even finished school yet. And she wants to have her own business. Do you think her husband will allow that?"

Laila looked away, staring out through the dusty window. I sensed her holding back something she wanted to say. What was she not telling me?

Furious, I asked again. "Will she still be able to have her own business?"

Laila slowly turned her head back until her eyes met mine. She bowed her head and softly said, "No, Madam." Seconds ticked by in silence, interrupted only by Aminah's involuntary sniffling. Why would a husband not want his wife to help support their family, especially when she could work inside her home? Surely her clients would continue to support her.

As if reading my thoughts, Laila answered those questions. "Madam, her future husband is 40 years old and lives far from here in a remote village. He is an uneducated farmer who is already married with several children. Aminah will be the second wife."

Laila's words left me breathless, unable to speak. In that split second, I saw Aminah's dreams shattered like a crystal glass flung against a brick wall, splintering into razor-sharp shards. My gut told me I had to stop this marriage from happening. My own eyes welled with tears as I realized how wildly her life had spiraled out of control. I crossed to Aminah and also wrapped my arms around her small, sobbing body.

I needed to come up with a plan to prevent Aminah from being sent to a distant outpost where her knowledge and skills would be wasted. In theory, Islam allows a man to marry up to four wives with the caveat that he treats each wife fairly and equally. In reality, as second wife, her responsibility would be to bear her husband more male babies and to take housekeeping orders from the first wife. I couldn't imagine Aminah living that way.

Maybe I could stage a direct intervention with her parents. On second thought, I could imagine her hostile parents berating me for interfering and screaming at me to mind my own business. Might *I* give her family money so I could adopt her? Crazy too, since I doubted I had enough money to offer what they might expect. But I had to get her away from her family and hide her so they couldn't find her. Suddenly, a flash of genius struck me. I would simply kidnap her and hide her in my house. My diplomatic immunity guaranteed that no one could search my house. It offered the perfect safe haven.

I couldn't take her with me *that* day because I'd need to do some serious planning to pull off this caper. I asked Laila to find out from Aminah when the wedding would take place. She told Laila it would take few months to make the arrangements. Great! I had time to work out a plan.

On the way home, I told Laila about my plan. Her eyes grew wide, and she shook her head forcefully. "*Nahi*, madam, *nahi*! You don't understand this culture. If you remove her from her family, you will turn her into an outcast. She will be disgraced. No one will ever want to marry her. You will ruin her life. Please don't!"

Of course, I didn't agree with her, believing that Amina's family had arranged her marriage to discourage her entrepreneurial ambitions. I didn't argue with Laila, but the weighty tension between us on the drive home kept further conversation at bay. That night, I spent hours plotting how I might carry out my intended kidnapping. It would be anything but straightforward, and logistical questions kept mounting. Finally, I opted to seek the advice of my female staff the next day at lunch.

"LADIES, I NEED YOUR ADVICE," I said to Muzhirah, Ayesha, and Anadia, once we'd settled ourselves at one of the square tables in USAID's cafeteria. "I'm thinking of kidnapping my young seamstress so she doesn't have to marry an old guy in the middle of nowhere to be his *second* wife."

Muzhirah immediately burst out laughing at my preposterous statement. "You can't do that. What would you do with her?"

"She can live in my house with me and keep sewing. I'd protect her with my diplomatic immunity!"

"You'd create an international uproar," said Ayesha. "The ambassador would have you shipped out of here on the next plane. Then what would happen to your seamstress? I'm sure *she* doesn't have a passport." Ayesha chuckled, shaking her head at my idiotic idea.

I'd been so occupied thinking about how to protect Aminah that I hadn't thought through the consequences *I* might face.

"But Aminah deserves to have a better life and a chance to use her talents!" I protested.

"Don't we all?" said Anadia, leaning into the table and speaking in a kind voice. "Brenda, I know that living in a culture so foreign and strange to you is a challenge. We know that sometimes you think the way we lead our lives is wrong and some of our customs conflict with your values. But remember, we've been living with our traditions for thousands of years, not just a few hundred years like you Americans. This is our way of life. We are not unhappy. You may think your seamstress is unhappy, but all of us have a duty to obey the elders of our families, and we take that duty seriously. Your seamstress has a duty to her family as well, and she *will* do what they ask of her."

Muzhirah, seeing I still looked doubtful, added, "Really, she will be fine, especially because she *is* so smart. For all you know, she will take her sewing machine with her and make fine *shalwar-kameezes* for all the women in her village. Who knows? Perhaps she'll start a sewing school for girls or a sewing cooperative for the women in her new village. And she will have babies to raise and love that will bring her so much joy. There is no more important role in the world for a mother than to guide her children to become good, productive adults. Just think, someday she may have four or five little ones as smart and as ambitious as herself, who will gradually transform that village. Each person contributes not only to making their family stronger, but their village, too. She *will* be fine."

"Really? You really think so?" I asked. They had flooded my mind with countless possibilities I hadn't considered. The scenarios they described didn't sound nearly as bad as where my imagination about Aminah's life had led me. I desperately wanted to believe that Aminah would be alright.

Anadia took one of my hands in both of hers. "Trust us, Brenda, each one of us had to go through the shock of our parents telling us they had picked a husband for us. At that moment, we all felt afraid, but each of us got used to the idea, got married, and here we are today."

Muzhirah pointed out, "Consider yourself lucky, Brenda, that you won't ever have that moment of terror to deal with, but good luck finding yourself a husband. If I had to do that on my own, *I'd* be terrified!"

We giggled together, knowing that as females, we'd created a lasting bond of friendship that surpassed our different religious and cultural beliefs.

THAT NIGHT, AT HOME, I apologized to Laila and told her, "I've decided not to kidnap Aminah."

I explained how my female work colleagues had guided me to a different understanding of Aminah's situation.

Her face lit up with a smile as she brought her hands together in prayer. "Thanks be to Allah!" We hugged, and then she added, "Madam, Allah will guide Aminah, and you too."

That night in bed, I realized how wrong I'd been to think I had the right to wrench Aminah away from her family and the life she'd been born to lead. Nor did I have any right to impose my values on a culture I did not truly understand. Just before I fell asleep, I prayed for Allah to watch over Aminah and me, and to find us both kind husbands.

Pakistani bride

UPDATES:

When I revisited Islamabad seven years after this story took place, I found the marriages of all the women in my former office remained intact and growing stronger. Neither Allah nor I succeeded in finding a husband for me. Considering the consistently high divorce rates in the United States, with 50 percent in first marriages and 67 percent in second marriages, I'm actually glad that I've remained single.

After the 9/11 World Trade Tower bombings in 2001, American sentiment significantly turned against Pakistanis. One of my former staff members called to see if the tragedy had affected any of my family or friends. I felt deeply touched that he had reached out to me. I told him no one close to me had been killed. He told me how most of the Pakistani people felt terribly embarrassed and ashamed of the people from their country who took part in the attack. As an afterthought, he asked if I'd gotten married.

In 2023, according to the World Economic Forum's Gender Gap Report, Pakistan ranked near the bottom at 142 out of 146 countries with gender parity of just 57.5 percent measured across four key dimensions: economic participation and opportunity, educational attainment, health and survival, and political empowerment. The previous year, it had ranked 145 out of 146.

Bride's henna

MAP OF PAKISTAN

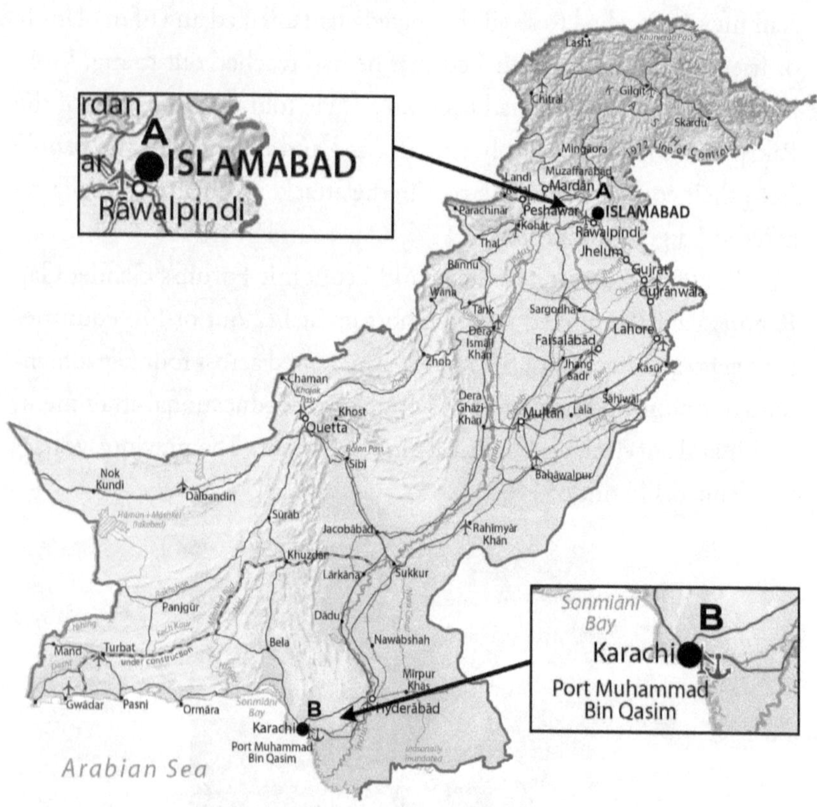

A : Islamabad - Capital City, My Home

B: Karachi - Chuck's Home

3

EARTHQUAKES, BOMBS AND MURDER!

PAKISTAN 1983-1986

THE HEADBOARD OF MY BED crashed against the wall, jolting me awake. *What the heck? Was someone at the foot of the bed shoving it forward?* The headboard slammed the wall again, and again, in consecutive waves. In the pitch black of night, terrified, I clung to the edge of the mattress being tossed like a dinghy against a rocky shore in a tempest. I wanted to scream out for help from the other guests. *Were they as frightened as me? Were their beds rocking like mine?*

My bed's wild romp ended after 15 seconds of sweat-drenching fear. Still, my heart raced as my brain searched for an explanation for this anomaly. Footsteps pattered quickly down the marble staircase from the second floor. Someone turned on a lamp in the spacious lounge outside my bedroom. Light seeped under the crack between the bottom of my door and the floor. I fumbled for the switch of the bedside lamp and turned it on. Above me, the triple-tier chandelier swayed like a pendulum.

I'd arrived in Islamabad, Pakistan, barely a week before, to begin a four-year assignment for the United States Agency for International Development (USAID). For the first month, until a construction team completed building the house the State Department had leased for me from a wealthy Pakistani government official, they'd assigned me to a room in their fully staffed guest house frequented by visiting diplomats.

Afraid and confused, I quickly threw on my robe. I sensed no further vibrations in the marble floor, cool on my bare feet, so I quickly joined the other six pajama-clad, robe-wrapped guests who had congregated in the lounge. Despite the seriousness of the moment, it amused me to see these professional colleagues not wearing work-related business suits and dresses.

"Damn, that was a good-sized earthquake," one man said.

I'd never felt the rumbling of an earthquake, though I'd lived in California for four years in the Sierra foothills east of San Francisco. We'd had one minor quake, but since I'd been driving in my car when it hit, I'd missed feeling the ground tremble.

"Are we sure that was an earthquake and not something else? Like a bomb?" I asked.

I knew that four years earlier, an angry mob of Pakistanis, primarily students, had breached the protective walls of the American embassy compound. During their violent attack, they burned all the buildings to the ground and killed two Americans and two local embassy employees. It had taken just a false radio broadcast from a religious Iranian cleric claiming Americans had masterminded the seizure of a sacred mosque in Saudi Arabia to incite the riot. I had no intention of participating in a replay of that catastrophic event.

"If it was an earthquake, there may be aftershocks," an older gentleman warned.

Suddenly, a female guest slapped her forehead with her palm. "You know what? I brought my shortwave radio so I could listen to the BBC news. Maybe they'll have a report on what happened." She raced upstairs to retrieve it from her room. When she returned, she placed the radio on the lounge's coffee table. Still shaken from the rude awakening, I sat on the floor close to the radio.

If an earthquake struck, I'd been taught the safest place to be was outdoors, away from any structure that might crumble. But if a bomb had exploded, I'd want to seek refuge inside a solid structure. I had no desire to go back to bed until I knew for sure what had happened. I presumed the others felt the same as we lingered around the radio, making small talk. The guest house cook, who occupied a small living area at the rear of the guest house, eventually appeared and offered us steaming cups of hot tea.

At 4:12 a.m., the pleasant speaking voice of a female broadcasting London's BBC news at noon announced, "We've just received word from Islamabad, Pakistan. An earthquake measuring 3.9 on the Richter scale has struck the capital region. The extent of any damage is unknown."

The confirmation of the seismic quaking of the earth brought me an unexpected sense of relief. Despite the fright we'd experienced, everything in the guest house remained intact and undamaged. Gradually, everyone drifted back to their rooms to catch a few more hours of sleep. While I waited for the adrenaline rush to wane, I reflected on the risks I knew I'd be taking by coming to Pakistan. Based on several factors, from health risks of tropical diseases to national infrastructure instability, foreign service officers received an additional 25 percent post differential in our pay, in recognition of the hardships of living in Pakistan. Earthquakes, though, I hadn't expected. How many other unknown risks might I face living on the opposite side of the globe from the US? Thankfully, that night, I felt no aftershocks.

THE DISCUSSION AT BREAKFAST the next morning and in the office continued to center on the earthquake. While eating scrambled eggs and fresh fruit in the guesthouse dining room, I started a conversation with the older man who'd warned of aftershocks. He told me his name was Chuck.

"Have you been in earthquakes before, Chuck?"

"Oh, a few over the course of a lifetime, I suppose."

"Any here in Pakistan?"

"Well, this one." I detected sarcasm in his voice from posing a question I already knew the answer to.

"Of course, I meant any other ones here?"

"They mostly happen in the northern part of the country. Small villages sometimes get wiped out. But not where I'm based in Karachi in the far south."

"What do you do for work?"

"What is this? 20 questions? What's *your* job here?" he asked.

The snideness of his comeback to my innocent question surprised me. I felt my cheeks flush with embarrassment. *Should I not have asked that question? Was he a covert operative with the CIA?* Diplomatically, I answered first.

"This is my first posting with USAID as the budget and accounting officer. I just got here last week, and I'm trying to meet people and figure out which offices they work in."

"Ha! Ha! So they've trapped you in this hellhole for four years. Damn." He shook his head and rolled his eyes, letting me know he felt for me. "Sorry to give you a hard time. I'm an auditor for USAID, inspecting programs here and in other countries in this region. I'm staying in this guest house for a few days while I review project documents kept in the office here."

It relieved me to see a smile break out on his face. His tough, steely exterior belied a soft heart after all. During our shared breakfasts and dinners at the guest house, I gathered tidbits and insights into Chuck's life. His four years of service in the Navy seemed to have etched a default expression of seriousness on his face. He showed the practiced discipline of a man who had been in the military. Although strands of gray highlighted his short, brown hair, the sturdy build of his body hinted at his commitment to regular exercise. I had little doubt that he could easily take down an adversary if challenged.

He rarely initiated conversations, but when I questioned him about working in foreign countries or about his personal life, he fully engaged in lively discussions. I discovered that at age 50, he'd arrived in Karachi earlier that year for what he intended to be his last overseas posting. Having joined USAID in 1967, he'd served the agency for 17 years at posts in Vietnam, Ghana, Morocco, Thailand, Panama, and Washington, DC.

"Yeah, my first post was in 'Nam during the toughest years of the war. My wife didn't want me to go, but I told her I wouldn't be going anywhere near the fighting. For that tour, my family remained in the States. After that, they came with me to the other countries. It was great for the kids to be exposed to the way other cultures live, and we had the chance to do some fun traveling as a family."

"Are they here with you in Karachi?"

"Hell no. This isn't the safest place in the world right now." *Did he think I needed a reminder of that?*

In response to the angry crowd setting fire to the embassy in 1979, the Security Office had enforced heightened security measures. Any vehicle entering the grounds of US government facilities had to stop outside the gates, open their trunks for inspection, and have the undersides of the vehicle scanned using a mirror attached to a long pole. They also assigned local security guards to stand watch around the clock at the gated driveways of USAID diplomats who lived outside the embassy compound.

"My wife would have come, but this isn't a place I wanted to bring my kids. Listen, it's just for another year—then I'm outta here. A couple more in DC and I'm done."

He sounded like a man biding his time in a place he really didn't want to be, and he didn't hold back on his cynicism. "Our government spends millions of dollars every year eradicating opium poppies from the farmers' fields here. Drug lords need the sap from the seed pods to make heroin. They pay the farmers far more for the poppies than any other crop they could grow. Why wouldn't they grow poppies? Once the poppies bloom, USAID send bulldozers into their fields to destroy the crops, but the farmers just reseed their fields the following year. It's like flushing money down the toilet."

A FEW DAYS LATER, on Saturday afternoon, I climbed the stairs to the guest house's flat rooftop terrace, an essential feature of nearly every house in Islamabad. It provided a convenient escape during the stifling heat of summer when sleeping inside became impossible. Families hauled cots up to their terraces to sleep under the stars in the relatively cooler outdoor night air. But I intended to use it to soak up some sun while writing in my journal. It surprised me to find Chuck comfortably settled in a chair on the terrace, reading a book. I sank into another of the cushioned chairs.

I explained to him how being outside on a breezy sunny day reminded me of my previous work as a whitewater river guide.

"That's something I've always wanted to do," he said. "What rivers did you guide on?"

"Mostly on the Stanislaus River in California's foothills north of Yosemite. The Army Corp of Engineers wanted to build a huge dam that destroyed the section of river we used for rafting to provide cheap water for agriculture corporations like Del Monte in the Central Valley."

"Sounds about right to me," he said, his tone laced with cynicism.

"We fought so hard to save the river. At our urging, our rafting clients wrote letters to their elected representatives. We organized lots of protest rallies against the Corp of Engineers. My boss and I, along with the owner of another rafting company, even flew to Washington DC to lobby senators and representatives drafting the Wild and Scenic Rivers Act. We didn't let up until the legislators agreed to include the Stanislaus River in the bill that sat on President Jimmy Carter's desk waiting to be signed on his last day in office.

"Then all hell broke loose as it appeared Iran might release the American hostages held captive for over a year. Carter diverted 100 percent of his attention to the hostages' release, so the bill that would have protected our wild and free Stanislaus never got signed, leaving *it* hostage to the damn dam builders." My voice trembled with the sadness and the anger of losing the river.

"Doesn't surprise me a bit. Sorry you couldn't save your river. Half the time, our government doesn't know what the hell it's doing." Something triggered inside him. He closed his book and sat forward, cheeks reddening before he spoke again.

"I'll tell you one thing. What our government did to those American hostages in Iran was unforgivable. There's no way in hell those poor innocent folks should have been forced to endure 444 days of torture and humiliation, confined like prisoners. Our military forces should have been in there on day one. For Christ's sake, the Iranians invaded *our* embassy." As he ranted, anger seethed with every word, his frustration palpable.

MY RECENT ORIENTATION with the State Department had included a module on what to do if one found themselves taken hostage. Since the late 1960s, hostage-taking commonly occurred with airplane hijackings, which averaged 40 per year. All but a few ended without loss of life. The instructor began his briefing with a warning.

"When you accept a position as a diplomat, understand that if you become a hostage, you are on your own. The United States does not and will not negotiate with terrorists. Do not expect the government to rescue you. Use the information I'm going to give you to increase the odds of your survival."

Wow! His opening remarks felt like a gut punch. I'd thought the opposite would be true. *Didn't we, as diplomats, enjoy special privileges in foreign countries that regular citizens didn't have? So wouldn't our skills, our knowledge, and our lives be worth the effort to save?* Apparently not!

Actions the instructor recommended included: don't confront or argue with your captor, do what they tell you to do, try to establish eye contact with them to build a bit of trust, if possible, because psychologically, it becomes much more difficult for a captor to kill someone with whom they've created a bond. Before going overseas, he stressed the importance of having a plan for exactly what we would do if taken hostage. I'd found this advice uncomfortably morbid, but he insisted it would help us and our loved ones if we knew exactly what each of us would do during my captivity, should the unthinkable happen.

I dreaded talking with my parents about potentially being a hostage one day. After explaining why we needed to have this conversation, I rubbed my palms together and told them my plan. "If I'm ever taken hostage, every day, *I'll* take time to remember the fun sleepovers I had with my friends in the bunk beds of the tree house you made for us, Dad, between the oak and elm trees out back. And every night, *I'll* say a prayer asking God to return me safely home to you."

After a few awkward seconds, Dad jutted his chin at Mom, letting her decide what their side of the deal would be. Her eyes became moist as she said, "Dad and I will remember how much fun we had when you took us rafting on the Stanislaus River. What a fun trip that was! We'll pray every day that you'll come back to us unharmed."

I never expected the relief I felt from knowing we'd created an invisible, unbreakable bond from heart to heart.

If Chuck had ever attended such a briefing, by now, he'd decided the State Department's advice was worthless crap. The plan of the soldier in him demanded drastic action.

"If anyone ever tried to take me hostage, I'd tell them to go to hell. Then I'd whoop their ass and make them sorry they ever tried to mess with me. No, sir, no one is going to take *me* hostage!" He made a victory fist pump before adding, "People are too damn afraid and weak these days to stand up to their adversaries."

His strategy left me baffled. Unless he carried a concealed gun, I couldn't fathom how he thought he'd stand up to an armed terrorist. It sounded like a recipe for disaster. Then again, *I* wouldn't want to take on an enraged Chuck.

A few days later, I gave Chuck a hug as he checked out of the guest house before boarding a flight back to Karachi. Beneath the man's prickly exterior, I'd discovered his vast knowledge of the world, his remarkable dedication to his work, and how he adored his family above all else. He'd been kind to me during the first two weeks of my new career. I looked forward to our paths crossing the next time he came to Islamabad.

A YEAR LATER, on December 4th, late in the afternoon, our USAID Mission Director unexpectedly strode into the Controller's office. "I'd like you all to come over here." He stared at the floor while we left our desks to gather around him. Something terrible must have happened. The grave expression on his face filled me with a sense of dread. When he looked up at us, his moist dull eyes revealed the grief he struggled to contain.

"I'm afraid I have some bad news to share with you. Yesterday, terrorists hijacked an airplane headed to Pakistan, demanding it to be flown to Tehran. We believe that three of our USAID auditors were on that plane returning home from an audit in Yemen." Gasps shattered the silence, as the Mission Director's nod only confirmed our fears. My heart sank as I recalled my conversation with Chuck. I prayed to God that Chuck was *not* one of the auditors on that plane.

"The embassy has received an initial limited report stating the terrorists have killed a male passenger who remains unidentified. I will let you know more when we get updated information. But right now, please join me in a moment of silence and hope for the safe return of our colleagues."

The fact a passenger had been killed sent chills through my body. There were absolutely *no* facts that pointed to Chuck as being the dead man, but in my heart, I knew if he was on that flight, it would be him. I returned to my office, closed the door, and sat staring blankly at the foothills in the distance through my window. As the reality of the situation set in, I put my head on my desk and sobbed. Overwhelmed by a sense of helplessness, anger exploded inside me. I hated the terrorists.

As news of the hijacking spread around the globe, a chaotic scramble by journalists competing for early details, some inaccurate, ensued. That night and the following day, I watched the BBC news coverage and learned that on December 3rd, 1984, four Lebanese hijackers affiliated with Hezbollah took control of Kuwaiti Flight 221 bound for Karachi, carrying 155 passengers and 11 crew. They ordered the pilot to fly to Tehran, Iran. Shortly after the plane landed, the hijackers, brandishing four handguns and two grenades, ordered all Americans and Kuwaiti citizens to move to the first-class section of the plane. Minutes later, a shot rang out from the front of the plane. Afterward, the hijackers carried the fatally injured body of a male to the plane's door and tossed the body out onto the tarmac.

The hijackers then threatened to blow up the plane if Kuwait didn't immediately release the Shia terrorists they had imprisoned the previous year. Meanwhile, the identity of the murdered hostage remained unknown. Two days later, on December 6th, the hijackers forced a second male hostage to the doorway where they executed him by shooting him six times in his back, causing his body to fall forward onto the tarmac.

The following day, all USAID staff crowded into the largest conference room in our building to learn more about the continuing saga playing out in Tehran. The Mission Director began by telling us the terrorists had released women and children but still held all the male passengers and the crew. He then said, "Unfortunately, I'm truly heartbroken to tell you that based on evidence obtained from the dead bodies by the Swiss embassy after the second murder, we now know that the first person killed by the terrorists was our friend and colleague Chuck Hegna. Two days later, they murdered another of our dedicated colleagues, Bill Stanton. A third USAID auditor is still being held captive."

Though my premonition had prepared me for this revelation, I stood frozen in disbelief. Chuck was dead!

MEMORIES OF CHUCK'S FEISTY SPIRIT and tragic death served as a constant reminder of the growing number of terrorists in the Middle East. During the next two years, other USAID missions in the Asia region invited me to help train their accounting staff. They needed guidance to transition from their manual accounting ledgers to USAID's new automated system being implemented globally. Eager to explore new countries, I readily accepted these short-term assignments.

However, Chuck's death made me increasingly uneasy about traveling to India, Nepal, Thailand, and Egypt, as news of terrorist attacks and plane hijackings continued to make headlines.

Prior to my arrival in Pakistan, I never entertained the notion that I might become a target of brazen terrorists. However, Chuck's death had smacked me with a harsh dose of reality. I decided that if *I* bore the ultimate responsibility for my safety, I would be wise to find ways to blend in with the Islamic people.

I chose to wear the country's traditional attire: a three-piece outfit of baggy pants banded at the ankle; a long-sleeved, below-the-knee-length dress; and a gauzy scarf worn over the head or draped over the shoulders. One of my local staff found me a secondhand copy of the Koran written in both Arabic and English that I stashed in my carryon luggage. After the tragic hijacking, the State Department allowed foreign service employees to travel with a regular US citizen's passport rather than their Diplomatic Passport if they felt safer doing so.

Shortly after my arrival, I began daily private hour-long lessons with Ahmed, the embassy's Urdu instructor. Most of the Americans in Islamabad had attended the Foreign Language Institute and passed their required language proficiency exam in Spanish or French before being posted abroad. So only a handful of American diplomats interested in learning Pakistan's complex national language looked to Ahmed to gain a basic spoken fluency.

But USAID sent me directly to Pakistan without requiring prior language training, so I had to sign an agreement to get that waiver. It gave me two years to achieve a higher level of spoken proficiency in Urdu to pass the grueling language exam, back in DC on my home leave. I told Ahmed during my first lesson that my least favorite class in school had been French. Back then, I never imagined I'd have a job that would require me to master a foreign language, certainly not one with an alphabet of strange symbols and where verbs *ended* the sentences.

Ahmed faced a daunting challenge to ensure my proficiency reached the passing level, but the stakes I faced couldn't have been higher. If I failed the exam, I'd be out of a job.

BESIDES ENSURING MY EMPLOYMENT, I realized the better I could speak Urdu, the easier it would be to conceal my American identity. One day, in the middle of a lesson, I asked Ahmed, "What would be the best phrase I could use if someone asked me to prove I'm a Moslem?"

Wrinkling his brow in surprise, he said, "Why are you asking me this?"

"In case I get hijacked or attacked by an angry mob of students. So they'll let me go."

Ahmed laughed, throwing his hands up as though I had missed the obvious. "But you have blue eyes, Brenda. That alone is a dead giveaway."

I knew that 99.9 percent of Pakistanis had brown eyes and dark hair, but I argued back.

"Some Americans in the United States with blue eyes consider themselves followers of Islam."

"In the US… maybe. But not here in Pakistan."

I frowned and looked away as he teased me. Once he realized that my request had been serious, he backtracked. "Okay, Okay. Here's what you should say—*Bismillah al-Rahman al-Rahim*. It means in the name of God, the most gracious, the Most Merciful. We say it before dressing, eating, working, even getting in a car."

I practiced saying it a few times until Ahmed nodded his approval. Then I committed it to memory.

IN EARLY 1986, a telex arrived from the USAID mission in Dhaka, Bangladesh, inviting me to provide two weeks of training for their accounting staff. Not that I needed an incentive to make the trip, but the American Controller of the Accounting Office doubled as an amateur astronomer. He owned a high-power telescope for viewing the night skies from his rooftop terrace. Since Halley's Comet would zoom past Earth for the first time since 1910, we planned my trip to coincide with the comet's closest approach during the first two weeks in April. This would be the first and only opportunity during my lifetime to view this fiery phenomenon. I felt lucky I'd get to witness the comet with an avid stargazer.

The Bangladeshi accountants quickly learned how to work with the new system. The only interruption of our work came one afternoon when a terrifying lightning storm passed over Dhaka. Ominous gray clouds obscured the sun, creating the illusion that night had come early. The sudden crackle of a brilliant flash immediately followed by reverberating thunder startled me. Suddenly, hailstones came hurtling down from the sky, pelting streets, buildings, and cars, mimicking the sharp, percussive strikes of someone banging on a snare drum.

I headed toward the office windows, wanting to watch the havoc being wreaked by the deluge on the street below.

"Brenda, stay away from the windows," shouted one of the local accountants, stopping me in my tracks. "This hail is really dangerous and can easily shatter glass." I noticed everyone had crowded into the center of the office's open bullpen. As the fury of the storm reached its peak, I could see hailstones the size of baseballs whizzing past outside. I thought of farmers working in their fields, hoping they'd had time to seek shelter. I felt certain that if any of those hurtling ice projectiles struck a person, it would instantly kill them.

Just as I thanked God for the safety of being indoors, a hailstone slammed into one of the office windows. The impact sounded like a small bomb flinging shards of broken glass into the office. I cringed, waiting for the next explosion. How many of our six windows would survive the onslaught? I'd never been in an active war zone, but hunkering down to wait out this storm must have been like waiting for incoming enemy fire. For several minutes, the siege of ice balls continued, but the storm spared the rest of our office windows from a direct strike. When, abruptly, Nature's spigot shut off the flow of hail, I rushed to a window and peered down at the devastation.

Three floors below, a layer of crystalline white hailstones covered the street. The violent pounding had shattered the windshields of two-thirds of the vehicles parked along the side of the road and left them dented with small craters. The offices on the opposite side of the street displayed exteriors pockmarked with broken windows. What a mess! Fortunately, carports behind the building shielded the vehicles of USAID employees.

I needn't have worried about how we would get back to the controller's house that night because, within 30 minutes, the humid 85-degree air temperature outside had melted the hail. Puddles of water filled the potholes, turning the street into a watery obstacle course. We threaded our way home through a maze of destruction—broken storefront windows, downed tree branches, overflowing drainage channels resembling small rivers—to reach the residential neighborhood where the controller lived.

During my stay in Dhaka, clouds shrouded the night sky dome on most nights, concealing any view of Halley's Comet. However, my last night there, April 15th, coincided with Halley's closest pass to Earth. A cloudless sky revealed a brilliant display of twinkling stars. After dinner, my host's family and I climbed to their rooftop terrace where he'd placed his telescope for an optimum view of the comet. Its route passed just above the horizon directly over the Libyan embassy next door.

We took multiple turns gazing at the comet and its tail. The telescope's magnification let us zoom in on each section of the comet: the nucleus, the coma, and the tail of dust and gases. While waiting for our turns at the telescope, we amused ourselves by joking about how the Libyans would react to our under-the-cover of darkness observation of their embassy. For all we knew, they might have thought we were spying on them (though our merriment and laughter easily countered that theory). For half an hour, I watched the comet's progress, then excused myself to pack my suitcase for my flight back to Pakistan the next day.

WHILE WE SLEPT PEACEFULLY that night, the US Air Force, the Navy, and the Marine Corps covertly carried out Operation El Dorado Canyon in retaliation for the Libyan sponsorship of terrorism against America troops and citizens. The US military had linked Libya to the bombing 10 days earlier of a Berlin discotheque, a hangout for US military personnel that resulted in the deaths of two servicemen and injured 79 Americans. The precise strikes on multiple locations across Libya by our military aimed to eliminate Libyan leader Muammar Gaddafi caused extensive destruction of crucial infrastructure. Nevertheless, he cleverly eluded capture.

When I strolled into their kitchen the following morning, the somber expressions on the faces of the controller and his wife immediately caught my attention. Before they even spoke, I could tell something bad had happened. They briefed me about the concerning news being aired on BBC TV.

The controller said, "Reports of the attack have gone global. All American embassies are on full alert for potential reprisals."

"Oh, crap!" I said, instantly fearing the predicament I faced. "You know, a few years ago, a mob of furious Pakistanis led by university students, stirred into a frenzy by an unfounded rumor, burned the embassy to the ground. *This* isn't some false claim. The entire world is seeing pictures of this attack! God only knows what they'll do now. I'm not sure that I should fly back to Pakistan today."

"I'm wondering the same thing. You're welcome to stay a few more days in Dhaka if things get out of control in Islamabad," the controller offered.

"How safe do you think *you* are?" My voice resonated with concern, a subtle recognition of his own vulnerability. "Damn! You live only 50 yards from the Libyan embassy. They know you're Americans. What's to stop them from attacking *you*?"

The controller shrugged his shoulders and exhaled deeply. The entire world waited in uncertainty. In hindsight, I wished we hadn't been pointing the telescope at their embassy last night. I didn't like either of my choices.

"Maybe I should call my office to see if they think I should return," I said.

We agreed that checking in with my bosses would be prudent, so once we arrived at his office, the controller booked a called to Islamabad. The Bangladeshi phone company estimated it would take half an hour for an outgoing line to become free. While we waited, I kept weighing the pros and cons of the two choices. In Bangladesh, I'd be with other Americans, but whether that would be a wise choice was debatable. Even with my Koran and ability to speak Urdu, as an American woman traveling solo, I'd definitely feel vulnerable flying back to Karachi, then on to Islamabad.

When we got the callback placed to my boss's office phone number, I halfway expected the mission would be closed or operating with essential staff only, so it surprised me when he answered on the third ring.

"Hey, Dave, what's going on in Islamabad? Are many people protesting? I'm scheduled on a flight back to Karachi this afternoon. Is it safe to come back there?"

My rapid-fire questions caught him off guard.

"Why wouldn't you come back?" he asked.

Baffled by his nonchalance, I said, "Well, pictures of our attack on Libya are being broadcast everywhere. Last time with no solid proof of American aggression, Pakistani protesters burned the embassy to the ground."

"It's been pretty quiet around here so far. I don't see any reason for you not to come back."

Dave's lackluster risk assessment of the situation in Islamabad left me unsure if I could fully trust his judgment. Even if he said everything seemed fine at the moment, I worried that despite his assurance, chaos could erupt at any moment. "When I get to Karachi, I'll call you again just to be sure things haven't gotten out of hand."

With the decision to return made, the Controller arranged for a USAID driver to take me to the airport. As I waited for my flight to board, the quandary of whether to go or stay lingered in my mind like a never-ending game of ping-pong. Self-doubt tormented me. Was I crazy to get on this airplane headed to Pakistan? A plane that anti-American fanatics could hijack? To transport me to a city where the angry voices of mobs filled the air, screaming blasphemies at America? Delivering me to a terrifying end of my life on Earth…? That's what happened to Chuck.

Part of me wanted to go to the check-in counter and buy another ticket for a flight back to the United States, where I would be safe. But what if Dave was right? There'd be no valid reason not to return. I'd never felt more frightened in my entire life than I did at that moment.

"Pakistan International Airlines flight to Karachi is now ready for boarding." The announcement echoed through the departure hall, causing a mad dash of people to swarm the entryway to the plane. I waited until nearly everyone had disappeared down the ramp. Then I stood and hesitantly walked onto the plane.

I ARRIVED BACK IN KARACHI that evening. As the plane descended into the country's largest city, I saw no signs of unrest, no burning buildings, no streets jammed with protesters. I took that as a good sign. Outside the airport, I found the USAID driver who'd been tasked with delivering me to our guest house in Karachi, where I would stay overnight. I asked him if there had been unrest in the city because of the bombing. He told me there had been a couple of small protests in a few locations. The route to the guest house we took avoided any potential hot spots, and I saw nothing out of the ordinary on the ride.

I didn't bother to call Dave the next morning because all the news outlets reported the country's urban centers remained calm. On board the flight to Islamabad, I mused how little attention the Pakistani people had paid to the Libyan bombing, or at least the lack of reaction it had provoked. Everything seemed normal.

During my Urdu lesson the next day, I said to Ahmed, "I worried there would be an extreme reaction by Pakistanis to the Libyan bombing, since TV and newspapers prominently featured images of the attacks. But everything seems quiet here. Why?"

"That's simple," he said in a matter-of-fact tone. "When they burned the embassy, the students were on break from their classes with ample time to indulge in mischief. However, now they're completely focused on taking their final exams with no time to spare."

All the Pakistani families I knew had a deep commitment to their children's education, with the kids themselves striving to outperform each other in pursuit of top grades. So Ahmed's explanation made sense. He felt confident that no delayed protests would arise after exams concluded.

A FEW MONTHS LATER, while reviewing and approving invoices to be paid, I felt a tremor cause our building to vibrate. I sat frozen at my desk, my concentration broken by the intensifying rumbling. It reminded me of standing on the platform above the tracks of a yet-unseen approaching train. The air pulsated with an invisible force, despite the absence of train tracks anywhere near our office.

The powerful tremors continued. My floor-to-ceiling windowpanes squealed as each wave compressed the glass, trying to bend it. I needed to escape. Through my open door, I heard my staff anxiously repeating, "*Zalzala!*"

Racing through the accounting office, I screamed, "We need to leave NOW! Everyone follow me!" Terrified as I descended the stairway already crammed with others fleeing from the shuddering building, I never looked back. My gut instinct told me I needed to get outside as fast as I could. By the time I dashed through the door into the parking lot, the tremors had nearly subsided. Catching my breath, I surveyed the staff gathered outside. To my utter shock, I discovered only the American staff had evacuated the building. Not a single one of our Pakistani staff had joined us.

Ten minutes after the earthquake ended, our head of security cleared us to reenter the building. Back in the accounting office, I demanded to know why my staff had defied my order for them to leave the building. I got a few sheepish looks, but no one answered me.

"I'm serious. If this building collapsed, it could have killed you. During an earthquake, you need to get *out* of buildings so you won't get trapped in rubble if the quake damages them."

No one said a word. A few shook their heads, believing I'd given them the wrong advice. Finally, Ali bravely stepped forward. "The reason we don't run or try to escape during an earthquake is because we believe if you get injured trying to escape, that injury will never heal. If you break a leg, it will be useless for the rest of your life."

His statement dumbfounded me. They would rather risk their lives than try to save themselves! Others murmured words to support Ali. I could see how deeply embedded this belief had become in their culture. None of *my* warnings would change their minds.

Ali continued, "Don't worry, Miss Brenda. We protect ourselves by standing in the frame of a nearby doorway or crawling under a desk. Allah will protect us."

Since experiencing the surprise of my first earthquake in Pakistan, I'd researched the impact of earthquakes in Asia. I learned that Pakistan lay in one of the highest seismic zones in the world, with Islamabad rated likely to suffer moderate-to-severe damage from earthquakes. For my staff's sake, I hoped Allah *would* keep them safe.

That evening, I discovered a large crack that ran from near the ceiling diagonally along the entire length of a wall in my living room. Another crack had formed on a wall in my bedroom. USAID had the owner call a building inspector to evaluate the crack. Since the fracture extended completely through this interior wall, chipping paint on both sides of it, I wondered on what basis the inspector had concluded these cracks to be superficial and harmless. If another earthquake struck at night, I wanted to be prepared. I practiced the 15 large strides I'd need to escape through the front door to the driveway in less than 10 seconds, hopefully with enough time to save myself.

OVER THE NEXT SIX MONTHS, the embassy issued a couple of notices asking Americans to be diligent when outside their homes and workplaces. They suggested parents drive and pick up their children from the American school because intelligence reports suggested terrorist groups had been tracking the movements of foreign diplomats.

Out of the blue, six months before the end of my four-year assignment, I got a telex from the boss I served under during my first two years in Islamabad. Back in Washington, DC, he oversaw post assignment scheduling for USAID Controller office staff globally. He asked if I had any interest in curtailing my assignment in Pakistan early to be transferred to the USAID mission in Barbados.

His message floored me. They wanted to send *me* to a tropical island paradise that other staff considered a dream assignment. I took a few seconds to be sure I wasn't missing any practical reason to stay in a land of frequent earthquakes, potentially deadly tropical diseases, angry protestors and terrorists, halfway around the world from home. Not a single reason to stay came to mind.

I wrote a telex back to my first boss: "Yes, I enthusiastically accept your offer to transfer to Barbados."

Brenda dressed in shalwar kameez

UPDATE:

Pakistan continues to have devastating earthquakes, many of which top 5.0 on the Richter scale. In 2005, a 7.6 magnitude earthquake in the northern Azad Kashmir area became the deadliest in Pakistan's history, killing at least 86,000 people.

The conversations I had with Chuck have stayed with me throughout my life. His death devastated his family, who subsequently sued the Iranian government under the US Antiterrorism and Effective Death Penalty Act enacted by Congress in 1966. The damages awarded to the Hegna family totaled hundreds of millions of dollars, yet their efforts to recover frozen Iranian assets held by the US government have yielded limited success.

I couldn't wait to get to my dream job in Barbados, but once I arrived, my heart filled with disappointment when I discovered the job differed significantly from what I had envisioned. Items cost nearly double in the capital city, Bridgetown, compared with similar items in the US. While I dreamed of feasting on a variety of fresh fish and shellfish, local flying fish provided the only plentiful and reasonably priced ocean dwelling food source. The residents ate flying fish fried, broiled, grilled, baked, and as fishcakes nearly every day of the week.

I discovered I could drive completely around this tiny island measuring only 21 miles long and 14 miles wide in less than half a day. After exhausting my options for adventurous explorations within a month of my arrival, ironically, I became a hostage (of a different sort) to its confined space.

Worst of all, shortly after arriving, I learned my first boss secretly hoped that by relocating me to Barbados, I'd be able to tackle the challenge of restructuring a completely dysfunctional finance department. After enduring six miserable months with no sign of progress, I resigned from USAID and returned home to the US.

MAP OF GUATEMALA

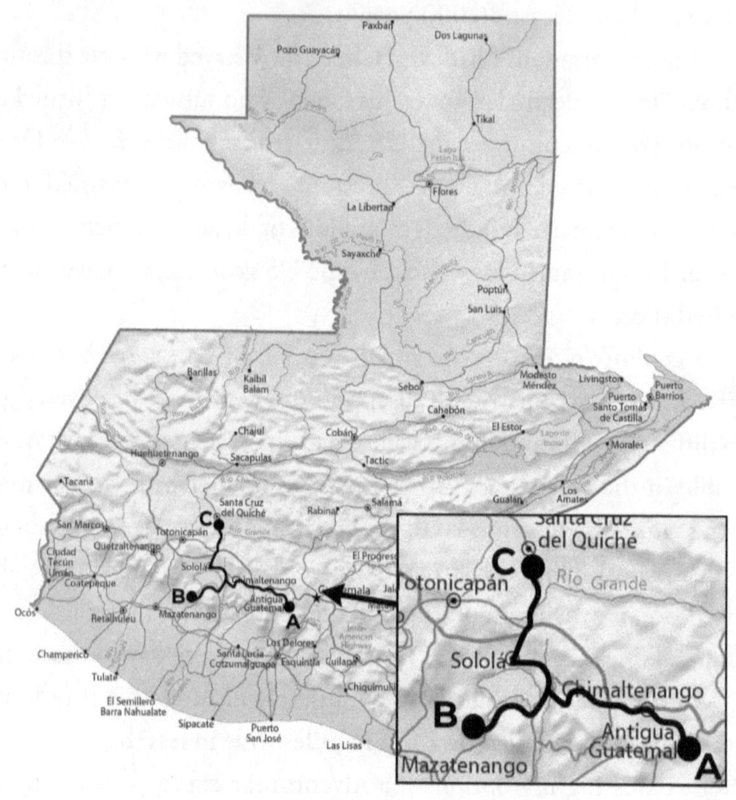

A: Antigua - Language School

B: Santiago de Atitlán - Home of Maximón

C: Chichicastenango - I Meet Josh Again

4

SHATTERED

GUATEMALA - 1988

"DON'T MESS AROUND with Maximón." They *all* tried to warn me.

The American embassy in Bolivia had sent me for two months of intensive Spanish study at the Language Institute in Antigua, a colonial village nestled in a valley surrounded by volcanos in Southern Guatemala. My local host family argued nothing good could come from my going to see him. "His village is a very dangerous place for foreigners to visit," they said.

The cheerful young woman behind the counter at the local bakery I often frequented after class shuddered when I expressed an interest in meeting Maximón. She handed me a chocolate chip cookie, still warm from the oven, and begged me to stay away from him. Even my Spanish teacher, Maria, sorely regretted ever mentioning Maximón to me. Foolish me. I chose not to heed their advice. My reckless disregard led to Maximón driving a knife through my heart. At least, that's what it felt like.

Since my stay in Antigua coincided with the holy days of Easter, Maria gave me a booklet describing the religious traditions of the Guatemalan people to read for one of my lessons. I learned most were practicing Catholics who observed the elaborate traditions of their faith. Just after sunrise on Good Friday, my host family and I joined hundreds of other Antiguans to celebrate one of their ancient traditions on an ancient cobblestone street near La Merced Church. Each family brought baskets overflowing with a variety of freshly picked floral species: blood-red rose petals, deep purple bougainvillea blossoms, blue hydrangea flowers, golden sunflowers, and other colorful local blooms.

We had just six hours to design and build an elaborate floral carpet covering every inch of the mile-long route the religious procession would follow. As the sun inched higher in the sky, the *jefe*, responsible for designing our 20-yard section of the carpet, vigorously conducted our 50 pairs of hands, like a maestro leading his musicians in a military march. Stooped over, I worked feverishly for hours, carefully spreading handfuls of petals and blossoms inside chalk-drawn shapes on the cobblestones, following the *jefe's* instructions.

As my back muscles tired, I paused to inhale nature's balm, the heavenly bouquet of fragrances that sweetened the surrounding air, then dutifully returned to my task. When our team completed filling the last remaining spaces with petals, I stood and proudly admired our portion of the carpet. Within minutes, I heard the first faint chants from the approaching procession. As far as I could see in each direction, flowers created an exquisite living carpet.

With the others, I backed out of the way, clearing the route. Shortly after noon, priests swinging brass censers wafting the aroma of burning frankincense reached the spot where I stood. The Guatemalans bowed their heads in reverence to their savior as a dozen black-cloaked bearers hoisted aloft a palanquin carrying a life-sized statue of Jesus nailed to a wooden cross. The crowd fell silent as the procession shuffled past.

While the Guatemalans faithfully worshipped Jesus, I'd learned from Maria's booklet they also shared an unshakeable, deep-rooted devotion to an odd-looking, four-foot-tall, carved wooden idol. Though this practice blatantly violated Christianity's second commandment prohibiting idol worship, the priests knew enough not to condemn the indigenous practice. They left Maximón in peace.

Those who believed in his omnipotent powers flocked to him with all kinds of requests. Some sought medical cures or protection from enemies; others begged for revenge against them. Many pleaded for help to find a suitable spouse or to be blessed with an unexpected financial windfall. They all believed he could make their wishes, whether beneficial or malevolent, come true. The price for his favors included generous offerings of cigars, moonshine whiskey, and cash. However, the locals also realized Maximón could be a devious fellow. He'd gained the reputation of being a trickster, promising one favor but sometimes delivering a completely different outcome.

Maximón fascinated me. I found it ludicrous that thousands of people believed a piece of wood could grant their wishes, yet they faithfully defended his powers. I badgered Maria with hundreds of questions about the idol. When she finally divulged that he lived in Santiago Atitlán, a small village on the far side of Lake Atitlán, I told her I felt compelled to visit Maximón.

She warned me, "As a tourist, you would be foolish to go to that remote part of Guatemala on your own. Rebel guerillas control that area. They might rob you or do much worse." Even so, I felt an inexplicable need to see this popular effigy.

The more I talked about Maximón, the more worried Maria became I might attempt my dangerous plan. I never would have set off on this journey alone, but she didn't know that. She had told me once that her favorite place in Guatemala was Chichicastenango, known simply as Chichi by the locals. A safe and attractive destination for both Guatemalans and foreign tourists, it nested between volcanic mountains 90 minutes north of Lake Atitlán.

Chichi's bustling outdoor market featured hundreds of vendor stalls packed with colorful Mayan textiles, jade jewelry, and leather goods. Tourists came to this market specifically to shop for intricately carved and painted wooden ceremonial masks used in traditional Mayan dances. Now married, raising two young children, the cost of a trip by Maria's family to visit Chichi would exceed the family's financial means.

A week later, knowing it was a long shot, I offered her a godfather deal. "Maria, I'd like to take you and your family for a weekend overnight trip to Chichi. I promise you won't have to pay for anything."

She squinted suspiciously at me. "But why?" she asked.

I spelled out my plan. "We'll stay in one of the nice guest houses. And remember you've raved about how delicious the tostadas, tamales, and chicken pepian stew are in the restaurants there."

"I don't understand. Why would you do this?" she asked again. Suddenly, a glimmer of understanding flashed across her face. "Because *you* want to visit Maximón." She raised her palms to her forehead in consternation, knowing I'd outwitted her.

"Well, yes actually. We'll be in the vicinity, and I wouldn't have to go alone if I go with your family."

Reluctantly, she agreed to confer with her husband, Jose, that night. As I had hoped, she couldn't refuse my offer.

The following weekend, with me sandwiched between Maria's young ones in the back seat of her family's road-weary automobile, we headed west on the four-hour journey to Santiago Atitlán. I marveled at the spring awakening of the verdant plains skirting the ashen slopes of Volcan de Agua. The volcano dwarfed everything surrounding it.

At a small village on the south shore of Lake Atitlán, Jose inquired about the best route to our destination. He learned the road *might* be passable with four-wheel drive, which, of course, his vehicle did not have. And though *banditos* often hid along our route waiting to surprise their victims, his informant felt that because women and children occupied our car, they'd probably leave us alone.

The rutted excuse for a road challenged the car's suspension as we passed through small craters that pockmarked the dirt track. Several times, I winced as the car's undercarriage bottomed out, scraping over the exposed tops of small boulders. Our excruciatingly slow progress eliminated any hope of a fast escape should we encounter anyone with evil intent. Even I began to doubt the wisdom of insisting on this drive to Maximón's village. But after a full hour and another bumpy eight-and-a-half miles, I breathed a sigh of relief when we arrived in Santiago Atitlán.

Jose pulled up to where a group of men sat outside a small café sipping beer and gossiping. He got out of the car to ask where we could find Maximón. Only after passing an intense interrogation did they provide him with instructions about how to navigate the narrow alleyways to the shrine. Five minutes later, we reached Maximón's home.

At the sound of car doors opening, two of Maximón's caretakers came out to investigate. Another round of questions ensued while my impatience grew. At last, they gave us permission to enter the dimly lit room. In the center, flanked on both sides by two additional caretakers, stood the garish idol.

A black felted fedora rested atop his head. The same style of shirt and pants worn by the village men dressed his wooden body. But his clothing hid, barely visible behind a rainbow mishmash of floral, polka-dotted and striped scarves hanging from his neck, offered as gifts by women desirous of his favors. The dozen flickering half-melted candles spread out on the floor in front of him accented the gaudiness of his appearance.

I asked if I could take a picture of the bizarre scene. His caretakers easily pegged me as a foreigner, pointing at the fancy Canon camera slung over my shoulder. "We give you special price, *señorita*. For you is 10 US dollars for one picture." I suspected the exorbitant price equaled exactly what it would cost for each of the caretakers to buy themselves a bottle of moonshine whiskey.

Determined not to fund their vice, I countered, "I'll give you five US dollars for a picture."

"Is not possible. Maximón doesn't like his picture taken. He allows one picture for 10 US dollars. Don't insult him. Maximón gets furious if anyone insults him."

Peeved by their extortion attempt, I paced around the room trying to rationalize paying that much for the unique opportunity to capture an image of the mysterious Maximón. It came down to now or never. I fetched a $10 bill out of my backpack and grudgingly handed it to Maximón's cronies. I carefully adjusted my camera settings to ensure I'd get a clear picture in the dim light, and took the shot.

Then, I made my big mistake. Skeptical that a hunk of wood could grant wishes, I decided to test Maximón's supposed powers. What could I request of him? Nothing of significance came to mind. Then I thought about Josh. Early in my two-month stay in Antigua, a free-spirited young backpacker from Oregon showed up to rent another room reserved for students in my host family's home. He'd taken a few months off from his house painting job to wander south through Central America.

We immediately hit it off, spending time after classes at the bakery devouring chocolate chip cookies, or in the square conversing in English, an activity forbidden when in the presence of our host family. We even took a day trip by bus into Guatemala City to see a soccer match between Guatemala and their archrival Mexico. After a disputed call by a referee, the game had to be stopped. Emotions erupted. Being trapped in the middle of a riot between angry fans of both teams petrified me. Finally, the police, with their snarling dogs, got everything, including my pounding heart, back under control.

After a week of hanging out together, I'd felt comfortable enough to invite Josh to visit me at my home in Bolivia. He hadn't planned to go as far as South America, but the chance to see Bolivia appeared to tempt him, though he shied away from making commitments. During his second week in Antigua, another young American couple, who reminded me of Woodstock hippies, rented the third student room in our house. They stayed only three days. They hadn't come to learn Spanish, only to take advantage of the cheap lodging offered by the Language Institute. When they left, Josh impulsively joined them on their journey south to Honduras. We'd become best buddies, and I'd hoped to get to know him better. His decision deeply disappointed me.

At that moment, I got the outrageous idea of asking Maximón to arrange for us to meet again. I whispered so softly only the idol could hear, "Maximón, if you have such great powers, prove it to me. Arrange for me to see Josh again." I surprised myself that I'd dared to make this ridiculously bold request. After saying farewell to Maximón and his caretakers, we continued on our drive to Chichicastenango.

We slept that night in a well-kept, century-old guest house near the market. So that Maria could get her children to bed at a reasonable hour, we ate an early dinner. After the long day of travel and the excitement of meeting Maximón, an early night sounded good to me, too.

The next morning, following a light breakfast of pastries and fruit, we spent a few hours wandering through the market. I bought three weavings and one of the carved Mayan masks. Maria bought some fabric and candy treats for the kids. At noon, I suggested we eat lunch before beginning our journey back to Antigua.

I picked a restaurant in a charming two-story colonial building. An interior courtyard with a dozen white linen-covered tables served as the dining room. Pots of flowering birds of paradise and blooming purple bougainvillea accented the space with color. The host who greeted us said, "I'm so sorry, but as you can see, we have no tables available at the moment. You might have to wait for half an hour." While we discussed whether to wait or go elsewhere, the host presented an option. "Actually, we could seat you now at a table inside a smaller room just off the courtyard, if you'd like."

Figuring it might be difficult to find a restaurant that wasn't crowded, we followed the host into the room. Three people sat at another table, eating from plates heaped with food. I gazed in their direction, right into the unmistakable blue eyes of the person I had been missing. What was Josh still doing in Guatemala? He should have been long gone. The hippies sat next to him. Stunned, my mind flooded with questions. What were the chances that our paths would cross in Chichicastenango, a place neither of us had mentioned wanting to visit, before he left? What were the chances that our paths would cross at *this* moment in the overflow room of *this* restaurant? Oh my God, did Maximón actually fulfill my request in less than 24 hours?

I told Maria I knew the people at the other table and excused myself to greet them. As surprised to see me as I was to see him, Josh rose and gave me a hug.

"I thought you'd be in another country by now." I said.

"We went up north to checkout some Mayan ruins, but now we're headed to Honduras. I never expected I'd run into you *here*."

"I came with my teacher's family to see a wooden idol the people call Maximón. They believe he's got special powers." But I said nothing about my audacious request. "Have you thought any more about coming to Bolivia?"

"I have. But I've gotta see how far south I can get and if I still have money." He pulled out his wallet and showed me he still had the scrap of paper on which I'd written my phone number.

On the way back to Antigua, a debate raged in my brain. Had seeing Josh again been just a highly implausible coincidence? Or had Maximón proven to me how powerful he was? How could a piece of wood cause two people's paths to cross? I'd heard about people who'd claimed they'd been cured of deadly diseases because their friends and fans prayed to God to save their lives. Was it possible that a critical mass of people believing in a desired outcome could actually generate enough energy to make it happen? Could prayers enable God to heal? Could Maximón really grant wishes? I wasn't sure what to believe. But I knew seeing Josh one more time left me elated.

I'D BEEN BACK HOME in Bolivia for two months when my phone rang.

"Hi, Brenda?" said a vaguely familiar voice.

"Yes. Who is this?"

"It's Josh, from Antigua."

I wasn't sure what to say. I honestly thought that I'd seen the last of my friend in Chichi, so I'd put him out of mind as an unneeded distraction. "How are you? *Where* are you now?" I asked curiously.

"Is your invitation still open?"

The sound of his voice flustered me with excitement. "Of course."

"Great! I found a really cheap flight from Panama to La Paz. I can be there in two days if that works for you."

He gave me the details for his flight. I told him I'd pick him up at the airport when he arrived.

MY MAID, NATI, prepared the guest room, and we shopped for food so she could prepare my favorite Bolivian delicacies: a traditional spicy chicken stew and boiled potatoes smothered in a spicy peanut sauce. From the moment Josh stepped off the plane, the natural beauty of the snow-capped Andes towering over La Paz amazed him.

For the next two days, I became his personal tour guide. We wandered along the narrow cobblestone streets of the witches' market in La Paz, whose shops displayed bottles of magical potions and dried llama fetuses, rumored to bring good luck. At midmorning, we snacked on savory pastries filled with chicken, peas, carrots, and pieces of hard-boiled eggs in a spicy sauce. Josh's feeble attempts to mimic my technique of taking a small bite from the tip of the pastry to sip out the juicy sauce before biting into the pastry made me laugh.

In my Suzuki Jeep, we traveled on rutted dirt roads to the perfect scenic location for a picnic on the flanks of the majestic triple-peaked Mount Illimani. Closer to the city, we caught the changing colors of the setting sun on the sandstone pinnacles in the Valley of the Moon. Once again, we found genuine enjoyment in each other's company. Time after time, he thanked me for encouraging him to come to Bolivia.

I expected he'd stay for at least a week, though he hadn't mentioned when he would leave. If it were up to me, he could stay forever. During dinner, on the third evening of his visit, we made a list of additional interesting activities to do in La Paz. Nati made us mate, the tea of coca leaves known for calming altitude sickness and gastric distress after a spicy meal. We sipped the brew while reminiscing about the places we'd explored that day.

Suddenly, like a switch had flipped, Josh's demeanor grew ugly. Unprovoked, he argued with me. "I've never known anyone so selfish, prejudiced, and egotistical."

Stunned, I asked, "Why are you saying those things? What have I done to make you believe I am any of those things?"

His barrage of insults continued. "How can you be so judgmental, mean-spirited, and dishonest?"

How could *he* actually believe any of what *he* was saying, after I'd generously opened my home to him, fed him, and showed him the wonders of Bolivia?

When he finally screamed at me, "I made a huge mistake to even come to Bolivia." my eyes welled with tears. I couldn't bear to listen to him tear me apart for one second longer. I told Nati I had to go to bed because I felt exhausted, then abruptly fled from the kitchen.

Locked in my bedroom, I muffled the sounds of my crying with a pillow. His brutal words had shattered my heart into a million delicate fragments that cascaded in a haunting melody I would never forget. How could this kind, appreciative man whom I'd developed deep feelings for suddenly transform into a raving monster? What had I done to set him off? Eventually, sleep stole me away from those unanswered questions.

I woke the next morning to an eerily quiet house. Passing the guest room, I peeked through the open door and saw the room was empty. When I entered the kitchen, the pitiful frown on Nati's face forewarned me of the bad news she had to deliver.

"He's gone, *señorita*." She held out a folded note. "He asked me to give you this."

Hesitantly, I took the note, unfolded it, and read, "Dear Brenda, I have no words to tell you how sorry I am. The terrible accusations that came out of my mouth last night weren't mine. I swear I have no idea where they came from. Nothing I said last night was true. That's not how I feel about you. You didn't deserve any of that. I'm too embarrassed to stay here any longer. I hope you can forgive me. Josh."

I teared up as I read his apology. The truth in his written words came from the caring heart of the person I'd found so delightful. I regretted Josh's hasty decision to leave before I could read his letter and speak to him. But had I been in his shoes, I might have done the same. I knew

I'd never see him again, and it was all my fault. My grief melted into a boiling anger because I knew exactly who *had* spoken those hateful words. The trickster had exacted his revenge on me for doubting his power despite the proof he'd given me back in Chichi. I suppose I deserved it. They'd all warned me not to mess around with Maximón.

Maximón with one of his caretakers

UPDATES:

I never saw Josh again, though I hope he's lived a productive, fulfilling life. I wonder if he ever thinks of our adventures together, as I still do now and then. To honor Maximón, I display my framed photo of him in the hallway outside my apartment. To this day, I can't fathom how Maximón's powers work, but I believe energy forces exist that are beyond our ability to comprehend them.

In 2018, *National Geographic* published a story about Maximón that exposed its readers worldwide to this odd deity. Since then, his caretakers, realizing that tourists will gladly pay 20 US dollars each to visit Maximón, have become more welcoming of the revenue stream tourists generate. The villagers still keep his location secret by moving him to a different location in Santiago Atitlán once every year, so those wanting to see Maximón, or make a request of him, must still hire a local guide to lead them to him.

A recent video on YouTube by the Outlawes called *MAXIMON The Drinking Smoking God / A Mysterious Guatemalan Journey* is worth watching to learn more about Guatemala's beloved idol.

MAP OF BOLIVIA

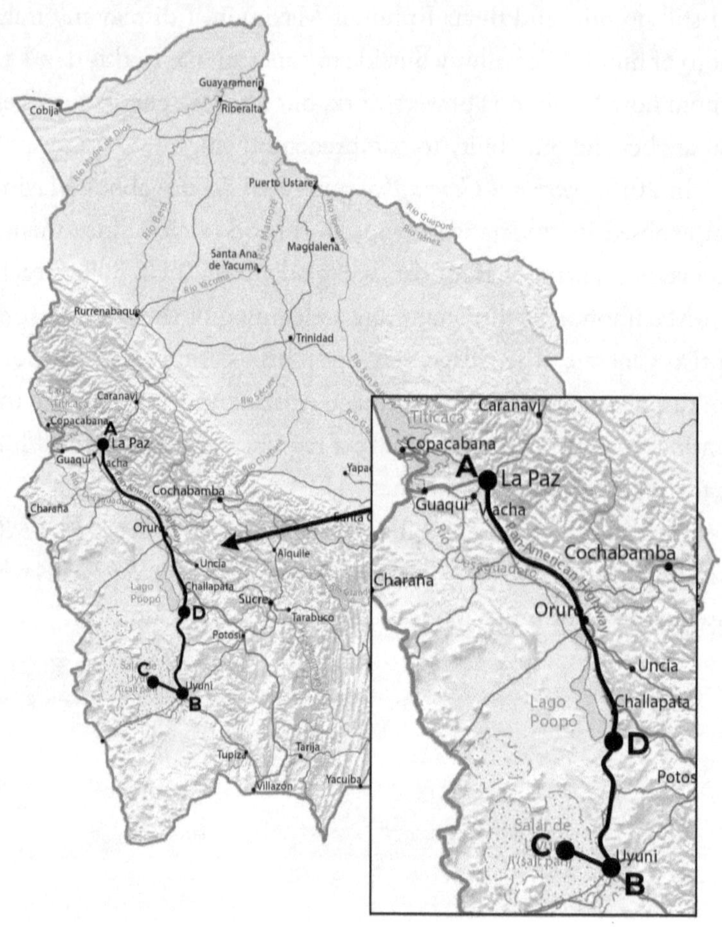

A : La Paz - Capital City

B: Uyuni - Village on Shore of the Salar

C: Middle of Salar - Two Dimension Experience

D: Camp by River Crossing

5

HEAVEN OR HELL?

BOLIVIA – MAY 1988

CAUTIOUSLY, I STEPPED onto the sparkling crystalline surface of this unusual geological formation that resembled frozen solid ice. But it wasn't. The hard-packed crust of salt topped an ancient brine pool, which in prehistoric times had been an immense lake.

FROM THE MOMENT I discovered the Salar de Uyuni existed, I knew I had to see this natural wonder for myself. Located 340 miles south of my home in La Paz, Bolivia, it would take two days of driving on a questionably passable dirt track to reach.

It didn't take long to find four daring friends willing to join me for the rugged trip. Shortly after I arrived in Bolivia in 1987 to work for the United States Agency for International Development (USAID), I befriended Ann, the vivacious and adventure-loving Economic Officer at the American embassy. In her, I found a kindred spirit who equally enjoyed spending weekends journeying off the beaten path to glacial ice caves or along the infamous "death highway," a narrow, one-lane, unpaved roadway that wound in continuous curves from high in the Andes to the Amazon River basin. It took all of a second for her to say "Hell, yes." She offered her "Built Wild" Ford Bronco SUV, known for its off-roading capabilities, for the trip.

Ann suspected she could tempt a young consular officer and his wife to explore this remote region with us. As soon as Ann described our plan to Larry and Mony, they eagerly signed on. Being avid campers, the dangers of crossing the windswept wilderness of the treeless high desert plains didn't faze them. They offered to use their Jeep as a second vehicle, since a trip through this unforgiving wilderness without a backup would be disastrous in the event of an automotive mishap.

Meanwhile, I enticed our anything-but-conventional USAID Regional Legal Officer, Alex, with plans for our trip over the long Memorial Day weekend. He frequently traveled from his base in Ecuador to other South American USAID offices to handle their various legal issues. I'd gotten to know him on previous visits he'd made to La Paz. We'd bonded over shared dinners, telling each other stories of our previous river rafting and hiking exploits. He readily agreed to tweak the timing of his upcoming trip to La Paz so he could take part in this crazy quest with us.

My pre-trip research revealed the Salar to be the largest salt flat in the world. It had a polygonal quilted surface covering 4,050 square miles (the size of the big island of Hawaii). Its crust stored 10 billion tons of salt, while the brine below held the world's richest untapped known source of lithium, an essential element in batteries used to power electronic devices. In contrast, the miniscule village of Uyuni in the southwest corner of Bolivia's Altiplano barely rated a dot on the map. The Altiplano covered a 500-mile-long by 80-mile-wide vast plain, spreading out between the two ridges of the Andes at an altitude of 12,000 feet.

The only practical time to undertake this journey would be during the dry season, when the dirt roadways would be in their best condition for passage. Unfortunately, the dry season coincided with winter in the southern hemisphere, lasting from May through August. When bundled in warm clothing, on the 12,000-foot-high-plains, daytime temperatures boosted by intense sunlight could be pleasantly tolerable. But after sunset, temperatures swiftly plummeted below freezing. Despite its high altitude and subzero coldness, it rarely snowed on the Altiplano, though the peaks that fringed the plain remained snow-covered year-round.

Into our duffel bags, we loaded layers of our warmest winter clothing. We made lists and double-checked everything we'd need for the road trip through the hostile, mostly uninhabited landscape. That included jerry cans of extra gas and drinking water, tents, sleeping bags, and propane-fueled cooking gear. We packed food and beverages that would provide simple yet filling meals we could prepare quickly. Our first aid kit was so well stocked it would have put any rural clinic's medical supplies to shame.

Since we'd be venturing into a region of Bolivia unknown to any of us, I searched for a local acquaintance to accompany us. The only person I could find who had actually been to Uyuni was Juan, the leader of a mountaineering club based in La Paz. He also possessed valuable skills for surviving in harsh weather. His knowledge of the route to Uyuni, and his ability to communicate with the local people, gave me confidence we wouldn't unwittingly get ourselves in trouble. Juan insisted we bring two pairs of sunglasses to serve as an extra layer of protection for our eyes against damage caused by the blinding solar reflections from the salt.

We left the warmth and safety of our homes in La Paz to spend the 1988 Memorial Day weekend plus two vacation days driving the country's only major north-to-south "highway," aptly named Route 1. The handful of other vehicles we encountered were all heavy-duty transport trucks. The treeless high plain offered unobstructed visibility for miles. We could easily track approaching trucks by the enormous billowing dust clouds that trailed behind them.

For two days, we bumped and bounced across the hard-packed dirt. Larry and Mony's Jeep lagged at least a mile behind to avoid sucking in the dust roiled up by Ann's Ford. In places, the rainy season had dissolved the road into a thick slurry of mud. Now in dry season, the sun had baked the remnants of muddy two-feet deep ruts into mounds as hard as brick, rendering the roadway impassable. To avoid those sections, we followed ad hoc detours carved into the adjacent desert by experienced truckers. On one detour, we passed close to a 20-foot-tall forked cactus tree while weaving through quivering tussocks of *puna* grass. Grown to a height of three feet, the dried mounds of sharp-edged blades bore a striking resemblance to giant grayish-brown porcupines, both species equipped with spines best left alone.

Our toughest challenges involved crossing the eight streams that flooded the roadway, varying from a few inches to three feet of swift-moving water. It had never occurred to me that bridges didn't exist in Bolivia outside of the capital and its few major cities. After engaging the four-wheel-drive functionality of our vehicles, we plowed into and through the swiftly flowing current, hoping to Dios we wouldn't get bogged down in a quagmire.

"God, I love driving on these dirt tracks," said Ann, bouncing in her driver's seat as the Ford dipped into and out of potholes. "It's such a great escape from the office."

I knew her job involved sensitive diplomatic tasks, so it must have felt freeing to leave those responsibilities behind. It certainly provided a refreshing break from my work.

Approaching a shallow stream with a completely visible bottom, Ann, fully confident in her vehicle's capabilities, declared, "I can handle this." Fearlessly, she stepped on the gas, and we flew down the sloped bank, spraying a wake of water from both sides of the vehicle before chugging up the opposite bank. That crossing didn't scare me.

When another deeper stream interrupted our progress, she stopped on its bank. Using my river-guiding skills to read the water for any dangers in the crossing ahead, I saw nothing that would cause a problem. However, Ann's pale and lightly freckled face displayed her concern as she skeptically wrinkled her nose. She removed her sunglasses to get a closer look at the water. "Ah, this one looks challenging. You want to take this one, Alex?"

"Yeah, sure, looks like fun!" When they got out of the car to exchange places, Alex, physically fit, with the genes of a daredevil, bounded to the edge of the stream to scout a crossing route. The brisk wind sweeping across the plain ruffled his brown hair and pinkened his cheeks before he climbed into the driver's seat. "Hold on, folks! Here we go." He embraced the thrill of this crossing like a matador taunting a provoked bull, charging at the water as if daring the current to stop us if it could. Ann, Jorge and I held on for dear life.

Later, when we reached the riskiest crossing, where the rushing water appeared both wide and deep, we waited until a transport truck approaching us in the distance arrived. As the truck advanced toward the crossing, it sped up rather than slowed down. We watched as the truck rocketed into the water. The engine strained, heaving the loaded truck forward, until it hauled up the sloped bank to where we waited. We asked for the trucker's help to plot a safe route through the water. The veteran driver pointed out the entrance and exit points. Jorge translated his advice to our drivers. "Floor the gas pedal and don't let up until you reach dry ground on the far side, like *banditos* running from the law. Anything less than full steam ahead," he warned, "and the current could sweep our vehicles off-track downstream."

For the first time since leaving La Paz, I worried we'd gotten in over our heads. As a river guide, I understood the powerful force of water. Here in the middle of nowhere, the last thing we needed would be for our land vehicle to become a floating boat.

Alex, hyped on adrenaline, took the wheel, let out a banshee whoop, and stomped on the gas. Ann's vehicle plunged into the water, causing a torrent of spray to fly in all directions. "Go, Alex! Keep going!" the three of us screamed. The car rocked from side to side as the tires fought for traction on the rocky stream bed. Alex hunched forward, white-knuckling the steering wheel, forcing the gas pedal tight against the floorboard. After 15 of the longest seconds of my life, the Bronco reached the exit point on the far bank, its tires gripping onto solid ground.

We let loose with excited cheers and got out of the car to watch Larry's crossing. Though in a lighter-weight vehicle, he too flew across the stream. The trucker stayed long enough to see we had crossed safely. Then he nodded his approval and waved a salute before climbing back into his truck. His wisdom had served us well as we careened through the current from one bank to the other.

Uyuni's few one-room mud-brick buildings appeared on the horizon late in the afternoon of our second day. Jorge had agreed to get us to Uyuni, after which he would catch the rickety overnight train that passed through Uyuni back to La Paz for an event he needed to attend. Our mini-caravan drew curious stares as we drove along the only street in town, trying to locate where the train would stop.

We found it just ten minutes before the dilapidated train chugged to a stop. Jorge grabbed his backpack, bid us adios, and climbed aboard the train. His final wave back at us gave me the impression that he might have been relieved to be parting company with our zany group. Now we were on our own to explore the Salar, before navigating ourselves back to La Paz.

We drove out onto the salt flats to set up camp. We all felt the need to put some distance between us and the settlement's locals, whose unwelcome scowls discouraged us from camping close to their *casitas* (tiny homes). Mindful that the night wind tearing across the endless open surface of the Salar would be wicked, we positioned our vehicles in a "V" formation to create an improvised windbreak. We set up our tents inside its sheltering barrier, while two cans of hearty beef soup warmed in a pot on the stove and day turned to night.

By the time we ate our meal, the frigid air had penetrated my multiples layers, causing me to shiver. "God, this soup tastes wonderful!" I said, sipping the steaming broth.

"Dip some bread in it and it'll taste even better," said Alex.

Following his lead, we all ripped a hunk from the crusty sourdough loaf.

After dipping her hunk in her mug to sop up some hot soup, Ann shoved it in her mouth, delightedly murmuring, "Mmm."

The near-gale-force wind had forced Larry to replace his signature cowboy hat with a wool beanie. He slapped his knee and said, "The only thing that could make this meal better would be a roaring campfire we could all hunker around."

"Hear! Hear!" agreed Alex.

On the second stove, a pot of water boiled that we used to end our meal with a cup of hot tea. It took us all of 15 minutes to finish eating, but we'd given our bodies a head-start on fending off the bitter coldness. Exhausted by two hard days of jouncing over roads resembling washboards, and shivering, I announced, "Before I freeze to death, I'm going to call it a day. See you all in the morning." I headed to my tent and immediately snuggled into my down sleeping bag, waiting for the chill that had reached my bones to dispel. Outside, the fierce wind roared all night long.

THE NEXT MORNING, intensely bright sunshine shone through the nylon walls of my tent, waking me to a spectacular day. The wind had calmed to a refreshing breeze, and a brilliant sapphire blue colored the cloudless sky. My mind revved with the anticipation of exploring the salt flats. Close to our camp, we noticed a *cholita* (local indigenous woman) sitting on the salt with her young children. The wind and sun had weathered her facial skin to the point she looked more like a grandmother than their mother. All around them stood three-foot-tall, white, cone-shaped piles of salt.

She explained that local workers "mined" the salt by scraping surface layers into piles to export to buyers both in Bolivia and beyond. She also told us that the "safe" track used by truckers hauling goods to villages in the southwest lay just a short distance beyond where we had camped. The flat level surface of the Salar was a trucker's dream. They could cover the 90 miles across the salt in a quarter of the time it would take to circle the lake on the rough dirt roads.

Though in the wet season, signs of the established track disappeared beneath the flooded surface. To avoid the risk of getting lost and falling into one of the open holes in the Salar's crust, the truckers returned to using the land route. However, toward the end of the rainy season, she told us trucking stopped altogether because the dirt roads became so muddy there were no passable routes.

When we told her we planned to drive out into the middle of the Salar, she wagged a short leathery finger at us, fervidly insisting that we stay on the track. She warned the crust varied dramatically in thickness, and the brine beneath in some places was as deep as 430 feet. We assured her we had no intention of straying off the track. When she pointed at our eyes, I donned my second pair of sunglasses to prove we understood the danger of possible blindness and permanent eye damage from not taking this precaution.

By midmorning, our vehicles sped along a barely discernible track, the shoreline shrinking behind us in the distance. Soon, the flat scene ahead of us contained nothing except two colors: blue above, white below. After an hour, we stopped to take pictures.

"I'm going to take a walk out in that direction," I told my friends as I wandered away from the group.

"Watch out for thin ice—I mean salt," yelled Ann.

Step after step, I advanced a hundred yards into the emptiness in front of me. Had an invisible curtain just parted, allowing me to step into a two-dimensional world? I stared at a scene split in half of just blue above and white below. I felt no sense of depth. Like a still life painting, nothing moved.

I took two steps forward, but the scene ahead of me appeared exactly the same. Another two steps changed nothing. Any sensation of time passing no longer existed. Ugly or beautiful ceased to have meaning because the deep blue and pure white remained infinitely unchanged. The concepts of right or wrong, good or bad, beginning or end, had no meaning in a dimension of just two colors. The scene completely lacked sound. I wanted to swallow the solitude and breathe in the peacefulness of this exquisite moment. I existed. Blissfully. Alone.

Gradually, my feeling of contentment faded. What *if* this was all that ever existed? What *if* nothing ever changed? Everything forever frozen on a blue-and-white vertical plane. No thoughts. No escape. Only an insanity of nothing. Could this be hell? Terrified, I needed to run from here, to break away from the sensory deprivation that shook me to my core.

I spun around, begging God to let me see my friends. With immense relief, I found myself back in my real world. I dashed back to where my friends gathered by our vehicles. The sound of their sweet voices and just being close to them filled me with euphoria.

We drove back to a small island we had passed earlier, where a few tall cactus plants somehow thrived in the middle of this barren environment. We spread a blanket on the surface of salt, which none of us could resist calling ice, and prepared our picnic sandwiches. Our conversation during lunch centered on the remarkably unique physical characteristics of the Salar. But each of us in our own way had sensed and become unnerved by the mystical, otherworldly aura that pervaded the surrounding landscape.

Ann said, "There's no sound out here except the noise we're making. It seems like we're isolated from the rest of the world."

"I agree," said Mony. "It just feels like time has stopped."

"I wouldn't want to have car trouble out here." Larry's words, meant to be lighthearted, missed the mark, leaving everyone feeling uneasy instead of amused.

We'd intended to camp another night at the edge of the Salar. Instead, we swiftly reached a unanimous decision that we'd seen enough of it. We'd start the journey back toward our own warm beds in La Paz that afternoon. Satisfied with our choice to leave the Salar in the rearview mirror, we climbed into our vehicles and headed north.

About an hour before sunset, we arrived at the trickiest and deepest of the stream crossings we'd negotiated with our trucker friend's help on the way out. Parked in the road ahead of the crossing, five cargo trucks obstructed the way forward. We pulled up behind the last truck in line and piled out of our vehicles to investigate the hold-up. We could hear irritated voices cussing and complaining. Ahead, stuck in the middle of the stream, a truck tilted at a precarious 50-degree angle. Obviously, no one could go anywhere until the idled truck could be removed.

One trucker told us the unlucky driver had driven partially off the upper side of the streambed's stone-lined track. At lower water levels, the truckers had built the solid footing specifically to prevent this sort of mishap. The truckers continued to argue about the best way to remove the truck. Finally, they agreed it would be much more difficult to winch the truck backward out of the water than to winch it forward to the other side.

Unfortunately, all the trucks at the scene were on the south side of the stream behind the stranded vehicle. They needed a truck traveling from the north to arrive. Given the lateness of the day, chances were there wouldn't be another truck arriving until the next morning. With nothing to do but wait, we prepared to camp right there next to the stream.

The wind sweeping across the Altiplano grew in intensity and dropped the temperature below freezing. While we still had a shred of daylight, we set up our tents in the open field off to one side of the road, sandwiched between large round tussocks of dry grass.

Ann, Alex, and I figured that if we all huddled together in my two-person tent that night, we might benefit from the increased heat produced by three bodies. Aching from the cold, we climbed into our vehicle, started it up and turned the heat control dial to maximum high heat. For some extra energy, we gobbled down a few things that didn't require cooking: some bread, cheese, granola, and chocolate bars.

Outside, the truckers intentionally lit some of the huge clumps of grass on fire. Initially, they exploded as intensely burning fireballs. The truckers stomped their feet on the ground in a circle around the dancing flames. They hoped to steal a tiny bit of warmth before the clump burned itself out with the quickness of a campfire's dry tinder.

As soon as one clump burned out, the truckers ignited another, repeating the process over and over. We watched as gusts caught sparks from the burning grass and carried them across the open plains. With such speed, they had no chance of landing long enough to ignite anything before the wind sucked the spark dry.

When the sun dipped below the horizon, the bone-chilling cold wrapped itself around us. The truckers took refuge inside their truck cabs. We climbed into my tent. The wind relentlessly slammed the side of the tent, absent any windbreak for protection. As I struggled to find sleep, shivering inside my down sleeping bag, I prayed for a humongous monster truck to come to our rescue. I slept in fits and starts.

I WOKE WHEN THE SUN finally cleared the top of the mountains off to our right. Bone dry from the lack of humidity in the air, I reached for my water bottle to wet my mouth. The damn thing had frozen solid—inside the tent! Crawling out of the tent, I instantly noticed that all the trucks from the previous night had left, including the one that had blocked the stream. Except for the howling wind, I'd heard nothing all night long.

Directly ahead, it shocked me to see a layer of solid ice encasing the stream from bank to bank. How low did the temperature have to fall to freeze swift-moving water? It had to have dropped *way* below freezing, with the wind chill factor added in. Without a doubt, that night took the record for the coldest night I'd ever slept outside (including even near the summit of Kilimanjaro). With the sun up, we didn't have to wait long for its warming rays to melt the ice. No one felt like eating breakfast in temperatures this cold, but we heated water for coffee and tea while the ice completed its vanishing act.

Though apprehensive about seeing a truck get into trouble crossing the stream the previous day, we wanted nothing more than to resume our journey home. We could spend hours waiting for another truck to lead us across the rushing current. Heads nodding in agreement, a quick conversation led us to a unanimous decision. We'd go for it on our own.

I said, "It doesn't look as if the water level or the speed of the current has changed since we crossed it two days ago. If we made it across then, we ought to be able to do it again today."

"I'm with you," said Alex. "I just hope that when they pulled that truck out of the water, they didn't displace any of the stones the truckers used to line the streambed."

We walked down to the edge of the water to study the route across. Alex and Larry mapped out their approach, with daredevil Alex agreeing to lead. Larry would wait until he saw our vehicle emerge on the opposite bank. Back in our cars, seat belts on, Alex revved the Bronco's engine and said, "You guys ready?"

"Let's do it!" shouted Ann from the copilot's seat.

The Bronco hit the water going 20 miles per hour, skimming the surface for a few seconds before its weight plunged its front end deep into the water. In the center of the stream, the water piled halfway up the side of the vehicle, forcefully trying to push us downstream, but the tires found traction as we bumped over the stones below, holding us on course.

"Way to go, Alex!" I hollered encouragement from the back seat when we reached the three-quarter mark across the stream. I no longer worried that we might have to take a swim in the frigid water to save ourselves if the Bronco got swept off track. I could tell from the shallowing water we would make it to shore safely.

Alex exhaled deeply and pumped his fist gleefully once we emerged onto the dry riverbank. "That's one hell of a way to get your car washed, Ann."

We waved for Larry to come across. He traced a perfect copy of Alex's route, reuniting with us moments later. With both vehicles safely across, joyfulness buoyed our spirits. We'd conquered the worst obstacle we'd face. With the Bronco's heat turned to max, we nibbled on snacks as we drove past distant herds of alpaca and their close cousins, vicuna.

The hours sped by as we stopped only for bathroom breaks and once to refill our tanks with gas.

AN HOUR AFTER SUNSET, the Bronco pulled into my driveway. I pulled my gear out of the back, thanking Ann and Alex for sharing this amazing adventure with me. "Just count me in when you plan another one," said Alex.

Little did he know I already had an idea for another adventure in the Bolivian Amazon jungle, an idea still in its infancy. For now, we had the time to savor the rewards of our just completed journey. I had endured the experience of stepping into a hellish second dimension, and I'd survived spending the coldest night outside, I could imagine. The prospect of entering a warm house filled me with delight. I couldn't wait to throw my exhausted body into a soft bed heaped with heavenly cozy blankets.

Salar de Uyuni

UPDATES:

Ann, Alex, and I planned several more adventures together, including that spark of an idea for a wooden dugout canoe trip down a major tributary of the Amazon. Ann and I have remained lifelong friends and enjoy reminiscing about our travels together and sharing our other travels with each other.

Nat Geo calls Bolivia's Salar de Uyuni "one of the most remarkable vistas in all of South America, if not on Earth." It has become one of Bolivia's most popular destinations, attracting 60,000 to 70,000 visitors each year, some of whom stay in world-class salt hotels costing more than $200/night. Visitors can now choose from over 100 different lodging establishments in and around Uyuni, based on their budgets.

The surface of the Salar has darkened because of droughts in recent years caused by climate change. After one heavy rainfall in 2021, runoff from the nearby mountains caused ugly algal blooms which discolored the Salar's surface water.

In 2023, Bolivia's government, which previously had been reluctant to allow foreign corporations rights to engage in lithium extraction from the Salar, inaugurated its first lithium processing plant. They also announced agreements with China and Russia for the material's exploitation and sale. The plant will affect the availability of water already made scarce by droughts, driving residents of small villages in the area from their homes.

Star Wars: The Last Jedi (2017) used locations from the Salar for the ending battle exterior scenes.

MAP OF BOLIVIA

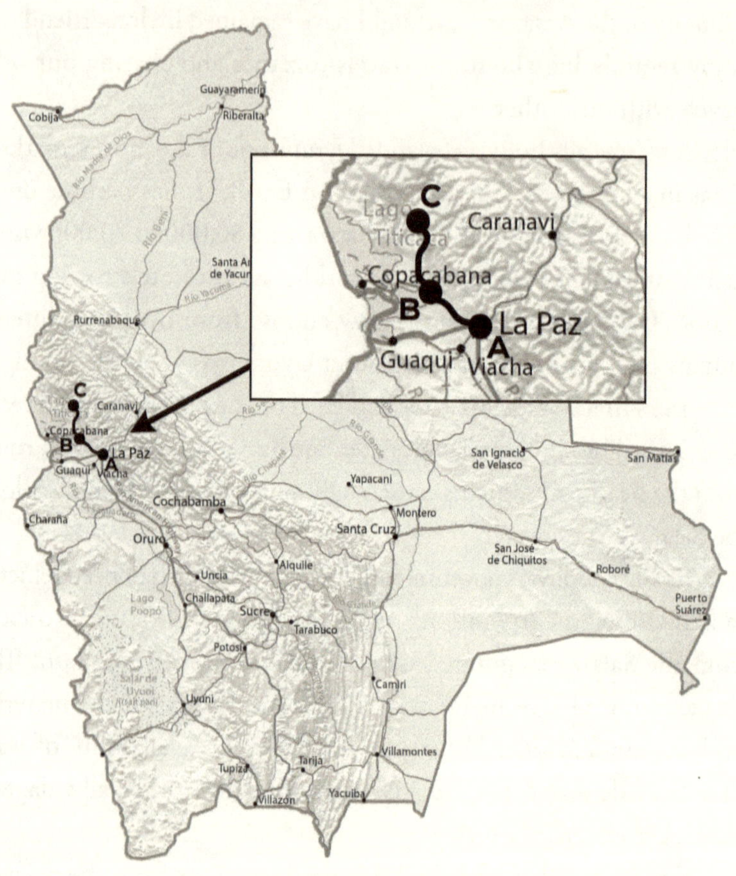

A : La Paz - Capital City, My Home

B: Huarina on Lake Titicaca

C: Sorata - Near Cave

6

GOING BATTY

SORATA, BOLIVIA - 1989

I CERTAINLY NEVER EXPECTED that within 24 hours I would find myself in a harrowing position 100 feet deep in the earth, struggling to squeeze my body through a claustrophobic passage. If I'd known, I might have reconsidered our weekend getaway with my four friends. We'd planned our escape from the crowded city of La Paz, built on the steep sides of a canyon eroded by the Rio La Paz that flowed from the expansive high plateau above it. This river in spring, fed by snowmelt, roared down through the center of the city.

To reach our destination, the sleepy village of Sorata, due east of Lake Titicaca about 95 miles northwest of the Bolivian capital, we first needed to follow the bumpy cobblestone road that led us 1,000 feet higher from La Paz onto the 12,300-foot-high plains of the Altiplano. Leaving the rarified air of La Paz to spend even a few days in the oxygen-enriched air of Sorata, 3,000 feet lower in altitude, would boost our energy and be a gift to our tired bodies constantly starved for oxygen in La Paz.

The intensifying pressure in my ears from gaining altitude muffled the sound of our Jeep's wheels clattering over the cobblestones as we climbed toward the Altiplano. After 15 minutes of yawning and rubbing behind my ears, the sudden burst of my eardrums unblocking brought instant relief from the throbbing pain and restored my hearing to normal. But almost immediately, I felt the pressure building again. In less than 20 minutes, we traded cobblestones for a rutted, muddy dirt track winding through the shoddier, teeming neighborhoods of El Alto and beyond to the vast desolate windswept plains of the Altiplano.

On one side, the plateau stretched westward, far into the distance. To the east rose the towering Andes, creating a nearly impenetrable barrier to the lowland jungle farther east. For the next four hours, we jounced over the hard-packed dirt road that led north. I rode with our US Naval Attaché, Jeff, and his wife Joy, in their Jeep. A military-style cut of his reddish-brown hair topped Jeff's tall, thin build. Already nearing the end of his 20-year military career at a youthful 42 years old, he displayed the controlled discipline of a career officer. When he spoke, he expected people to listen.

By contrast, Joy's warm smile and graceful charm irresistibly drew people to her. She preferred to dress in stylish vintage clothing, giving her a glamorous look that complemented her outgoing personality. Her shoulder-length, wavy, light brown hair framed high cheekbones and intense blue eyes.

Since Bolivia is one of two landlocked countries in South America, initially, I found it strange that the United States government would send a naval officer to a country with no access to an ocean. But cocaine cartels had built production factories in the jungles, using rivers to transport coca leaves to the cocaine factories by boat. Jeff consulted with Bolivian law enforcers to monitor and disrupt the flow of the raw materials to the jungle factories. He also advised his local counterparts about safe boating practices on Lake Titicaca. I'd met the couple at embassy social events. Joy and I had become good friends.

Our US Air Force Attaché, Brent, and his wife Leslie followed behind us in their four-wheel-drive vehicle. We'd opted to take two vehicles to avoid being stranded in the rugged highlands should a mechanical problem arise with one of the vehicles. Brent maintained his muscular build with regular workouts. His neatly combed, light blond hair, smooth unblemished skin, and dazzling blue eyes could have fooled anyone into thinking he worked as a highly paid male model.

Leslie reminded me of a small-town homecoming queen. Tumbling, carefree, light brown curls and an innocent shyness marked her natural beauty. Her cheeks glistened in an endearing pale blush. When she stood close to Brent, her shoulder tucked snugly under his arm, as if the two fit together like jigsaw puzzle pieces.

Brent and Jeff worked together on several projects including tracking the progress of the US government's ill-conceived coca eradication project, using aerial monitoring to measure the hectares of voluntarily destroyed acres of coca bushes and to detect and intercept drug shipments before they could leave Bolivia.

The success of the US-backed coca eradication program depended almost solely on convincing the farmers in drug-producing countries to stop growing the coca bushes. Dried coca leaves were an essential ingredient in the recipe for manufacturing cocaine (their problem). Meanwhile, the US failed to commit significant funding to educate and rehabilitate drug users in the US (our problem). The Bolivian farmers weren't fools. They gladly agreed to accept money for cutting down mature coca bushes that were nearing the end of their productive life, promising to grow substitute crops such as maize, coffee, cacao, or bananas. But the typical peasant farmer earned just half the revenue from growing alternative crops than he could earn from growing coca. So, within a year or two, they replanted their steep hillside farms with new coca seedlings.

Bolivians scorned Americans who worked with the DEA and other agencies involved with coca eradication and confiscation. Jeff and Brent found their jobs stressful because of the constant potential for danger. They took advantage of every chance to escape from the city to relax in idyllic remote villages. When they invited me to go along, I immediately accepted, eager to explore a part of Bolivia I'd not yet seen.

At the halfway mark, our route skirted the southeastern shore of Lake Titicaca, where dozens of boats moored along the shore. Constructed of colorfully dyed bundles of reeds, their bows and sterns curved upward, reminiscent of Viking ships. The center of the larger, more expensive-looking boats featured brightly decorated canopies to protect goods and people from scorching sun rays or rain. We pulled off the road to stretch our legs at a spot with a clear view out over the lake, where Jeff went into lecture mode to share his knowledge of the lake with us.

"Well, folks, you are looking at the highest commercially navigable lake in the world at 12,500 ft above sea level. It's also the largest lake in South America, covering 3,200 square miles. This southern section belongs to Bolivia; Peru claims the rest."

"How deep does it get?" asked Brent, gazing out over the deep blue water.

"Just over 900 feet, but the average depth is closer to 350 feet."

"How far is it to Peru from here?" asked Leslie.

"To the far end of the lake is about 120 miles, but if you're in a boat, you'll enter Peru about halfway across."

Doubting the sturdiness of the reed boats, I said, "I'm not sure I'd want to attempt a crossing in one of those." I could imagine being caught in the middle of this lake in the fierce winds of a sudden squall.

Surely the waves would crash over the pontoon-like sides, swamping and dooming the boat and its passengers to a watery grave.

Jeff continued, "These boats only travel between villages along the shore, and you've probably noticed no one is swimming in the lake because the water temperature is around a chilly 55 degrees. By the way, the local people believe that anyone who falls into the water should *not* be rescued but left to drown as a sacrificial offering to the Earth Goddess *Pachamama*."

Given the fatalistic outlook of the local people, I felt completely satisfied admiring these reed boats with my feet planted on *terra firma*.

"Too bad it isn't closer to lunchtime. We could get *trucha*," said Joy. Jeff frowned and shook his head. Once, Joy had told me that despite Jeff's encyclopedic familiarity with all creatures living in water, he chose not to consume any of them.

"Maybe we can stop and get some on the way back," Joy hinted a second time. She raved about the mouthwatering Titicaca *trucha* she'd eaten nearby in the village of Huarina, where a few popular restaurants specialized in grilling a white fleshy species of trout living in the lake. Fresh fish was nearly impossible to find elsewhere in Bolivia, so Joy's description enticed Leslie and me. We seconded her suggestion, which irritated Jeff.

He beckoned to us. "Let's get going. It's still a long way to Sorata." We climbed back into the vehicles and continued north. Less than an hour later, we arrived in the village of Achacaci, where we made a right-hand turn off the "good" road onto a much rougher one leading northeast toward our destination. Not only was this dirt track narrower, but in places, the drivers had to swerve to avoid dropping into foot-deep ruts. Our route seemed more like an off-road motorbike obstacle course than a route for vehicular travel.

After reaching a saddle between two much higher peaks, the road began its descent, carved into the side of the eastern flank of the mountains. As the track paralleled the valley far below, our progress slowed. The steepness of the terrain demanded that Jeff brake continuously. For the remaining 34 miles of the journey, our map showed we would lose 4,200 ft in altitude, an average gradient loss of 2.4 percent. Whenever he could, Jeff released the brakes to prevent them from overheating, and we coasted downhill, gradually picking up speed.

I'd always had an easier time clearing the pressure in my ears when *gaining* altitude, but they stubbornly refused to unblock when *losing* altitude. Twenty minutes into the descent, the sharp ache in my ears brought tears to my eyes. I tried yawning, massaging the back of my ears, pinching my nose and blowing, but nothing relieved the pressure. I wondered if my head might explode. The three of us hadn't spoken for a while. Our eyes remained riveted on the treacherous road, scanning the distant serpentine ribbon for signs of approaching trucks. Finally, I had to admit the pain was excruciating.

"Do your ears hurt as much as mine do right now?" I asked Jeff and Joy.

Joy turned around and saw me clutching my ears and the pained expression on my face.

"Oh, dear, why didn't you say something? I have something I think will help." She dug into a pocket of her daypack and pulled out a white tube.

"I never travel at high altitudes without this. Just put a few drops in each of your ears. It will amaze you how quickly it will unblock them." She handed me the tube. I read the label. The name of the liquid manufactured in Bolivia was Otalex. I felt torn about using a drug not manufactured in the United States, but the intolerable pressure in my head, along with Joy's endorsement of the product, erased any doubts. I uncapped the tube, tilted my head, and squirted two drops in each ear. The sensation of the cool liquid filling my ear canal instantly brought a sense of relief. Almost immediately, I noticed a slight lessening of the pain. I waited for the dramatic hiss of pressure releasing from my eardrum that I'd expected, but it never happened. Within 15 minutes, I could hear normally, and the pain had vanished.

"Where did you get this stuff?" I asked Joy. "This is like a magic potion."

"They sell it over the counter in any pharmacy here. We usually put a couple drops in our ears before we leave the house when we know we're going to be at higher altitudes. It also helps with changing altitudes on airplane flights."

Delighted with this new discovery, I couldn't wait to buy my own tube of Otalex. Just as my ears cleared, we arrived at the place on our map that showed, over the next four miles, we'd be losing altitude rapidly via 17 notoriously hair-raising switchback turns. Looking out the window, I could see the road crossing back and forth along the steep mountainside making gradual forward progress, the way a sailboat's tacking maneuvers work when it sails into the wind.

Sheer cliffs towering skyward on the left and a sheer drop-off into the valley on its right made this road so perilous. The bumpy roadbed provided just enough width for our Jeep. A calamitous disaster would surely befall two vehicles attempting to pass on this stretch. As Jeff tackled the switchbacks, I held my breath at each 180-degree turn.

We discovered that the wise engineers who designed the road had taken advantage of the naturally occurring wider spots to construct pull-offs, where one vehicle could wait for an approaching vehicle to pass. Luckily, we only encountered one truck, whose driver had seen our two vehicles descending. He'd pulled over to allow us to pass safely.

Once past the switchbacks, the road leveled out, and the angle of decline lessened as we drove through a fertile terraced valley leading to Sorata, a small village of a few hundred people. At one time, Sorata had served as a gateway to the Amazon basin, linking gold fields in the high plains with lowland rubber plantations. At an altitude of 8,786 feet, it nestled against the spectacular backdrop of two of Bolivia's snow-capped 21,000-foot peaks, Illampu and Ancohuma.

As we approached the center of the village, Jeff muttered, "Now we just have to find our hotel, but that shouldn't be too difficult since there aren't many buildings large enough to accommodate multiple guests in this place."

"I think it's that stone building up ahead." Joy pointed to a two-story colonial, constructed of stone and clay bricks. Jeff turned into a gravel lot on one side of the building. Beyond the lot, a garden with vibrant blooms and enticing fragrances greeted weary travelers. A few moments later, Brent and Leslie pulled in beside us.

"Let's check this out," said Jeff, hoisting his backpack and duffel bag. The rest of us followed as he climbed a set of rock slab stairs onto a veranda and opened the door on which hung a welcoming wooden sign with red letters: "*Bienvenida.*"

In the reception area, behind a polished wooden counter, stood a plump woman whose weathered skin creased in wrinkles, making it difficult to gauge her true age. Her thick black hair, plaited in a single wide braid, extended to below her waist. Her equally dark eyes gleamed as she enthusiastically greeted us.

"*Ola. Cómo están todos?* How can I help you?"

Jeff stepped forward. "We have a reservation for three rooms—two doubles and a single for two nights," he said.

Before he could give his name, the woman asked, "You are Americans? Five of you, yes?"

"That would be us," Jeff said. Our behavior and clothing instantly gave us away.

The woman plucked three keys from a rack where eight keys dangled. She handed Jeff two keys, then jingled another, waiting to see which of us would claim the single room. I reached for it. "*Bueno.*

Get yourselves settled, then come back to our dining room just behind reception for a welcome drink before dinner."

I opened the door that matched the number on my key, and stepped into a bare-bones room lacking charm but containing the essentials: a single bed covered in a dated off-white chenille bedspread, a three-drawer dresser, and a table lamp on a stand next to the bed. Late afternoon light streamed through a large window draped with white, gauzy curtains casting shadows on the beige walls. A well-worn bath towel and face cloth rested on the end of the bed, to be used in the shared bathroom down the hall. I left my clothes folded in my duffle, placing it on the floor out of sight on the far side of the bed. Removing only my pouch of toiletries, I placed them on the dresser. Then I walked back down the hallway to the dining room.

Seated at a table for six, I found Jeff and Brent already sipping mugs of cold *Paceña* beer, having delegated *their* unpacking to their wives. When I took a seat at the table, the woman who had checked us in hurried over to take my drink order.

"I'd love a pisco sour." I assumed that even in a small village they would have the makings for the national drink of Bolivia.

"Of course, *señorita.*" She turned and scurried off.

"You're going for the hard stuff, hey?" Brent teased.

"Better tasting than what you're drinking." I nodded with disgust toward their mugs.

A few minutes later, the woman placed a frothy citrusy-sweet cocktail on the table in front of me. I smiled and said, "*Perfecto, Muchas gracias!*" The drink, made from pisco, a liquor distilled from fermented Muscat grapes, lime juice, simple syrup, and egg white, combined and vigorously shaken, always tasted refreshing to me. When Joy and Leslie joined us, they saw my pisco sour and ordered the same. As we enjoyed our drinks, the tantalizing aromas of dinner being prepared wafted from the kitchen, making my stomach growl in hunger. I'd eaten nothing but a few snacks in the Jeep on our way here. That explained the lightheadedness that came from drinking on an empty stomach. But I enjoyed feeling mellow now that we'd arrived in Sorata safely.

We thought we had the small hotel to ourselves, until three hunky men in military camouflage fatigues and heavy-duty leather hiking boots, weighed down with fully loaded backpacks, tromped into the dining room. Tanned, muscular, and sporting short, military-style haircuts, they exuded airs of supreme confidence. I wondered if they were members of a US government special ops team of some sort. Jeff and Brent, who immediately recognized them as soldiers, sat up, curious to find out where these men came from and what they were doing in Sorata.

The moment the one in the lead spoke, his British accent revealed their homeland. "Hello, I'm Colin. Pleased to meet you. These chaps are Chad, and Andrew here is our team leader." The two behind Colin nodded politely upon being introduced. From the insignia on the men's berets, Brent identified them as his counterparts.

"Glad to meet you. I take it you're with the British Royal Air Force. I'm Brent, US Air Force." With a friendly smile, he extended his hand for a hearty handshake, establishing an instant rapport. Brent introduced the rest of us and explained we'd come to Sorata to relax and do some exploring in the local area.

"Why don't you pull up some chairs and join us for a drink?" Jeff said, making some extra room by shifting his chair closer to Joy's.

While the other two nodded their willingness, Colin replied, "Listen, after the 10-mile hike we've just been on, we don't want to stink out these lovely ladies, so let us ditch our gear and grab a quick shower first. Then we'll take you up on your offer, mate."

Half an hour later, cleaned up and having changed into more comfortable navy Henley thermal shirts and khaki pants, they returned.

"Can we treat you to a cold mug?" Brent asked, holding his own aloft.

"Believe me, we would kill for a strong porter, but technically, we're on duty, so we'll stay with the soft stuff," Colin explained.

"On duty?" asked Brent. He and Jeff seemed surprised. "What's your mission here? That's if you're allowed to tell us?"

"Not a secret op, if that's what you're thinking," said Colin, grinning. "We're part of a team doing research on acute mountain sickness, AMS, and its impact on the human body. There are seven of us here in Bolivia. We all landed in La Paz two days ago. Half of us immediately came here to a lower altitude to acclimatize, while the other three and our team doctor have established a research base at 16,000 feet on Illampu, that ice-covered beast of a mountain just south of here. We're just biding time here until we join them in two days."

"Damn, that's high. Good thing you're all in good shape," said Brent

"Have to be if you want to be part of a mountaineering unit," said Andrew, who stood taller and lankier than his mates. His weathered complexion, and the pale sunglass-protected skin around his eyes, offered proof of the many hours he spent outside exposed to the natural elements. As the leader of the mountaineers, his serious, practical demeanor would be invaluable in the rarified air of the high Andes. He continued, "Originally, this mission called for us to scale a few of the highest peaks in Peru, but the Shining Path terrorists have been too unpredictable and, frankly, more dangerous for us than attempting to summit those peaks."

Jeff noted that the Bolivian government also monitored the communist guerilla movements for any sign that their revolutionary ideology might be spreading across the border. "I'd say you made a wise choice to carry out your research here in Bolivia," he said. "What are you expecting to learn from your study?"

"RAF wants to measure how much of a difference a short acclimatization at a lower altitude makes before making an ascent to a final high-altitude destination." Chad explained. Without a beret atop his head, wavy light blond hair brightened his face and softened his features. The sleeves of his Henley bulged around his bicep muscles. "Our roles on this assignment? We're just bloody lab rats." His clean-shaven face broke into a wide smile, revealing perfectly aligned white teeth.

As he talked, I gazed into his sky-blue eyes, never expecting to encounter such a handsome man in a remote village like Sorata. His charming British accent only added to his appeal. The irresistible magnetism I felt for him brought back memories of my high school years. Along with a hundred other love-struck girls, I'd had a hopeless crush on the cute and super-talented star pitcher of our school's baseball team. To me, he resembled a dashing young movie star.

I couldn't help myself back then or now. "Chad, I could listen to your accent all day," I told him.

"Well, you ought to. You folks across the pond have bastardized the English language. I don't know what language you're speaking. Maybe American? But it sure as hell isn't proper English." He lobbed the insult at us in a joking, fun-loving way, inviting a debate.

Jeff took him on. "Maybe we've improved the mother tongue. Seriously, who would consider a *bumbershoot* a more suitable description for an object to keep you dry in rain than an umbrella? What the heck is a bumber, anyway? Everyone understands umbrella..." he said, pantomiming a canopy over his head.

Joy interrupted before Chad could defend himself. "Why in the world do you call an apartment a *flat*? Tires can be flat. So can a pancake, or a road through a desert. But apartments are three-dimensional residences!"

As the Brits guffawed at our arguments, I couldn't resist adding, "*I* want to know who decided the word *loo* is what a toilet should be called."

"Guess we've hit a raw nerve," Chad conceded. "You can just keep speaking your American and we'll speak our English!"

THE MEN SAT WITH US for a dinner of local specialties that included a tomato-and-onion-based spicy chicken stew served over vegetable rice. After indulging in a serving of sweet custard flan floating in a pool of caramelized raw sugar, our British companions excused themselves. Colin said, "We're pretty knackered."

"OK, tell us what's knackered means in American?" Leslie teased. "It sounds like hammered, but since you guys haven't been drinking, I need a translation."

"Good one, Les!" cheered her husband, while Jeff, Joy, and I gave her a thumbs up.

"It means we're pooped. Do you know what that means?" Chad wisecracked. He noticed me grinning. "No. Not that we need to use the *loo*!" He glanced at me and winked. "We've got a 5 a.m. wakeup call for a training run before breakfast, so we're turning in early." I melted at his obvious flirtation as they trudged out of the dining room.

WHEN THE SERVER CAME to clear our table, Brent asked him, "What places or things should we visit while we're here in Sorata?"

After sizing up our group, the server asked, "Are any of you afraid of being in narrow spaces?"

"Why?" I asked, wanting to know what he had in mind.

"A nearby village holds a hidden grotto that is a secret to most people. They call it *Gruta de San Pedro*. You must enter a cave and follow it deep into the earth, where it leads to an underground lake. But in places it's quite narrow. Never go by yourselves, only with a local who knows the route to the grotto. Incas supposedly built secret passages used to transport gold from mines in the high plains to Cuzco or to lowland plantations. You wouldn't want to get lost. Our legends also say conquistadors buried treasures somewhere deep in the cave."

The possibilities of buried treasure and secret passageways had us excited.

"How do we find this place?" Jeff asked.

"The entrance to the cave is just over six miles northwest of here. With a four-wheel-drive vehicle, you'll be able to manage the rough track. It'll take you about 30 minutes. Or you can hike there through our scenic valley in about two hours."

The purpose of our weekend getaway centered on relaxation. So, when Leslie silently mouthed "Drive?" we all nodded vigorously.

"In San Pedro, there are only a few small houses. Keep an eye out for a wooden sign on the right-hand side of the track with an arrow that says *gruta*. Pull off the track and park by the sign, then follow the dirt path up the slope. The villagers will see you coming and will send a guide to lead you into the grotto."

"Sounds like we've got a plan for tomorrow," said Jeff.

THE NEXT MORNING AT 8 A.M., the scrumptious smell of sizzling bacon coaxed me from a pleasant dream of mountain climbing with a certain blonde RAF officer. In the dining room, we took seats at a table offering a carafe of Bolivian roasted coffee and a full pitcher of freshly squeezed orange juice. Ripe grapes, oranges, papayas, and bananas filled a fruit bowl. The server hurried over. "*Buenos dias!* How did you sleep?" The lower altitude made breathing easier, so all of us had slept soundly, waking refreshed.

"This morning, we have an omelet made with local goat cheese and herbs, banana pancakes, or quinoa porridge. All come with bacon and toast. You'll want to eat a hearty breakfast if you're going to the grotto."

As I devoured my flavorful cheese omelet with salty, crisp bacon, it occurred to me there might be a warning in the server's statement that we should eat a hearty breakfast. Had he subtly implied we might not be eating again soon? Why would he think that? Was he worried we'd get lost in the cave? What *if* we got lost in the cave? Who would rescue us? I tried to rid my mind of those questions to focus on our group's discussion about the things we needed to bring on our exploration.

Headlamps and extra batteries topped the list. Full water bottles. Rope and a couple of carabiners Jeff had stashed in his Jeep that could be helpful in getting over rough spots. Granola bars we'd brought with us from La Paz for extra energy. Cameras and extra film.

"Good morning, mates," Colin's cheery voice greeted us as the RAF team entered the dining room dressed in field ops camouflage. They slung their backpacks off, piling them out of way in a corner. "Mind if we join you?"

They snugged another four-seat table up to ours, and we shuffled our chairs close together so everyone had space at the table.

"How was the early morning training exercise?" Brent asked.

"Just a five-mile cross-country trek this morning," said Andrew, pouring a cup of steaming joe from the carafe on the table. "Pretty steep terrain up and back. Worked up a bit of an appetite."

After the server took the Brits' order, Chad, sitting across the table from me, asked, "So, what are *your* plans for the day?" With his eyes locked on mine, I felt compelled to answer.

"We're going to explore a cave that opens into a cavern with a lake deep underground where treasures might be buried."

Chad's eyes opened wide with curiosity. "Where is this cave?"

"Roughly six miles away from here in a tiny village."

Chad glanced at Andrew like a child, determined to convince an adult that doing what he wanted was absolutely necessary. "Andrew, you probably don't realize that I'm an avid spelunker in my spare time. I've been exploring caves since I was a kid. Any chance we could check this cave out?"

"You could come with us," I blurted out, not bothering to check with the others in my group. The presence of an experienced survival expert climbing around underground with us would undoubtedly enhance our safety. I recounted what we'd been told about the cave.

"I'm in," said Colin, turning to see if Andrew would approve the outing. Andrew took his time before answering.

"In this situation, I'll grant permission. I'm not keen on anyone getting hurt, so if I think it becomes dangerous, I'll call it off. We'll make the jog over there with light packs." Turning to us, he asked, "How are you getting there, and what time are you planning to leave?"

Brent responded, "We're planning to drive there in one of our vehicles. We could take both our Jeeps if you'd like to come with us, to save time."

"Thanks, but we should be able to knock that off in an hour if we jog. Besides, that run will count toward our daily exercise regimen."

We agreed they would depart immediately upon finishing their breakfast and we would follow, rendezvousing with them 60 minutes later at the cave.

WE BUMPED AND BOUNCED along the rutted, single-lane, dirt track, spewing a thick dust cloud in our wake. When we'd covered five-and-a-half miles, we caught up with the RAF guys trotting at a brisk pace down the center of the track. To give them a hard time, Jeff beeped the Jeep's horn repeatedly. They stepped off the road on to the higher shoulder to allow us to pass. Jeff opened his window to hassle them. "Another half mile, guys, better step it up!" I felt bad when our trailing dust cloud obscured them from view.

Despite being the backseat passenger, I spotted the crude wooden marker first. "Look up there on the rise. Does that sign say *gruta*?"

"Sure does," said Jeff as he approached the marker. He cautiously steered the Jeep off the track onto to a flat grassy spot just beyond the signpost.

We piled out of the vehicle and retrieved our gear from the back, waiting to spot the RAF team. When they saw us, Chad and Colin instantly broke into a sprint, both determined to be the first to reach us. Of course, I rooted for Chad to win the race, and he did.

A narrow footpath led through an overgrown field to the base of a 100-foot rock cliff. All eight of us carrying packs stocked with the needed essentials plodded single-file up the trail.

"I don't see anything that looks like an opening to a cave," said Brent, surveying the base of the solid gray rock wall in front of us.

In the distance, on a trail running parallel to the cliff, I spied a young boy carrying what looked like tiki torches headed in our direction. The village's covert grapevine apparently worked.

"Hey, guys, we've got company." I said, pointing toward the boy. "Suppose he's our guide?" As he came closer, I could see he clutched three torches in one hand balanced against his shoulder. In his other hand, he carried a one-gallon plastic jug. His crude torches amounted to soot-smeared tin cans nailed to wooden poles an inch in diameter and three feet long.

"*Hola, me llamo Jose.*" Dressed in threadbare dirty clothes, with uncombed hair that needed a cut, his still hairless face and shy grin belonged to a boy no older than 10.

After introducing ourselves, he led us 50 yards farther along the foot of the cliff to a three-foot-wide crack in the wall just wide enough and high enough for a person to squeeze through. There, he handed the torches to three of the men to hold. Crumpled, filthy-looking cloth rags filled the cans. Jose uncapped the jug and poured a clear liquid over the rags. From its distinctive oily scent, I identified it as kerosene.

After recapping the jug, Jose struck a match against the rock wall, then carefully eased the lit match close to the top of the torch Colin held.

"Watch it, chap!" Colin shouted, extending his arm far away from his body.

"*No hay problema,*" Jose assured him as the match lit the kerosene fumes. The soaked rags ignited, producing a flame that burned without consuming the rags, the way a hurricane lamp's flame slowly consumes the wick. He took the lit torch from Colin and used it to ignite the torches held by Jeff and Brent, explaining the cans had to be held upright to avoid spilling the fire. Because we didn't know how long the torches would stay lit, we chose to save our headlamps as backups.

Jose, with a torch in hand, waved for us to follow him as he disappeared sideways through the crack. Andrew and Chad fell in behind him. Jeff, holding the second torch, lit the way for Joy and me, while Brent carried the third torch for Leslie. Colin volunteered for the sweep position. Once through the entrance, the ground angled steeply downward, but the passage widened slightly, allowing for easier going. It took only two minutes for darkness to completely engulf us.

"Goddamn, it's dark in here," muttered Jeff.

The glow from the torches barely illuminated the boundaries of the passage. I relied on my hands to guide me along the walls and my feet to identify obstacles along the path. Those holding torches warned us about sharp outcrops protruding from the walls and small boulders jutting from the ground. We inched along, descending into the silent bowels of the earth.

I'd kept my anxiety about climbing into this black hole under control until I realized how many million tons of rock hung suspended just inches over my head. Suddenly, I froze. What if an earthquake hit while we were in the cave? What would it feel like to be obliterated in the blink of an eye under the weight of all that rock above me?

"*Stop it. Banish those thoughts!*" I said to myself, though a sudden burst of adrenaline had already caused my heart to beat faster. Even with second thoughts racing through my mind about entering the cave, I couldn't just turn around and bolt because getting around the bodies behind me in the confines of this narrow passage would be impossible. Trapped, with no choice but to continue moving deeper into the earth, mounting misgivings caused my queasy stomach to churn.

Ahead, I heard Andrew say, "How the hell are we supposed to get through this? This kid is a beanpole. Sure, he can wiggle through, but there's no way any of us are going to fit through this opening."

"For sure. That's a dodgy move, mate," Chad agreed.

Beads of sweat formed on my forehead. Were they solely from fear? Or had the temperature actually warmed as we pushed deeper into the cave? An image of the raging underground infernos in Hades flashed through my mind. Hearing the doubts expressed by the macho RAF members at the front of the line made me regret what we'd gotten ourselves into. Jeff crowded closer to speak with Jose in Spanish, then translated what he'd learned.

"This is the narrowest part of the descent, but it's not too long. We're going to have to go through flat on our stomachs. Jose will go through first, covering his torch with a snug-fitting wooden cap for the few seconds he needs to get through this tight spot. On the other side, there's a chamber big enough for all of us to gather. Once he helps Andrew and Chad get through, he'll come back for the rest of us."

"Good luck with that," said Chad. "I'll believe it when I see it."

The space ahead of us went pitch black. Then I heard the scraping noises of Jose's body dragging over dirt. *We must be nuts*, I thought as I nervously swayed from side to side, imagining trying to force my body through the tightly confined space I'd yet to see. I shivered with dread at the task I'd have to perform.

A few seconds later, when Jose uncapped his torch beyond the crawl space to light the chamber on the far side, Andrew declared, "Bloody hell. The little stinker got through."

"You're up, mate," Chad told Andrew. "If *you* make it, I'll follow."

"Bugger off."

With four bodies ahead clogging the passage and blocking my view, I could only guess what was happening, but I heard Jose's voice from the far side, coaxing the rest of us to follow. "*Venga. Venga.*" I heard Andrew shed his pack and position himself prone on the ground. The dim light from the torch on the far side served as a beacon.

After sizing up the challenge, he said, "The space that's constricted looks to be about four feet long. The trick will be to keep as flat as possible inside it. I'm ready to tackle it." He grunted as he squirmed his way through the opening.

Chad hollered, "Hey, Andrew, I'm sending your pack through!" as he pushed it into the tight passage.

"Got it, mate," said Andrew.

"Here's mine coming through," said Chad, shoving it into the hole. He turned around to those of us still behind him and said, "See ya on the other side." Then he squatted and launched himself into the opening.

When Chad reached the far side, I heard the two giving each other high fives over their success. Then Jose crawled back to our side. He took Jeff's torch, capped it, and held it close to his side as he slithered back through the opening. Jeff stretched out on the ground, groping with his hands and feet as his body disappeared into the downward-sloping shaft. "Damn it," he cursed, his voice muffled deep inside the narrow passage. "Keep your head low to the ground," he growled. "I just whacked my head on a rock jutting from above." A minute later, as he emerged into the chamber, the opening glowed again.

Now Joy stood in front of the tiny opening. "This doesn't look like much fun. How did you guys ever get through this?" I could hear the fear in Joy's voice. With only the light from Brent's torch lighting our side, we could barely make out the contours of the space we were in.

"Come on, hon. You can do this!" Jeff said, helping to persuade his wife. "Once you get down on the ground, you'll be able to see how to do it. I'm right here to help you."

"Jeff, I don't know if I can do this," said Joy.

"You can, and you will. I promise. It's really not that bad."

I helped Joy slide off her pack. Only when she kneeled on the ground did I get my first shocking glimpse of the tiny opening. It sent chills down my spine, surpassing the terror of even my worst nightmare. The rectangular opening measured no more than 18 inches high and 36 inches wide, just about the size of a cheap casket!

Jeff said, "Lie flat on the ground and you'll be able to see it's not that long. First, pass me your pack." Still kneeling, Joy shoved her pack deep into the hole until she felt a tug from the other side as Jeff pulled the pack through. "Great! Now, put your arms out in front of you and wiggle yourself into the opening. Once you've got your shoulders inside, I'll be able to reach you and help pull you through." Joy trembled as she stretched out on the ground, put her arms into the opening, and squirmed forward. "Good job, hon. I got you. Keep wriggling," said Jeff, as his wife closed the gap between them. "Trust me, Joy."

I watched as her hiking boots disappeared, and moments later, light once again shone through the opening.

I heard Joy tell the group on her side, "I'd like to ask the first guy who climbed through that passage what the heck he was thinking. How did he know he'd be able to get back out?"

"Ah, but that's the thrill of spelunking," said Chad. "We've just *got* to know what's beyond."

"Maybe you do." Sarcasm colored her response as she brushed the dust from her clothes.

I stared at the tiny opening, not knowing whether to laugh at the irony of trying to wiggle my body through it like an animal burrowing into the earth to find shelter, or to cry, thinking of all things that could go wrong. What if I got stuck in the middle, unable to move forward or retreat? What if I suffered a panic attack in the claustrophobic enclosure? And again, I thought of an earthquake that might encase my body for eternity right in this spot. I took a few deep breaths. Everyone else had made it through, and my body was no larger than theirs. Besides, I didn't have a choice.

Brent helped get my pack off and gently urged me to lie flat on the ground with my face directly in front of the opening. At the other end of the tunnel, Jeff's face grinned at me.

"Brenda, you got this. I'm gonna help you." He extended one of his arms into the passage and said, "Stretch your arms out toward me." I closed my eyes and reached into the hole. "Good. Now slide your body forward."

My heart pounded so loud I expected to hear its echo bounce off the stone walls surrounding us. I thought to myself, *This is absolutely freaking nuts.* But I pushed against the ground using the toes of my hiking boots. I felt the uneven surface below my belly as I inched forward. A moment later, I felt Jeff's hand grab my left arm just above my wrist. He gently tugged on it, aiding my own efforts to get to the other side.

The others cheered as my head emerged into their space. A few seconds later, I could stand up. The 20-second downhill crawl didn't seem so impossible now, though I knew as we left the cave, gravity would work against us.

I asked Jose in Spanish, "How many more of these narrow spots are there?"

"*Nada mas,*" he answered.

"Thank God!" I fist-pumped, relieved to have the scariest part of the descent behind me.

Jose instructed, while Jeff translated. For the last group, Brent needed to pass his torch back to Colin. Brent and Leslie would come through next before Jose would go back for the third torch, and Colin, temporarily left in darkness, would scurry through last. Getting the last group through went without a hitch.

Before we set off again, Jose explained that the descent would become steeper, though the passageway would be wider. In formation, we set off, careful to avoid rocky obstacles in our path. The lower we went, the warmer it became. I shed my sweatshirt, but still beads of moisture formed on my head and body. Without warning, something invisible swooped past only inches over my head. I ducked into a protective curl. "What the heck was that?"

Leslie squealed as it whizzed by her.

"Just missed me too." Brent said, "Its wake of air swept across my cheek!"

"Aw, you're not scared of a tiny black bat, I hope." Chad laughed. "Don't worry—they won't fly into you." Then, imitating the voice of a ghoulish vampire, he added, "Und dey vont bite you und suck your blooood. Hah. Hah. Hah." As soon as he finished teasing us, three more of the creatures zipped past us.

"Man, they fly fast," I said. "In the dark, you can't see or hear them coming until they're right in front of you."

Chad explained, "The little buggers weigh practically nothing and can fly up to 100 miles an hour in open spaces. No doubt we're disturbing their sleep with our torchlight and the noise we're making. Bats are night creatures. After sunset, they become active. During the day, their favorite '*hangouts,*'" he said, making quotes with his fingers, "are in the nooks and crannies of caves."

As we continued deeper into the earth, I noticed a damp grayish-white substance covered the upper surfaces of rock outcroppings we used to steady ourselves on the uneven footing. Only after I had placed one of my hands on it did I realize the coating was bat poop! The tiny stealth-bombing poopers appeared to be multiplying the further into the cave we went.

The passage suddenly opened into a massive cavern so vast that the light from our three torches couldn't penetrate the darkness far enough to reveal its boundaries. We stumbled our way down a boulder-clogged steep banking. In the spacious opening, the audible sounds of thousands of flapping wings, invisible in the blackness above us, echoed throughout the chamber. A single bat or two I could deal with, but I felt grateful to be spared the sight of the colony of bats circling above us.

Jose led us forward until we stood eight feet above the near edge of the lake. From there, he motioned for us to follow as he led us gently downward along a path on the water's left bank. The small radius of light we traveled in made it impossible to see the far side of the lake or where it ended.

"How long is this lake?" Jeff asked Jose, who simply shrugged his shoulders. The humid air temperature had reached an uncomfortable level akin to what I'd expect on a sunny day in the tropics or if we had stepped into a hot sauna. Sweat poured down my back, soaking my T-shirt and the back of my shorts. The cover of low light spared me embarrassment from the expanding spots of wetness.

"What d'ya think? Should we keep going to see how far this body of water extends?" Chad asked. As the only spelunker among us, it didn't surprise me he was pushing to explore further.

"I have a better idea," said Leslie. "Why don't we take a break and drink some water and eat a snack? Aren't you guys sweating?"

The clear water below us beckoned to me. Feeling my body overheating, I suspected the cavern's water might be refreshing. I inched my way back the way we'd come, searching for a pathway down to the water's edge. When I reached lake level, I squatted and swished my hand through the crystal-clear water. It felt warm, but not as warm as the air. I desperately wanted to cool off.

What creatures might live in a lake deep underground, I wondered? With no sunlight, I doubted there would be any large creatures. But parasites? Bacteria? Viruses? Given the size of the bat population, surely some guano had found its way into the water. Did I really want to immerse myself in water of questionable quality? I decided on a compromise.

I sat on the sloped ground and took off my sneakers and socks, putting them higher on the slope behind me. Then I stood, balancing on my left foot, still planted on solid ground, while I dipped my right foot into the water. Aaaaaaah, that felt amazing! I put some weight on my right foot, eight inches deep in the water, to see if the lake's bottom felt slippery or mucky. A slight cloud of sediment rose and swirled around my ankle, but quickly settled. I felt the firmness of the bottom beneath my feet as I stepped into the lake.

I waded knee-deep into the water. I could hear the others chattering away about bats and speculating about the size of the cavern. The Brits poked fun at Jeff and Brent, who trash-talked them in return. They positioned all three torches together, attempting to amplify the brightness of the light where they had gathered, while dark shadows mostly obscured my location. No one seemed to notice I had wandered away from the group.

I had a fierce desire to submerge my whole body in the lake, but then I'd be stuck wearing soggy clothes until we returned to the hotel. Unless… I took my clothes *off*. My prudish New England upbringing frowned on skinny-dipping, but that didn't mean I'd never done it. Would my American friends be shocked to see me swimming naked in the lake? Did I dare to disrobe in the presence of these handsome RAF officers? Actually, they wouldn't be able to see much at all if I stayed in the deep shadows.

I returned to land, where I quietly and quickly peeled off my clothes, then proceeded back into the lake. I submerged myself until only my neck and head remained visible above the surface. The velvety smooth warm water surrounded me, allowing me to feel magically suspended in nothingness. I had no regrets about my decision. Before I could bask for long in its calming embrace, Joy's concerned voice echoed through the cavern.

"Hey, Brenda, where are you?"

"Where'd she go?" asked Leslie.

I knew I had to reveal my location so the group wouldn't panic. Reluctantly, I splashed the surface of the water with one hand while waving my other arm over my head. "I'm over here."

It took a few frantic seconds for them to home in on the direction of my voice. Looks of surprise turned to envy as it became clear what I'd been up to.

"Are you okay?" Brent shouted.

"I'm fine," I said with a hint of mischievousness. "The water's delightful. Come on in."

Though part of me wished they hadn't heard me, another part filled with joy when Chad said, "Right, mates. That's a bloody brilliant idea!"

It only took that gentle prod to persuade the Brits to strip off their clothes and pitch their muscular bodies into the lake. They frolicked like delighted kids in a swimming pool on a sweltering summer's day.

"Downright cracking, I'd say," added Colin, playfully splashing Andrew with a spray of water.

Doubtful at first about our antics, my American friends finally couldn't pass up the fun. Given the Brits' uninhibited display of nudity while they prepared to enter the water, Jeff addressed them with the tone of an overly protective husband, "Okay. Okay. We're coming in. But be gentlemen, will you, and divert your gazes so the ladies have some privacy."

The two husbands, along with the Brits, politely turned away while Joy and Leslie removed their clothes and walked into the lake. With eight naked charges now frolicking in the lagoon, Jose perched himself atop a large boulder, like a lifeguard, though *I* doubted he knew how to swim. Did he think we'd lost our minds?

With all of us in the lake treading along the silty bottom, we muddied the surrounding water. The combination of murky water and low light thoroughly concealed our bodies from sight. Best of all, the cooler water made the humid air feel perfectly comfortable.

"Let's just stay here. I'm really loving this," said Joy. "I have no interest in hiking farther into the cavern in this oppressive heat. I just wanna hang out with the bats in this relaxing oasis."

"I'm all for that." Leslie agreed, softly clapping her hands.

"Guys, take a torch and go exploring, if you want," Joy said. "We'll just wait here until you get back."

"Not a good idea." Andrew shot a warning glance at Chad. "We're all staying together."

Even Chad, who earlier had seemed adamant in his desire to hike farther, agreeably conceded without argument.

Perhaps because Jose felt hot, or hungry, or bored, he hollered a warning to us. Jeff translated his words. "He says we have to be careful that the torches don't burn out because this is an enchanted cave. Anyone left behind in its darkness will disappear forever. I guess he doesn't realize we have our headlamps as backup."

"Heck, we've only been down here for a little over an hour," said Brent, checking the time on his waterproof aviator's watch. "We still have plenty of time. Those torches should last for at least a few more hours."

Jeff hollered back, thanking Jose for his advice, letting him know we weren't ready to leave yet. Jose shrugged off Jeff's response.

Joy thoughtfully pointed out, "If he's really worried the torches are about to burn out, he wouldn't just sit there. He'd be gathering the torches and threatening to leave without us." We all agreed she was right.

As we blissfully floated in the water, an eerie thought raced through my mind. "Hey, guys, what if Jose *did* suddenly bolt with the torches? Do you think we could get out of here on our own?"

"Whoa! That sounds like a plotline from a Spielberg movie," said Jeff.

"You mean like that Indiana Jones movie—with hidden treasure and angry bats?" asked Colin.

"Exactly! But I think our movie should be a spy thriller," I said.

"Like an Indiana Jones meets James Bond adventure!" said Leslie.

These ideas excited Chad. "I can see it. This cave would be the perfect setting for a top-secret rendezvous between American CIA agents and British MI6 operatives."

Even the normally reserved Andrew added his take to the plot. "And their mission must involve Russia, wouldn't you say? Maybe a covert plan to disable their nuclear launch system?"

Joy chimed in, adding her idea. "But what they don't know is that KGB agents are hot on their trail and have already hired a local boy to help foil the meeting."

"You mean like Jose?" Jeff smirked, nodding to where Jose sat, completely disinterested in our chatter.

"Exactly!" I said gleefully. "He could lead the allied spies into the cave, wait until they're totally absorbed in their planning, then, without warning, snuff out the torches, leaving them stranded in complete darkness."

Andrew quickly shot down that scenario. "Nah, Spies would never be so careless. They'd bring powerful searchlights and other caving equipment."

"Well, what if, while the spies are working, the boy sneaks out of the cave to the waiting KGB spies? They hand him some sticks of dynamite and order him back into the tunnel to place it in the narrowest crawl space. When he exits the cave, BOOM! The explosion demolishes the passage out of the cave." Leslie shivered at her own suggestion.

"Too implausible," said Jeff. "Sure, the blast leaves them entombed, but they survive. One of the British spies, though, is an expert caver."

"That's right!" Chad beamed. "The blast fills the air with dust and riles up the bats. But he knows the bats will navigate toward fresh air and could lead them to another exit point deeper in the cave."

"Not *everyone* likes his plan, though," Colin noted with a wink at Chad. "They worry it will be a fool's errand and they'll end up dying in the depths of the cave where no one will ever find their bodies."

As our plot grew thicker, Leslie abruptly interrupted us. "Hey, guys, where's Jose?"

He was no longer perched on top of the boulder. He'd disappeared without making a sound. "Where the hell did he go?" said Brent. "All the torches are still here. He's got to be down here somewhere. Anyone see him?"

All eyes strained, searching the shadowy darkness beyond the circle of wavering torchlight for any sign of Jose.

"Jose, *donde esta?*" shouted Jeff. "*Ven aquí ahora!*" Despite Jeff's order for Jose to make his presence known, the cavern remained silent except for the gentle fluttering of the invisible bats above us.

As we called out, his name echoed off the walls of the cavern. We needed him to lead us out of the cave. Suddenly, I worried the movie plot being hatched in our imaginations might be more credible than we realized. I wasn't the only one alarmed by Jose's disappearance. After a minute that felt like an hour, a ghostly figure emerged from the blackness, walking toward us. When it stepped into the cone of light cast by our torches, we realized with great relief that Jose had returned.

"He probably had to pee and went to find some privacy." Chad speculated on the cause for his absence, while Jose reclaimed his seat atop the boulder.

The momentary scare killed any desire we had to resume script plotting. I could feel how wrinkled my fingers had become from spending so much time in the water, so I thought about getting out of the lake, but I didn't want my naked body to be the focus of everyone's attention. It had been easy to be the first to slip into the lake unnoticed by the others, but how could I tactfully remove myself without baring my assets?

Without warning, I felt a slight vibration deep underground, as the earth briefly grumbled. Like stampeding cattle, we splashed and scrambled to exit the lake. Getting out of the cave became my sole priority. I didn't care who saw me, as I hastily threw my T-shirt over my head and pulled on my underwear and shorts. The reverberation had shocked us. The others in our group also finished dressing with the speed of firefighters readying to respond to an alarm.

"Let's get the hell out of here while we can," said Jeff, grabbing his day pack and waving for Jose to lead the way.

Once Jose distributed the torches, we hustled back the way we'd come. I wanted to run, but knew I needed to watch where I stepped. In my haste to escape, I didn't want to sprain an ankle or break a leg. Ascending the slope away from the lake into the narrower passage, we again riled the bats that swooped past our heads as though to encourage our departure. Sweat dripped down the side of my face from the mix of anxiety and the heated air. My clothes, already soaked from dressing my wet body, became more uncomfortably saturated with the salty fresh sweat from my body.

Except for an occasional warning to watch our step when passing through a tricky section, we trekked in silence, each of us focused on moving as quickly as we could. We finally reached the low side of the tight squeeze. To exit, we needed to slither uphill against the gravity that had assisted us on our way in. We paused long enough to listen to Jose's strategy to get us back through the dreaded obstacle.

Jeff translated his instructions. "Listen, guys, we've all been through this obstacle before, which means we can all get through it again. Jose will take two torches through first, because, remember, the passage on the other side is just narrow enough for moving single file. Andrew will go first. Then me and Joy. Andrew will take a torch and lead our first group up the path. It's a straight shot back to the entrance. Colin, Brent, and Leslie will go in the second group."

That left me in the final group, being one of the last to break free of the cave's clutch. I thought about protesting, but decided to suck it up. Teaming with the only expert caver of the group and our guide, who possessed an intricate knowledge of the cave, brought me a sense of comfort. But every minute that passed, I felt the cave closing in around me, stifling my breath. I craved the spaciousness of the vast valley outside and longed for the breeze to brush against my overheated cheeks.

Jose grabbed and capped two torches and quickly disappeared into the darkness of the narrow passage. Seconds later, we saw the soft glow of light on the far side. Then Jose slithered back into the chamber where we waited.

"Let's get on with this," said Andrew as he dropped to a squat, then launched his body forward up and into the narrows. Jeff only waited long enough to lose sight of Andrew's boots before following him.

"Joy, come on, hon," Jeff called from the upper side. "Just like before, get flat, arms stretched forward, head down, and squirm toward me. It's easier coming uphill."

Joy showed no fear as she followed Jeff's instructions. We watched her progress quickened once Jeff tugged at her arms to help drag her through the crawlspace. Jeff yelled back to us, "We're clear. On our way out." Colin led the way for the second group. On the way in, we'd spent at least 30 minutes navigating this obstacle. Now we resembled a group of lemmings hellbent to escape this cave.

"All clear." Brent signaled once Leslie made it through.

"Righto. On my way," Chad answered. He winked at me. "Don't worry, Brenda, I've got your back. I'll help pull you through." Then he was gone.

Lying flat on my belly, arms stretched out ahead, I wiggled my body forward. Seconds later, I felt Chad's powerful hands firmly grip my wrists. He tugged gently but forcefully, hauling me toward him until I had space to stand up. Even in the dim light, his blue eyes seemed to sparkle. I wanted to give him a big hug for his help, but realized with dismay that the front of my wet T-shirt was now smeared with muck from my belly crawl. I settled instead on a simple compliment. "Thank you so much for your help, Chad. I can't believe how strong you are!"

"My pleasure, Brenda, anytime."

We stood in darkness, connected by an invisible spark as Jose capped and brought the last torch through. With the torch uncapped on our side, Chad said, "How about we get out of here?"

My heart pounded, being so near Chad, but I couldn't bear to stay underground for one moment longer. I nodded. "Let's do it."

After 15 minutes, we emerged safely into daylight. The brightness forced me to squint. We found no evidence that suggested the KGB or anyone else had been stalking us. Jose seemed overjoyed by the 10 US dollar tip we gave him for being our guide. I wasn't the only one with a muddy mess on the front of my shirt and shorts. We all sported the cave's grime like a badge of honor for achieving our goal.

Later that evening, bathed and dressed in fresh-smelling clothes, we gathered for dinner in the hotel to celebrate our adventure. The Brits would leave before dawn the following day to join their team members already at high altitude. As we recalled the events of our time in the cave, it all sounded rather implausible. "Who's ever going to believe we did these insane things?" I asked.

"What does it matter, really?" Chad replied. "*We* know what we did, and if it remains only a memory between the eight of us, that's bloody well fine with me."

I nodded. "We shared an intense experience that has bonded us forever, even if we never cross paths again. It's been a true privilege, gentlemen, to share this time with you."

"Hear. Hear." We clinked glasses in a last toast.

Woman and child with llamas in the high Andes

UPDATE:

Lake Titicaca is drying up. After a 2023 winter heat wave and a recent lack of rainfall combined with high levels of solar radiation which drives evaporation, the drop in the water level of the lake is drastically affecting tourism, fishing, and agriculture.

The Gruta is now a tourist attraction. The village has blasted out the narrow squeeze. Now there's an enlarged pathway, large enough to walk standing up to the lake, strung with electric lights all the way to the water. The owners have brought in six-person paddle boats visitors can rent to paddle around the lagoon. The cave's bat population, including a rare local species, has been decimated.

Sadly, my American friends and I lost contact with each other after we departed from Bolivia. I never expected to hear anything from our RAF friends, but I can say Chad's blue eyes still twinkle in my memories.

Andes Mountains in Bolivia

MAP OF TUNISIA

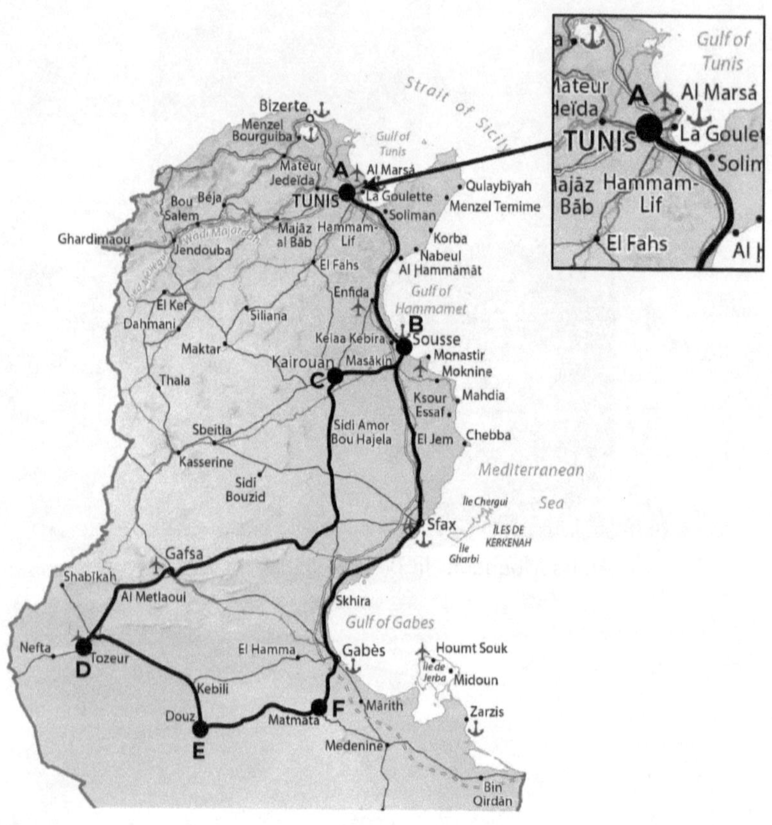

A : Tunis - Capital City

B : Sousse - Beach Resort

C : Kairouan - Start of Eid

D : Tozeur - Youssef's Home

E : Douz - Edge of the Sahara Desert

F : Matmata - Troglodytes

7

IN THE LAND OF
THE TROGLODYTES

TUNISIA – APRIL & MAY 1990

ANY HOPE I HAD of enjoying the exotic sights and enticing aroma of spices in the ancient bazaar ended abruptly when a hand forcefully grabbed and squeezed my butt. Shocked by this violation, I instinctively swatted at the offending hand. Trapped within a boisterous mob that jammed the narrow alley, I could barely move. By the time I maneuvered around to confront the pervert who had dared to molest me, the men close enough to have committed the dastardly act feigned innocence.

Frowning at them, I shouted, "No!" I twisted sideways, and motioned for them to pass. No way I'd give those men a further opportunity to grope my body. Still, I continued to be jostled by the throng of local residents, mostly men in crumpled shirts drenched with sweat, pushing and shoving their way forward, hurrying to pick up needed goods from shops in the Tunis bazaar on their way home. I inched forward along the cobblestone alley that echoed with the sounds of vendors hawking their goods and haggling for the best prices.

Suddenly, I felt claustrophobic, shaken by the stream of shoppers sweeping me with them in a direction I wasn't sure I wanted to go. The concierge at my hotel had given me a map with the layout of the bazaar, but I certainly didn't want any of those men to perceive me as being lost or frightened. I'd only progressed a couple hundred yards into the enormous market when I realized it had been a terrible idea to venture into its maze on my own.

I worked my way to one side of the alley, then quickly retreated the way I'd come. On my way to the bazaar, I had paid no attention to the men gathered outdoors at sidewalk cafés, but now on my return with a heightened awareness of danger, I noticed groups of them inhaling vaporized hashish through a communal hookah pipe. I realized that these stoned-out-of-their-minds men derived enjoyment from jeering at me as I passed by them. The smirks on their faces and tones of their voices conveyed their contempt for an unescorted foreign female. I ignored them and hurried to reach the safety of the hotel. I collapsed on a sofa in the lobby until I finally caught my breath and the tension in my body dissolved.

THIS HAD BEEN MY FIRST NON-WORK DAY since I'd arrived in the capital city of Tunis for a two-month long assignment with USAID's mission in Tunisia. My USAID host, Martha, had left me on my own to take care of her Saturday chores. During my first week in this country, I spent most of my time in the company of other

American diplomats. Martha picked me up from my hotel and drove me to and from the office each day.

She also arranged for us to attend several dinner parties at the homes of her work colleagues. During one dinner conversation about how the toe of Italy sits only 200 miles from Tunis, one guest nearing the end of his four-year assignment remarked, "Watch out, Brenda. You'll find these Tunisian men have the worst philandering tendencies of Italian men with the worst chauvinistic attitudes of Arabic men." I should have taken his warning more seriously.

For my first solo outing, I thought about spending the day visiting the ruins at Carthage a few miles northeast of Tunis, but the hotel concierge recommended I stay within walking distance of the hotel.

"Madam, I think you'd enjoy an exploration of the souks in our outdoor market nearby." His voice filled with enthusiasm as he described the different sections in the market. "Each souk has colorfully decorated shops and boutiques tightly crammed together offering tempting displays of similar products. So, while one souk sells only meat, another sells only fish. Others sell fabrics, spices, jewelry, perfumes, leather goods, medicinal plants, and handicrafts. All these souks interconnect by cobblestone alleys, some dating back to the 13th century."

I took his advice, thinking I could look for trinkets to give my friends and colleagues as gifts on my return to the United States. I *never* expected in public places men would harass me by grabbing my flesh in the market or catcalling insults at me in Arabic. The events of the day had intimidated me and left me reluctant to explore more of the city's attractions on my own.

THAT NIGHT, I ATE ALONE in the hotel dining room. My uniformed server, a handsome Tunisian with short black curly hair, dark eyes, and an engaging smile, offered me a menu.

"Madam, my name is Youssef. May I get you a drink?"

His command of English impressed me. "Yes please, I'd like a bottle of sparkling water, no ice." While he fetched my water, I scanned the menu. He returned with a tray that held not only my water but a plate of Tunisian olives marinated in a spicy oil and warm, crusty slices of a baguette.

"Do you have any questions about the menu?" Youssef asked politely.

"There are quite a few dishes that sound appealing. What would you recommend?"

I'd discovered in my travels I should heed the advice of locals when it came to food.

"Do you like seafood?"

I nodded, thinking that the grilled lemon shrimp skewer might be tasty.

"I think you might like our squid. The chef here cooks it perfectly." He raised his right hand to his mouth, kissed his fingertips, then lifted them in delight.

The only squid I'd ever eaten had been deep-fried, tasteless, chewy rings as rubbery as an elastic band. Youssef saw my alarmed look.

"Madam, we have the best squid in the world in the Mediterranean waters close to Tunisia. Our chef first grills it, then sautés it with spices and vegetables. It will melt in your mouth."

Though hesitant about choosing the squid, Youssef's pitch made me decide to try it.

He smiled and said, "You won't be disappointed. I promise."

Tunisians typically gathered for their evening meal at 8 p.m. By their standards, I'd arrived two hours early. Since Youssef had no other guests to look after, he lingered at my table. I learned he'd mastered English while attending a school for hospitality management in Europe. He dreamed of becoming the general manager of a hotel. When he inquired about my day, I described my failed attempt to explore the market. He shook his head and frowned with disappointment that my outing had not been pleasant.

When he set the plate of squid in front of me, the lemony, garlicky scent of it set my mouth watering. My knife easily sliced through the local delicacy. Youssef paid close attention to my reaction as I took my first bite, watching for any signs of delight or disappointment. As promised, it melted in my mouth, with a taste similar to chicken piccata, only much more tender. "This is exquisite!" I said, readying my fork for another bite.

"Told you." He grinned.

This delightful dinner helped to salvage what had otherwise been a dreadful day.

AFTER SLEEPING SOUNDLY, I woke feeling fresh and energetic. I determined not to let the inappropriate behavior of the local men put a damper on my explorations of their city. After consulting with the hotel concierge, I headed to the boarding station of a small train that ran between Tunis and the popular tourist attraction nearby, the ancient ruins of Carthage.

In the third century BC, Carthage was one of the busiest port cities on the Mediterranean Sea, serving as the political and trade center of the North African empire, inhabited by half a million people. A few centuries later, the Romans conquered and destroyed much of the city. Conquered for the second time in the seventh century by the Arabs, they later abandoned it.

The train ride took 30 minutes to reach the Hannibal stop. A few other tourists also got off the train. Ahead of us lay the weathered clay-brick ruins of Roman baths, houses, a chapel, cemetery, and partial remains of intricate mosaics. Acres of ruins dotted the landscape. The area spread wide open for exploring. Since no paths marked a route through the remnants of what had once been a bustling metropolis, I picked my way through, around and over still-standing structures, stopping to take photos of ornate columns and colorful mosaic designs.

Except for a few tourists strolling among the ruins in the distance, the ancient expanse of partial shells of buildings remained deserted. I felt liberated being away from the busy center of Tunis and its hookah-smoking stoned men. Here, a gentle salty breeze blowing off the sea caressed my cheeks and ruffled my hair. The squawks of seagulls soaring through a cloudless blue sky occasionally pierced the silence. Perched on a stone wall, I attempted to envision the former city bustling with people and animals navigating its streets, conducting their daily affairs without the aid of modern technology.

After that peaceful interlude, I continued my exploration of Carthage. As I turned a corner and began walking down a passage secluded by high walls, I noticed a man approaching from the opposite direction. It seemed odd that on such a warm day, he was wearing a long coat. He didn't look like a tourist either. When only 15 feet separated us, he flung open his coat, exposing his fully aroused naked body.

I screamed, "No! Get away!" twirled around, and raced in the opposite direction. Reaching a wide-open area, I quickly glanced back to see if he was pursuing me. Gasping for breath, and with my heart still pounding, I felt a wave of relief wash over me when I realized the pervert was nowhere to be seen. Disgusted and angered by this man's lewdness, I walked back to the train. I had hoped to visit many attractions in this country, but if Tunisian men blatantly disrespected women the way I'd experienced two days in a row, my expectation seemed well on its way to being dashed.

THAT NIGHT, YOUSSEF'S FACE lit up when I entered the dining room. He led me to a table and helped seat me. "Miss Brenda, how was your day?" he asked while handing me a menu.

His brow wrinkled when he saw the frown on my face. I shrugged my shoulders.

"What happened?" His eyes reflected genuine concern as he patiently waited for an explanation.

"I can't go anywhere in this country without being harassed by the men. Today, in Carthage, a creep exposed himself to me. Really gross."

Youssef hung his head in exasperation at hearing my revelation.

"Miss Brenda, I'm so sorry. These men are ignorant. They think they can do anything they want with women. I apologize for their rudeness."

I felt guilty categorizing all Tunisian men as assholes, when Youssef clearly did not fall in that category. "You don't need to apologize for them. You're not like them."

Then, to change the topic of conversation, I said, "I'm starved, and I already know what I want for dinner. More of that delicious squid please!"

Youssef laughed and winked. "A fine choice, if I say so myself."

He chatted with me when not serving other diners, making sure that my second dinner of the chef's Tunisian-style squid matched my enjoyment of my meal the previous evening. As I finished eating, Youssef approached me and stood fidgeting as if unsure whether he should voice his thoughts. Finally, he spoke.

"Miss Brenda, if you'd like, I would be happy to accompany you to see the sights in our city when I'm not working. If you are in my company, the men will not bother you, I promise. But only if you would like."

It had taken him courage to suggest this to a female foreign diplomat. Holding his breath, he waited to hear whether I'd accept or reject his help.

"Youssef, that is so kind of you. I'd hate for you to have to use your free time to be my bodyguard."

"I don't mind. Really, it would be my pleasure. I get through my shift at 10 p.m. If you meet me in the lobby, I will take you to a nice café close by. We can talk about the places you'd like to see in the city and make a plan."

Later that evening, we sat at a sidewalk table drinking coffee and eating sweets, while I peppered him with questions about the best attractions in and around the capital. I told him, "I can skip anything that is typically touristy. I'd rather get to know and see the authentic Tunisia."

He seemed pleased that I wanted to know his country on a deeper level. Youssef also told me about his family that lived in an oasis southwest of Tunis. I didn't say it, but the idea of visiting an oasis intrigued me.

We began a list of sights to visit. On his next day off, as soon as I got through work, we'd take an evening stroll back through the souks, where he could also help me bargain for reasonable prices on anything I might want to purchase. The following weekend, we'd take the train past Carthage to the quaint seaside village of Sidi Bou Said, known for its cobbled streets and picturesque blue-trimmed white houses. There we could savor its claim to fame, *Bambalouni*, a delicate, fluffy fried donut bathed in honey. Afterward, we'd take a walk along their sandy beach.

As Youssef walked me back to the hotel, I noticed the Tunisian men sitting outside the cafés we passed showed no interest in me. No one leered or catcalled as they had when I passed by them alone. With Youssef, I felt safe. I looked forward to his company on our future outings.

WHEN I ARRIVED IN TUNISIA, a country with a predominantly Islamic population, their holy month of Ramadan had already begun. Muslims observe this month with fasting, communal prayers, reflection and offering charity to others. They are required to fast every day by abstaining from food and drink from before the first light of dawn until the setting of the sun. At the end of Ramadan, they "break" their fast with a three-day-long celebration of feasting called *Eid al-Fitr* with their extended families and communities.

What I hadn't realized was that I'd have six days off in a row in late April, including the three religious holidays of *Eid*, two weekend days, and the May 1st International Labor Day holiday. By then, Youssef had already escorted me to most of the places in Tunis I'd wanted to see. About a week before the start of *Eid*, after being seated at my table in the hotel dining room, I told Youssef, "I have six days off from work next week, and I really don't feel like sitting it out here in Tunis. Do you know of any companies that offer tours I could take to see other parts of Tunisia?"

I saw Youssef wince and guessed he didn't approve of my taking off on my own, even if it was with a tour group. He explained, "During *Eid*, most individuals take time off from work, and it might be challenging to find any tours operating during that period."

Realizing the dilemma I faced, my lips curved into a disappointed pout. When he returned with my entrée, I noticed a sparkle in his eyes.

"Miss Brenda, I've been thinking of going home to celebrate *Eid* with my family. Would you like to come with me?"

Would I like to visit his home in an oasis and celebrate the feast of Eid with his family? What a fantastic idea! But what would my colleagues at work think of me gallivanting around Tunisia? Would it shock his family if he showed up with an American female diplomat?

I concealed my initial excitement by asking logistical questions.

"Youssef, can you get six days off? How would we get there? Wouldn't we shock your family if you showed up with me?"

"I have seniority here at the hotel and haven't gone home for *Eid* for two years. So yes, I can get that time off and maybe a few extra days. And don't worry—I'll get a message off to let them know you are coming."

Suddenly, a worried expression swept over his face as he turned away. When he faced me again, he said, "Actually, I'm not sure this is a good idea."

"Why?" I asked, secretly not wanting to lose this opportunity.

"My home is in a rural part of the country. We have no electricity, no proper bathroom like you are used to, and we sleep on mattresses on the floor. I'm not sure you would be comfortable."

"Youssef, believe me, I've endured much worse conditions in African jungles. I'll be fine. But how would we get there?"

"If it were just me, I'd take a bus, but because of the greater number of people traveling for *Eid*, the buses will be overcrowded, noisy, and stifling."

I scrunched my nose at that dreadful description. After considering other options, I asked, "Well, is there anywhere I could rent a car?"

He slowly shook his head. "That would be too expensive, like around $300 American dollars for a week."

That sounded like a deal to me. A private vehicle would give us the freedom to explore wherever and whenever we pleased. Though that amount must have felt like a fortune to Youssef, I could easily afford it.

"Youssef, I'll pay for the car."

Eyes wide open in disbelief, he said, "Really? You want to do that?"

"Yes! I'll even pay for our hotel rooms and meals when we aren't staying with your family. It'll be a grand adventure for me, for both of us."

"Since you don't have a license to drive here, I'll have to drive."

"Which I'd prefer, since you know where you're going. I'm happy just to be a passenger so I can take in all the surrounding sights."

Spontaneously, we'd found a win-win plan. Youssef could spend *Eid* with his family, and I'd have a chauffeur/tour guide to take me sightseeing around Tunisia. At that point, I didn't really care that my USAID colleagues might find the idea of a single female diplomat taking off on a road trip with a young Tunisian hotel worker scandalous.

IN THE DAYS BEFORE OUR TRIP, we plotted out a route that would take us in a loop around the northern half of the country. On the morning of our departure, Youssef arrived at the hotel in the vehicle I'd given him money to rent. A late-model car it was not. Superficial dents from never-repaired past mishaps blemished its white body. Despite the high mileage of 150,000 kilometers recorded on the tracker, the interior of the car remained tidy, and its engine functioned properly. We loaded our suitcases in its trunk and headed south.

On the first day of our trip, we drove through Hammamet and Sousse, both offering high-end resorts on the Mediterranean Sea catering to wealthy Europeans wanting a relaxing beach vacation. In Sousse, we stopped at one resort to take a peek at its pristine white sands. What I never expected to see were several female guests shamelessly sunbathing topless!

"This country is Islamic. How can they do that?" I asked Youssef.

"It's true that Tunisia prohibits nudity in any form. However, privately owned resorts allow bathers to expose their bodies while on their grounds and beaches. The women from Europe don't want any tan lines to show." Youssef shrugged and arched his eyebrows at the incongruity of the practice. Yet he didn't seem to mind gazing at the well-endowed naked women.

From Sousse, we headed west through rolling hills and vast fields brilliant with millions of bright red poppies in full bloom. At one point, I asked Youssef to stop so I could wander out among the colorful flowers. These red poppies, a different species than opium poppies, had become a symbol of remembrance after World War I. As a child, I remembered learning a poem about these poppies that started, "In Flanders fields the poppies grow. Between the crosses, row on row. That mark our place."

I sat down in the middle of the field and asked Youssef to take a photo of me surrounded by the gently swaying sea of scarlet. In just a matter of days, these vibrant blooms would disappear until their reappearance at the same time the following year.

Our destination that night took us to the fourth-largest city of Kairouan. We arrived in time to visit the Grand Mosque just before they closed to prepare for *Eid*. We walked through the ancient market's maze of hundreds of narrow alleyways within a walled compound. As people scurried to find their last-minute needs for the following days' celebrations, everyone seemed to be in a festive mood. They sensed their month-long fast would end in just a few hours.

Ramadan officially ends when the religious leaders sight the new crescent moon. In anticipation, we all waited as the sun set for the start-of-*Eid* decree to blare from the speaker atop the mosque. As soon as the proclamation sounded, the faithful wasted no time in savoring their tasty dinners before hurrying to the mosque to pray. Youssef and I found a cozy little restaurant inside the souk, where we ate a deliciously spiced couscous mixed with diced dried fruits and nuts.

That evening, joyful residents crowded into the streets, greeting friends and neighbors at a city-wide celebration party for all. Groups of musicians gathered at street corners playing traditional Tunisian folk music on drums, sitars, flutes, and violins. Youssef and I found a bakery selling the traditional almond sweets made especially during Ramadan. We bought a box of them to take to Youssef's family but devoured two of the sweets right there. Then we threaded our way through the celebration back to our hotel.

WE GOT AN EARLY START the next morning on our drive south to Youssef's family's home in Tozeur. We encountered few other vehicles on the road, but we started seeing more camels as the landscape transitioned to desert. My imagination conjured the picture of an oasis as a tiny pool of life-saving spring water surrounded by a couple of palm trees in a vast, lifeless expanse of sand. That impression likely came from a cartoon I'd seen of a half-dead man crawling across the scorching sand, hands outstretched toward a shimmering spring, only to discover it had been a mirage.

My faulty impression of an oasis changed as we got closer to Tozeur. We rode with the windows down as the daytime heat soared, grateful for the warm breeze circulating through the car. We passed through tiny villages, where we saw groves of coconut palm trees being grown as a primary source of revenue for the rural farmers.

Suddenly, Youssef pulled off to the side of the road.

"I'm thirsty. How about you?" he asked.

I nodded. But it puzzled me, as no sign of liquid appeared anywhere in sight. I asked, "Where are you going to find us something to drink?"

Youssef pointed up. High in a palm tree towering above our car hung a cluster of coconuts. Of course! I knew the hollow inside the coconut contained a natural and nutritious water.

"How are you going to get up there?" Was he going to throw stones at the cluster, hoping to hit and jar one of them loose?

"I'll show you."

He strode over to the trunk, kicked off his shoes, and then shinnied up the trunk. He'd obviously done this before because he looked totally at ease, even while dangling dangerously high on the trunk. When he finally got close enough to reach the cluster, he grabbed and twisted one coconut free.

"Watch out down there," he shouted, then let the fruit fall to the ground, hitting with a dull thud. After releasing a second coconut in a freefall to the ground, he scrambled back down to where I waited. Although a machete would have been more useful, he pulled a jack-knife from his pocket to shave off the top of the green fibrous outer skin. Beneath, he located the three soft "eyes" at the top of the shell. He poked an opening through one of the soft spots into the hollow and handed it to me.

I took a swig of the clear sweet liquid that, despite the heat of midday, tasted cool and refreshing. After our short "water" break, we set off again. The closer we got to Tozeur, the more camels we saw roaming about.

Seeing my fascination with the furry desert dwellers, Youssef provided me with a few interesting facts about camels. "They look sort of clumsy, but they can gallop as fast as a horse and easily carry 200 pounds. So, the Tunisian nomads use them to transport passengers and cargo. They also get milk, wool, meat, and leather from them. They even collect their dried dung as fuel for cooking fires."

I gave him a thumbs up. "They're pretty resourceful to use every part of the animal."

"Camels can drink up to 50 gallons of water at a time, and it's possible for them to go for 10 days without a drink. Most foreigners think they store water in their hump." He chuckled. "But that's where they store extra fat."

"What does their meat taste like?" I asked.

"It's considered a delicacy for us, often prepared only on special occasions. You've never tried camel meat, I take it?"

"Nope. But I'd try it if I had a chance."

"Tell you what. I can ask my mother to make a stew of camel meat while we're there so you can see for yourself."

APPROACHING TOZEUR, we drove by a few large palm and olive plantations irrigated by water from the spring-fed lake. A population of 5,000 lived in the 2,600-acre oasis. Driving through the town, Youssef waved to or briefly chatted with several residents, exchanging *Eid* greetings. When we pulled up in front of Youssef's modest clay-brick home, his mother and sisters ran out to meet us. His mother hugged him tightly after missing him for two years, while his sisters chattered between themselves as they fixed their gaze on me. Their ankle-length, loose-fitting, beige dresses covered their bodies, and they wore matching beige scarves that covered their heads.

Youssef's mother finally released him and gripped my wrist to lead us into their home. Her forehead, cheeks, and chin bore the traditional tattoos of Tunisia's southern nomadic tribes. She welcomed me with genuine pleasure, excitedly speaking in words I didn't understand. I handed her the box of almond sweets we'd brought for her family. She bowed in acceptance, grateful for the gift we offered. Youssef took on the role of translator for the questions his mother and sisters asked about me.

"They want to know what you think of Tunisia, and what kind of work you are doing."

"You can tell them I am charmed by their country, especially since you've been acting as my bodyguard." I laughed, wondering how Youssef would translate those words. "You can tell them what we've seen. Just tell them I work with computers for the American government."

The women of the family had prepared a feast ahead of our arrival to celebrate the second day of Eid. We sat in a circle on a tightly handwoven wool Berber rug. Youssef's mom ladled out mounds of fine-grained couscous mixed with diced vegetables and spices, which she covered with a hefty portion of a simple favorite lamb stew cooked with potatoes, onions, and peppers. She balanced a wedge of dense semolina bread on the side of each bowl, useful for soaking up the extra brown, aromatic broth remaining at the bottom. It delighted me to see his family's joy at having Youssef at home with them for *Eid*. I felt grateful I could help to make this reunion possible.

During our feast, Youssef, sitting on my left, turned toward me. His serious expression reflected a hesitancy that made me nervous. "Miss Brenda, during the *Eid* celebrations, it's customary for girls and women to decorate their hands with henna tattoos. My *sisters* think you should have a henna design on your hands. They would be delighted to make a design for you. But you can say no. There's no pressure for you to do it."

I studied the deep orange dyed patterns on the hands of the girls and their mother, while the sisters' eager eyes focused on me, awaiting my reply. I'd had a delicate lacey henna design drawn on my hands during a wedding I'd attended when I lived in Pakistan, so I knew that skin stained with the maroon henna paste would fade in a few weeks' time. *What the heck? While in Tunisia, why not do as the Tunisians do?*

"Tell them it would be an honor to have them decorate my hands."

They giggled delightfully as Youssef translated my answer. When we finished eating, the sisters quickly made up a batch of henna paste by mixing henna powder, ground fine from the leaves of the henna bush, with water and a bit of sugar. It needed to cure for a couple of hours before they applied it to my skin. When the golden sunset faded to black, we moved outside where the cooling air temperature offered relief, and we ate the traditional sweet treats made for *Eid*.

The family had placed a twin mattress for me in the small room shared by the sisters. The three of us plopped down on it to begin the henna ceremony. They used a kerosene lamp to illuminate the space where they would be working. The girls communicated using charades to determine how much of my hand I wanted to be covered with a design. I agreed to a solid geometric design on my fingertips and a spiral symbol on the backs of my hands with nothing on my palms.

Using a small bristled brush, they took turns painting each of my fingers with the rust-colored paste. The design completely covered my nails and extended in a V shape down to my middle knuckle. They chattered while they worked, but I saw the determination in their eyes to complete the design without making a single mistake. When finished, they raised my hands to display their artistic creation.

It looked like I'd been making mud pies! They wrapped both of my hands in clean rags to keep the henna in place until it dried and to prevent it from staining my clothes or bedding. Soon after, we crawled under the sheets and fell asleep.

THE NEXT MORNING, Youssef's family admired the design the sisters made on my hands. It certainly looked more attractive once they removed the dried henna, but I wondered if the solid orange-stained areas, much darker than I remembered the Pakistani henna design being, would take longer to wear off. Youssef's wide grin reflected his pride at my willingness to take part in their tradition.

That day we invited Youssef's sisters to come with us as we did a day trip to visit hot springs and the ruins of ancient villages along the border of Algeria. They appreciated the rare treat of going in an automobile to these locations, where neither had been before. On the way, we drove through a bleak desert landscape, passing by several small nomadic compounds. At a few, we stopped to greet the herders, caring for their goats and camels. The further south we drove, the sparser the vegetation became, but whenever we came to a spring, area nomads used the precious water to grow small garden patches.

We had no way to measure the scorching temperature, but in the early afternoon, with the sun directly overhead and no trace of shade anywhere, I found it unbearable. I estimated it had to be 90 degrees or hotter. When I complained, Youssef and his sisters laughed. "Hot for you, maybe, but this is the most pleasant time of the year for us." As physical proof of my body's struggle in the blistering heat, Youssef watched a few drops of sweat fall from my forehead onto my shirt.

Realizing I'd had enough of the heat and desert ruins for the day, he mercifully steered the car in a U-turn, heading east back to El Hamma. Even with all four windows rolled down, and Youssef driving reasonably fast, and despite the sun's rays now shining from behind us, the air circulating through the car still felt as hot as an oven. My imagination wandered as we sped back through the same desolate landscape.

How could the nomads live in such sweltering conditions when 90-degree temperatures were pleasant? Luckily, I wouldn't be around when daytime temperatures would climb well above 100 degrees. A silly thought darted into my mind. *What would a nomad do if dropped into a three-foot snow bank in below freezing temperatures? Just thinking about snowbanks seemed to make the air around me feel a few degrees cooler.*

Youssef's mother had a surprise waiting when she waved at us to hurry inside the house when we returned from our journey. Another feast lay spread out on the Berber carpet. As we took our places, a pungent aroma that made my mouth water filled the room. Youssef said, "My mother has prepared a special dish in your honor, Miss Brenda." He pointed at the large kettle containing chunks of meat in a gravy-like brown sauce. "This is a stew of camel meat!"

Touched, I put my hand over my heart in gratitude and then blew a kiss her way. She laughed at my odd gesture, then returned a genuine smile, seeing she'd made me happy. For this meal, she'd prepared a pea-sized variation of couscous by rolling the moistened semolina wheat flour in her palms. After cooking the pieces, she tossed them with hot spiced oil. I gratefully accepted the first bowl she filled, then waited for the others to be served. *So* curious to find out how camel meat tasted, I dug my spoon into the center of the mound in my bowl, capturing a chunk of the meat drenched in its sauce.

The savory, lightly salted sauce tasted delicious, but when I bit into the meat, it had the tough texture of gristle. I chewed on it for a while, making no progress in shredding it into smaller morsels I could swallow. The meat itself had no distinct flavor that I could discern. When I realized there was no way I could swallow the rubbery chunk in my mouth, I panicked. Removing it from my mouth, I feared, would be the ultimate insult to Youssef's mother. Yikes! I didn't know how to get myself out of this bind.

While I wracked my brain for a solution, I kept my eyes lowered and scooped a few pieces of the couscous onto my spoon and shoveled them into my mouth. What a burst of flavor! The large couscous pearls delighted my tastebuds. I wanted more of those. About then I noticed other family members gnawing on chunks of meat that they held with their fingers.

Immediately, I pulled my chunk from my mouth and pretended to gnaw it, mimicking the others. A few seconds later, I ditched the inedible meat back into my bowl. Now having an empty mouth, I went after more of the scrumptious couscous coated with brown sauce. I politely smiled when I picked out a few more pieces of camel meat, sucked the sauce off, and nibbled at them before replacing them in my bowl. No one seemed to notice that I wasn't a fan of camel meat. Phew!

AFTER TWO DAYS VISITING IN TOZEUR, the time had come to continue our journey back toward Tunis. Once we'd stowed our belongings in the car, I bid Youssef's family a heartfelt farewell. As we pulled away from his home, I leaned my head and arms through the open window, waving goodbye to his family with my orange-tipped fingers, one last expression of gratitude for their warm hospitality.

Since I'd expressed a desire to stand at the edge of the Sahara Desert, Youssef took us on a slight detour to the village of Douz, famously referred to as the gateway to the Sahara. Douz hosted an annual camel festival and market to celebrate the traditions of the desert culture with camel racing, traditional music, and dances. On the outskirts of the village, we followed the road to its end at the fairgrounds. There, a row of bleachers faced out over the vast empty expanse of desert. Truly humbled by the shocking sight, I climbed up on the bleachers and sat there in wonderment, trying to take in the scene's enormity. Just fine grains of sand, shaped by the wind into rippled dunes, sprawled out in front of me as far as my eyes could see.

Youssef, who grew up in the desert environment, couldn't understand my fascination with the monotonous landscape and wanted to continue our journey. But I sat there for at least half an hour mesmerized by the Sahara's dimensions, just trying to comprehend the vastness of its 3.3 million square miles, nearly the size of the United States. The Sahara Desert covered one-third of the African Continent. Compared to this desert, I felt about as significant as a few of its grains of sand.

Youssef leaned against the side of the car with a glum look on his face. Not wanting to make him wait any longer, I hollered to him, "I'm ready to go!" as I climbed down from the bleachers.

He perked up and hollered back, "You're really going to love our next stop!"

What other place could ever compete with the magnificent natural wonder I'd just witnessed?

The route we followed skirted the boundary of the Sahara Desert. We passed several enormous sand dunes just off the road. Though he hadn't planned to stop, the proximity of the dunes proved too enticing not to take a mini-break.

"Bet you've never skied down a mountain of sand." He tipped his head sideways, sure of his assumption.

I shook my head. "But I've skied down plenty of snow-packed mountains."

"Let's go," he said, already climbing the dune in front of us.

I followed. Moving forward proved slow and laborious, as if pushing against an invisible force. With every step I took, the sand beneath me gave way, cutting my forward progress in half. Youssef shouted encouragement from where he stood on top of the dune. I kept trudging, feeling the burn in my calf muscles. Finally, I crested the 100-foot high mound.

"Now comes the fun part," said Youssef. "Take a step down, dig your heels in, and just let your shoes glide along the surface of the slope and enjoy the ride. Oh, and if you feel you're losing your balance, make sure you lean backward, not forward."

Giving only those brief instructions, Youssef leaped off the top. As he gracefully skied down the slope, using his outstretched arms for balance, he gained speed. I focused intently, mentally trying to capture the precision of his technique. Just before reaching the flat land at the bottom, he leaned back into a sitting position to slow his speed. I applauded his exciting performance as he stood and brushed the sand off his clothes.

He shouted up to me, "Are you ready to try it?"

"Yup." Instead of the leap forward Youssef took, I cautiously side-stepped off the top and began my descent sideways down the slope. My technique combined surfing and skiing moves, which gave me better control over my speed. After the first tense seconds, I relaxed and enjoyed the plunge. I slowed my descent at the bottom, with no need to finish the ride on my butt. We high-fived to our success, then resumed our drive.

"Our next stop is in Matmata, where the troglodytes live. What do you know about them?"

"I never heard the word until I came here."

"For centuries, these people have lived underground in 'cave' homes.

Living this way protects them from the scorching heat in summer and the chilly winds of winter."

"Do their roofs ever collapse?" I asked. "I couldn't imagine living my whole life in a dirt cave."

"Since it rarely rains in this area, floods are not a worry, and the dry packed ground is very stable."

Youssef laughed at my misconception. "First, they dig a large circular pit in the ground about twenty feet deep, which becomes an open-air courtyard. Then they carve individual rooms horizontally into the walls at the bottom of the pit. Afterward, they whitewash all the earthen surfaces to seal in the dirt and brighten the interior of the rooms."

As we approached Matmata, in the distance, I could see what looked like a crater in the otherwise flat plain. "Is that hole the pit of a cave home?" I asked.

"It is. But we're going to stop at a hotel built underground so you can see what it's like."

The concept of homes built into the ground intrigued me. At the hotel we descended into the courtyard, down a sandstone stairway carved into the side of the pit. Stepping through an opening into the lobby, I immediately noticed how much cooler it felt inside. What a difference from the adobe homes at ground level heated like ovens by the intense sun during the day. The lobby, with a bright white ceiling and walls decorated with natural-toned Berber textiles, had the feel of an ordinary hotel lobby.

A clerk standing behind the registration desk asked how he could help us.

"Do you serve drinks in the hotel? And is there a vacant room that we could look at by chance?" Youssef asked.

"Yes, of course. We have a bar just through that passageway to the right." He pointed to an opening off the main hallway straight ahead. "And I do have one room I can show you if you'll follow me."

He led us through a tunnel deeper into the earth. On either side, we passed closed wooden doors protecting the privacy of the occupied rooms. He stopped in front of one door and unlocked its latch before pulling it open so we could enter. He lit several lanterns that brought the room to life.

The 10-foot by 10-foot room, also completely whitewashed, contained a queen bed covered with a handmade linen bedspread in a geometrical pattern of vibrant colors. Spread on the floor, along the sides of the bed, handsome wool Berber rugs gave the room a homey feeling. Except for the lack of a window and a shared bathroom outside the room, it could have passed for a room in any decent hotel. I regretted we had not thought about staying in these unusual accommodations.

The desk clerk led us back to the entrance of the bar, where we sat on counter stools and ordered soft drinks. Chatting with the bartender, we learned that in the original 1977 *Star Wars* film, George Lucas had filmed locations in Matmata, including this hotel, and in other villages bordering the Sahara Desert to depict the fictional desert planet Tatooine, a beige-colored desolate world inhabited by human settlers and a variety of other life forms. He borrowed the planet's name from the real Tunisian village called Tataouine. Now I could hardly wait to rewatch *Star Wars* when I got home to find the scene shot right in this bar.

The bartender gave us directions to another private cave house located down a dirt road that passed close to it. He said the owner would allow us to take pictures from above down into his courtyard. The home appeared to be absent of occupants when we stopped and walked to the top edge of the pit. After a quick photo, we continued north toward the Gulf of Gabes.

The rest of our journey took us along the coast and through villages and towns that catered to beach-resort vacationers. The views of the gulf sparkled in the sunlight, and for people wanting to stretch out on lounge chairs or place beach towels on the sand to relax and work on their tans, these resorts fit the bill perfectly. But I considered these resorts ordinary and uninteresting. God knows I'd seen hundreds of beach resorts on the Florida coast while visiting my parents' winter condo. For me, the purpose of traveling meant exploring to discover unique or fascinating people, places, and objects that I could learn from. The first four days of our trip had provided so many enriching activities that I didn't mind just taking in the water views on our last two days.

ON MY FIRST WORK DAY back in Tunis, my host Martha's eyes widened with surprise when she caught sight of my henna design. "What have you done to your hands?" she demanded, while a few of the Tunisian staff in the office winked or nodded their heads in silent approval.

"I had them decorated for *Eid*." Her horrified look caused me momentarily to rethink the wisdom of allowing the sisters to stain my hands. With a shrug of my shoulders, I admitted, "I guess some foreigners might assume I've contracted a dreadful disease." The thought of the misconceptions I might unintentionally cause made me laugh.

MY FINAL OUTING before leaving Tunisia was a Memorial Day celebration held at the North African American Cemetery in Carthage. I felt ashamed that I knew nothing about the American soldiers who had fought World War II in Northern Africa where they died to protect freedom for America and her allies. In the 27-acre cemetery, meticulously maintained by the American Battle Monuments Commission, simple white crosses in perfectly aligned rows as far as you can see mark the graves of 2,841 American soldiers as a testament to their sacrifice.

Wide pathways divide nine grassy rectangular plots and lead to four reflecting pools where the paths intersect. An American flag flies high over the tranquil final resting place of these heroes.

American employees and contractors stationed in Tunis carpooled to the cemetery for this memorial service, held every year. To start the ceremony, a military band marched to stand in front of the outdoor seating area, playing "The Star-Spangled Banner" as we stood, to join our voices in singing our anthem. Speeches by an American general, a top official in the Tunisian government, and our ambassador acknowledged the supreme sacrifices of these soldiers and promised to maintain the cemetery in perpetuity. The ambassador ended his speech, vowing that, "The brave souls resting in this cemetery will never be forgotten."

Now that I had seen this cemetery, I knew I could never forget it. I thought of the red poppies swaying in the field I'd wandered into and wished I could go back and pick one of the vivid blossoms to place on each grave. Gratitude overflowed within me. The band started to play its final song. We stood and sang, "God bless America. Land that I love." Suddenly, I choked up.

My heart grieved for the brave young men who eagerly enlisted to serve their country in a foreign land far from their loved ones, who paid for their service with their lives, and for their families who would never again see their sons or brothers or fathers. Here, the remains of true patriots who never made it home to their loved ones lay buried in foreign soil.

Because of them, I finally understood and appreciated the amazing privilege of freedom they had fought for. No longer would I take my citizenship for granted. I returned home with many fond memories of my time in Tunisia, but none as powerful as the pride of being an American honoring the long-dead soldiers who fought so that, decades later, I could enjoy living in freedom.

Brenda in a field of poppies

UPDATES:

George Lucas brought fame to the troglodyte cave homes in the Matmata area by using them as filming locations for *Star Wars*. However, in the following decades, many families have abandoned these cave homes, as they seek better opportunities in urban settings. Many that are unused have fallen into disrepair. The few remaining troglodyte families swear they will not leave their homes or way of life.

I learned the hard way that one should never put henna paste on their fingernails unless they want to have curious minds asking why part of their nails are orange! As expected, the orange-stained skin of my hands faded to normal skin color after two months. But the deep orange stain on my nails remained as intense as when the sisters applied the henna. I had to wait nine months until my nails grew entirely out. Even my doctor expressed alarm until I explained that the stain was from henna.

The Sahara Desert is HUGE! But it's not flat. Sand dunes towering nearly 600 feet high in some places can shift by several yards each year in this constantly changing landscape. The climate is HOT and DRY. The highest air temperature ever recorded in the desert topped out at 136 degrees Fahrenheit in 1922, but the average high temperature spans between 100.4 to 104 degrees Fahrenheit during the warmest months, while sand temperature can easily reach 176 degrees Fahrenheit. Most of the desert gets less than .8 inches of rainfall in a year. Rain never falls in 10 percent of the desert.

The highest point in the Sahara Desert is at the peak of an extinct volcano (11,204 feet) called Emi Koussi in the Tibesti Mountains in northern Chad. From space astronauts consider it the most recognizable landmark on earth. Today, fumaroles at its base release gases and vapors that create hot springs. There are additional smaller volcanoes located north of Emi Koussi.

The Sahara Desert

MAP OF SRI LANKA

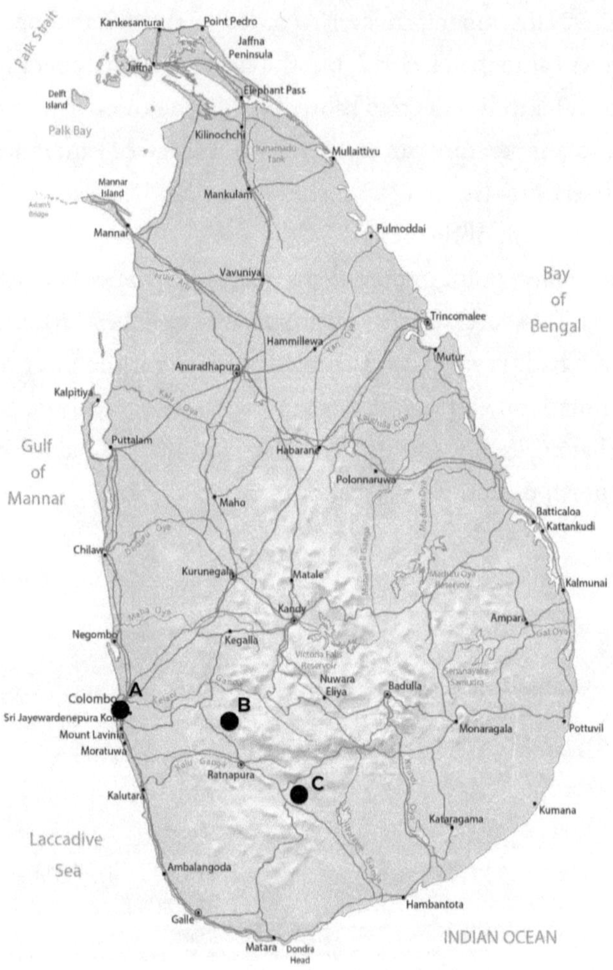

A : Columbo - Capital City, USAID Office

B : Site of Hash House Harrier's Run

C: Opata Estate - Rubber Tree and Tea Plantation

8

MIDNIGHT MAGIC

SRI LANKA - JULY 1990

I HAD THE SENSATION of arriving in La-La Land, though my ticket listed my destination as Colombo, Sri Lanka. I'd completely lost track of time after spending nearly 24 hours inside three cramped jets, catching only a few brief cat naps. The fuzziness in my brain from the exhaustion of an 8,500-mile flight compounded by a nine-and-a-half-hour time difference clouded my thinking. I desperately needed more sleep. But when I gazed down at the tear-shaped forested tropical island, rimmed by turquoise water rising from an ocean of deep navy, the excitement of landing in a country known for its natural beauty, delightful climate, and exceptional tea forced me to stay alert lest I miss one second of new exotic sights and sounds of the capital.

My host, Wayne Butler, the Controller of the United States Agency for International Development (USAID) mission in Sri Lanka, had arranged for a USAID driver to meet me at the airport. He delivered me to the Ramada Inn, my home for the next month. The front desk clerk handed me a registration form to complete. Still groggy, I asked for the day and date. She graciously answered, "Yes, madam, it is Tuesday, July 3rd." I didn't need to ask the time since the hands of a large wall clock behind the counter revealed it was 10:05 in the morning. She summoned a bellhop. The uniformed young man carried my suitcase to a spacious room overlooking a garden bordered by purple flowering jacaranda trees and sweet-smelling roses in a rainbow of colors.

After quickly hanging my clothes in the closet, I plopped down on the bed. I really needed to sleep, just for an hour, before heading over to meet Wayne and his Sri Lankan Finance Office staff. My one-month contract required me to teach them to convert their paper ledgers to USAID's new proprietary accounting software. I'd just sprawled out on the bed, eyes shut, feeling comfortably relaxed, when an irritating sound coming from somewhere in my room abruptly interrupted my reverie. I pinpointed the noise coming from a telephone resting on a wooden desk on the opposite of the room. In my exhausted stupor, I lunged for the phone. Who in the world knew they'd find me in *this* room?

"Hello?"

A husky, confident-sounding voice boomed, "Hey, welcome to paradise! I just wanted to check that you'd arrived safely. We're all thrilled you've agreed to give us a hand."

"And I'm thrilled to be here. But I'm really jet-lagged, so if it's okay with you, I'd like to take a quick nap before coming into the office."

"Believe me, I completely understand. That flight straight through from the US is a ball buster. Just give the office a call when you're ready and I'll have someone pick you up."

Wayne's bluntness surprised me, but the tone of his cheerful, welcoming voice put me at ease.

"Great, I just need about an hour. Then I'll come in."

He chuckled knowingly, as if privy to a secret I'd yet to learn, but my exhaustion prevented me from making further inquiries. I read him back the phone number he gave me, then thanked him, hung up the phone, and dove back onto the bed.

I'D ONLY BEEN ASLEEP for what seemed like five minutes when the damn phone trilled again. Grumpy from having my sleep disturbed, I answered the phone.

"Hey, are you okay?" Wayne asked, sounding concerned. "Since you never called, I thought I'd check on you."

I realized I'd must have been asleep longer that I thought. Embarrassed, I asked, "What time is it?"

"It's quarter to five. We're all getting ready to head home."

"Oh, no! I'm so sorry!"

Instantly, a pang of guilt washed over me as I realized I'd completely missed the entire first day of my contract. Before I could offer an explanation, Wayne said, "Don't worry. I didn't expect you to make an appearance today. It surprised me when you said you would. Today you just needed to rest."

Though I'd never met Wayne, I wanted to give him a hug for not being angry with me.

"Hey, tomorrow the office is closed for the 4th. Since I'm the token American in our Hash House Harriers group, I got assigned to set the trail for our run tomorrow. How'd you like to help me out? You'll get to see some of the countryside. It'll take us a couple of hours to design the route before the run starts at 3 p.m., but we won't do the run since we're setting the route. The runners should complete the run in 30 to 40 minutes, and then we'll socialize for another half hour. Afterward, we can catch some dinner."

I'd never heard of the Hash House Harriers, but I imagined one might be a heroin addict, stumbling towards his hidden stash of drugs.

As a USAID officer, I couldn't believe Wayne would have any connection to illegal drugs. Besides, his offer sure beat sitting alone in a hotel on an American holiday in a strange country.

"Sure. Sounds like fun!"

"Great, I'll pick you up in front of the hotel at 11 a.m."

I SKIPPED SUPPER and went back to sleep until the sun rose the next morning. A much-needed hot shower got my blood circulating and invigorated me. Only when my stomach growled did I realize how famished I felt. Before Wayne arrived, I took advantage of the hotel's complimentary breakfast buffet. One side of the buffet table offered familiar Western breakfast fare, while the opposite side featured the curries, rice, and noodles that Sri Lankans favored for their first meal of the day. I filled up on fluffy scrambled eggs, crunchy hash browns, and crispy bacon.

Promptly at 11 a.m., Wayne drove up to the front door of the hotel in a late-model white Land Rover. He got out of his vehicle, approaching me with his arm extended, and squeezed my hand in a hearty welcome. "It's really great to have you here with us. Our IT guy, Namal, has a hundred questions for you, but let's not talk about work today. Let's have some fun." He opened the passenger door of the Land Rover so I could climb inside and placed my backpack on the back seat. It surprised me that the interior of the 40-year-old confirmed bachelor's car could be so spotless, though two giant stuffed black plastic trash bags in the back compartment caught my attention.

As he pulled onto the city boulevard heading southeast, I studied my colleague. His hair, caramel brown peppered with a few early strands of white, framed a handsome, clean-shaven, tanned face. He wore multi-pocketed khaki shorts and a T-shirt bearing the image of an American flag with the words 'Home of the Free' that hugged his fit broad chest.

"I should have told you to bring sunscreen and water, since we'll be outside all day. My bad." He grimaced. "But I brought enough bottles of water for both of us."

"Not a problem. I put sunscreen on this morning, figuring my skin would need protection from this tropical sun, a lesson I learned the hard way as a river guide in Africa."

Soon, we left the city behind as we wound our way through tropical forests interrupted here and there with cleared land for villages so small that we passed through them in less than 30 seconds. All the while, we gradually gained altitude.

"So, tell me, Wayne, what exactly is a Hash House Harrier?"

He laughed, amused by my lack of familiarity with the group.

"Aw, it's a bunch of wild-ass expats, mostly Brits, who get together once a month to do a run through the countryside, then celebrate by drinking beer, lots of beer!"

Oh, no! I silently kicked myself for not asking more about this outing before accepting Wayne's invitation. I detested beer. Ordinarily, this type of outing would never appeal to me. I consoled myself with the thought I *only* had to help Wayne set the trail; I had no interest in running or drinking beer.

About an hour after leaving the hotel, we arrived at a small quarry where Wayne parked his car in an open clearing. He retrieved the two huge garbage bags, handing one to me. The bag weighed much less than I expected. Wayne unknotted his bag to reveal tiny dots of shredded paper.

"I'm sure you've heard the fairy tale about Hansel and Gretel," he said.

I nodded.

"Well, today I'm Hansel and you're Gretel, and these are our bags of crumbs. The embassy generously saved the pulverized remains of shredded 'official business' telexes for us."

We walked to the edge of the clearing and discovered a narrow path leading into the forest. Wayne scooped a handful of paper dust from his bag and sprinkled just enough of it along the path to be visible, but sparsely enough to require careful attention to avoid wandering astray. The forest trees had tall branchless trunks that spread out in a canopy high overhead. It reminded me of a birch forest one could find in New England, but these trees had brownish-gray bark.

The spacious opening beneath the canopy made walking easy. After 10 yards, Wayne stepped off the path and headed through the woods, dropping random handfuls of paper every couple of yards.

"Do you know where you are going?" I asked, concerned that he didn't appear to be using a map.

"Nope. It's my first time here too. One of the Harriers recommended this spot."

I questioned our sanity for venturing into an unfamiliar forest, but Wayne's unwavering confidence that we'd have no trouble completing our task silenced my doubts. I trotted after him, my arms wrapped around the unopened second bag. As we made our way through the forest, Wayne purposely included zigs and zags on our route. He also created dead-ended diversions that would confuse the runners, causing them to have to backtrack to search for the true trail.

Melodious chirps, tweets, and warbles filled the air with birdsong. A gentle, earthy-scented breeze rustled the tree leaves. Every so often, Wayne would ask my opinion of which direction I thought we should head. He wanted his course to be tough enough that the runners would have to work hard to complete it, but not so hard that they might get lost. His mischievous grin offered proof that he thoroughly enjoyed designing this course.

After 20 minutes, the forest transitioned into a grove of ancient rubber trees. Wayne explained because of the absence of any fresh cuts in their bark, farmers no longer tapped them for latex. On we trekked until the rubber tree forest opened at the edge of a rice paddy. Our random meandering through various landscapes reminded me of Dorothy's quest to find Oz, but I certainly didn't expect to find a wizard living out here. *Where* were *we headed? Already on this short walk, I added a rubber tree and a rice paddy to my growing list of new discoveries!*

Wayne wanted to set the trail so that it would cross the paddy, further challenging his fellow Harriers. In the small pond-sized paddy, farmers had built up soil berms in long parallel rows that crossed the pond from shore to shore, so they could walk into the paddy to harvest the rice grains when they ripened. Looking down on the paddy from above, it resembled the contoured design of an old-fashioned washboard.

Unfortunately for us, we approached the paddy at a right angle to the parallel berms, so instead of walking along one eight-inch-wide ridge to cross the paddy, like a gymnast prancing on a balance beam, we had to step across the 18-inch-wide rows of water filled with sprouting rice shoots. Had the berms been solid, it would have been easy. But the top surface of some berms measured just four inches wide. Other berms had long gaps where up to two feet of soil had crumbled away into the surrounding water.

Wayne had used nearly all of his bag of paper dust getting to the paddy, so I gladly handed him my full bag before attempting to cross across the berms. It would be a test of coordination and balance, even without the bulk of the full trash bag to manage. If anyone fell into the water, I hoped it wouldn't be me.

We had roughly 30 berms to cross. Wayne fearlessly led the way. I watched as he teetered to keep his balance on each berm. It didn't help that he had feet several sizes larger than mine. I followed a few berms behind. Halfway across, Wayne planted his forward foot on a berm, but when he shifted his weight forward, a section of the berm under his shoe collapsed. He scrambled, side-stepping onto a more solid section of the same berm, but not before dragging one sneaker through the water, soaking it.

"Watch out!" he shouted. "The soil here isn't solid. I'm going to walk along this berm until I find a solid place for you to cross."

I walked parallel to him on the berm I occupied. Suddenly, a soup-bowl-sized croaking frog launched out of the water, landing with a thump on the soil right in front of me. It startled me, but I kept my balance.

"Whoa! You didn't warn me monster frogs live in rice paddies."

"Sorry! I didn't want to scare you, but I suppose you should also know if you see any snakes that are gray with orange bellies swimming in the water, they're venomous. I've been keeping an eye out but haven't seen any."

"What! You've got to be kidding! You're telling me, as we stand in the middle of this rice paddy, there are poisonous snakes surrounding us?"

Was this man totally nuts? What was he thinking? It wasn't only me he'd be leading into danger. How could he even think of setting a trail for the Harriers through this perilous terrain? We needed to get out of this paddy. Now!

"Don't worry. We're going to be okay. They're probably more afraid of us than we are of them. Let's just keep moving. We just have a few more berms to go."

Now, with heightened senses, I watched for any ripples disturbing the calm water and listened for the faintest rustling amidst the rice shoots ahead of me. I also looked for patches of the most solid ground on the next berm before stepping across onto it, while staying close behind Wayne. With stubborn determination, he still scattered paper dust onto every second berm as we approached the far edge of the paddy.

The width of the last trough of water, from the final berm to solid ground, had to be double the distance between the other berms. Wayne knotted and tossed the trash bag onto the solid bank ahead, then leaped across the water, landing safely. He turned to face me.

"You can do this. Take my hand." He bent forward, extending his arm toward me.

I inhaled deeply, then launched myself forward, grabbing his hand. He yanked, effortlessly pulling me over the trough, safely away from the reach of snakes. I let out a long sigh of relief.

Just six feet from where we stood, a single-lane dirt track ran parallel with the side of the paddy. Wayne unknotted the trash bag. "We should head back now since we've used half of the paper. We can follow this road for a bit, but the question is—which way do you think we should go?" He stared for a few seconds down the road in each direction. "To the right or to the left?"

"You're asking me?" I couldn't tell if he really didn't know or whether this was a joke meant to tease me. "Wayne, *this* is where *you* live. I arrived yesterday, remember? I'm still jet-lagged and disoriented."

"Yeah, I know. It's just that I have a horrible sense of direction. I thought maybe yours might be better than mine."

"So, you're telling me we're lost?" I threw my arms up in despair as the reality of our situation became clear. Using the skills I'd learned as a river guide, based on the position of the sun and the direction from which we'd approached the paddy, I figured that by following the road to our right, we'd at least be heading in a direction back toward the quarry.

"I think we need to go to the right." My bold response caused Wayne's brow to furrow.

"Hmm. I kinda think we should go to the left."

"Let's go to the left, then." I took a swig of water to moisten my parched mouth.

"No, I trust your instincts more than mine."

So do I, based on our adventure to this point. The man barely knew me, so how could he trust me to get us back to safety? No doubt he possessed a high level of intelligence, but honestly, it seemed he lacked a common sense gene.

"Let's go to the right," he said.

"I'll go in any direction except back through that paddy!"

We headed down the road, strewing the paper dust crumbs. Once clear of the paddy, I suggested turning to the right to wander back through the forest, to complete the loop we'd been creating. I got no argument from Wayne, who cheerfully carried on with his Hansel role. After a while, a small hut appeared in a clearing. Half a dozen chickens skittered across the bare ground in front of it. Gray smoke rose from an outdoor fire pit ringed with stone. The hut's door stood open.

Stepping into the clearing, Wayne bellowed, "Hello! Anyone home?"

A woman dressed in a well-worn drab yellow sari appeared in the doorway. She let out a loud scream when she saw us in her yard. An older man came running out of the woods behind the hut, shouting at us. Wayne dropped the trash bag and held his hands up to show he meant no harm. The man stopped yelling. I stood off to the side, amused at Wayne's comical attempts to get directions from them on how to find his car. He acted out the motions for blasting stone and chopping it in chunks, then pointed in different directions. After a few repetitions of Wayne's charade, incredibly, the man deciphered Wayne's strange movements and pointed toward the far side of his yard.

"*Namaste.*" Wayne bowed to the couple in gratitude. We retreated into the forest in the direction we'd come. To save the couple from a bunch of Harriers running through their yard, we backtracked 50 yards from his clearing before Wayne continued laying the paper trail. Fifteen minutes later, we spotted Wayne's car, just as Wayne used the last of the paper dust.

He turned to me, grinning. "We did it! Never had *any* doubt. High five?"

He stepped toward me to allow our hands to slap together in celebration of completing our assignment; then he checked his watch. The race would start in 30 minutes. For now, we could kick back and relax.

"It's a good trail. It's gonna take them 45 minutes at least," Wayne predicted.

"*If* they don't get bitten by snakes," I said. The overly serious tone of my voice made Wayne chuckle.

A few minutes later, a stream of Jeeps carrying the Harriers drove into our clearing, kicking up a cloud of dust. Some of Wayne's colleagues greeted him with wishes for a happy Fourth of July. Others joked they considered him a traitor to the British Crown. He introduced me to his buddies, explaining that I'd been the co-designer of the path they would soon be running. The crowd, largely Brits including two women, were joined by a Swede, an Italian, and a German. They shared a jolly camaraderie, featuring good-natured back slaps, spirited chatter, and plenty of boisterous laughter.

At 3 p.m., Wayne gave a piercing whistle to grab everyone's attention. He reviewed the race rules and pulled from the pocket of his shorts a sample of the paper dust for them to see.

"This is what we used to mark the trail today. Beware of the rabbit holes out there. Try not to get lost. Oh. Yeah. And beware—there might be some wildlife out there." After that last tip, he glanced at me, acknowledging he'd heard my plea for him to warn the Harriers about the snakes.

"Okay, any questions…? Everyone ready…? Get set… Go!"

A dozen runners took off on the wild chase to win bragging rights for finishing the course first. We could hear them hooting and hollering for several minutes as we sat on the tailgate of Wayne's Jeep. He started to tell me about some of the staff in his office I'd be meeting the next day. Primarily, I'd be working with a bright young Sri Lankan man named Namal, who had extensive experience working on Wang mini-computers, the platform that USAID's new accounting system ran on. He'd been working with the accounting staff, but since he didn't know the accounting system well, my job would be to serve as a conduit for the flow of information between both offices.

To our great surprise, two runners gasping for breath interrupted our conversation. Only 20 minutes had passed!

"What the hell? You shouldn't be back here yet," Wayne said.

"We followed the trail all the way," one of them replied.

"Did you go across a rice paddy?" I asked.

"What? No, we just ran through the forest."

"Something's wrong, Wayne," I said. "How could they have missed running at least half of our trail?"

"I know. They took off on the right path, and they came back on the right path. Somehow, they crossed from the outgoing trail over to the incoming trail. Hey, guys, come with me. I want to figure this out."

No one else arrived back early, so Wayne figured the mix-up occurred about 10 minutes down the path. He left me behind in case others returned early. I watched as the three men took off running down the path.

Twenty minutes later, the three men returned.

"You're not gonna believe this, Brenda, but at one point, the two trails pass within just eight feet of each other. This guy," he pointed to a brawny Brit, "happened to catch a glimpse of the paper dust and convinced his buddy here to follow the return trail."

The burly Brit glared at Wayne. "I think *you* get a fail in trail setting."

Wayne wasn't having that. "I think *you two* get a fail in following the trail!"

In the distance we heard pattering footsteps heading our way. Moments later, the front runner of the group that completed the entire trail raced into the clearing to claim his victory. His face registered shock when he saw the two shortcutters relaxing in camp chairs sipping beers.

"What the bloody hell? How? You never passed me…"

One of them playfully taunted the real winner. "I guess you missed the shortcut."

"What bloody shortcut?" he bellowed.

To keep the rising emotions in check, Wayne tried to calm everyone by explaining what had happened. He finally convinced the first two runners to concede that their colleague who'd completed the entire trail would be the winner. Over the next 15 minutes, the rest of the Harriers straggled into the clearing. Wayne counted heads to confirm everyone had finished the race. From the back of a Jeep, a few men pulled two coolers chock-full of bottles of beer buried in ice, and a bag of six-ounce plastic cups. The time for partying had arrived.

The president of this Harriers group, a feisty Brit, still in excellent shape despite his gray hair, stepped forward to begin the toasts. Wayne had warned me that whenever the group toasted the accomplishments or screwups of a Harrier, he or she had to step forward. The toastmaster would fill their cup with beer, which they had to chug down without stopping. They called this liquid toast a down-down. If a Harrier either couldn't swallow all of his beer in one shot, or chose not to drink it, they were required to pour it over their heads.

From the looks of this group, I presumed very little beer went to waste.

"To start us off today," the president said, "the first toast will be to the renegade turncoat Americans who insisted on rebelling against the Crown a few hundred years ago, and whose holiday of independence they celebrate today!"

A chorus of "Hear! Hear!" rang out. A few Harriers pushed Wayne toward the toastmaster.

The toastmaster nodded in my direction and asked, "Isn't your female associate an American, too?"

Oh no, no, no! Wayne promised I wouldn't get dragged into this beer bash. Now they were calling me out. No way could I guzzle six ounces of beer, but neither would I pour that rotten-smelling sticky beer on my head and clothes. How could I avoid this?

"Young lady, come here and get your beer," said the toastmaster.

I stared at Wayne, waiting for him to save me. He didn't.

Instead, he said, "Come on over here, Brenda. We've gotta celebrate the 4th!"

The group started chanting, "Brenda! Brenda! Brenda!"

I had no choice but to join Wayne and somehow endure the toast. With cups full, the toastmaster shouted, "To the Americans!" To which the group repeated, "To the Americans!"

Wayne lifted his cup and bellowed, "To the home of the brave and the FREE!" Immediately, he tipped his cup and swallowed its contents in five seconds.

I mustered up hidden courage and made the bold choice to chug the beer.

"Happy 4th everyone," I said, then tipped my cup. I sipped continuously, taking 20 seconds to drain my cup. It left a horrible taste in my mouth, but I got through the ordeal. I wondered how soon I'd feel dizzy. I started toward Wayne's Jeep to take my place on his tailgate.

"Just a moment, young lady. Come back here. You're not off the hook yet. It has come to my attention that, without a doubt, the individuals responsible for setting the trail today displayed an unprecedented level of incompetence unrivaled in the history of our club. This failure must not go unpunished!" declared the toastmaster.

Wayne mounted a challenge. "Whoa, just a minute. We set our

trail perfectly. All of you, except these two chaps, followed it and had a delightful run. God only knows why they strayed off the trail, cheating the course in a failed attempt to win the race. It's they who deserve punishment, not us."

The crowd heckled Wayne's excuse-making. "All in good time, sir," replied the toastmaster. "Step forward to accept your punishment, both of you."

Crap! Not again. I did not sign up for this! If they were serving up frozen strawberry daiquiris, I might accept that punishment. But more beer… yuck!

Though Wayne put up a dramatic show of faux disgust, I suspected he would eagerly accept the punishment doled out to us. Again, he tipped his cup and drank his beer in a few gulps. When the toastmaster handed me my cup, I stalled, deciding between the two evils. If I drank it all, I had no doubt I'd become tipsy. If I poured it over my head, I'd be wearing sticky, stinking clothes for at least a few more hours. I really wanted to toss half the cup of beer at the toastmaster and the rest at Wayne!

Instead, I raised the cup to my lips and groaned, "On my first day in this country, this is the treatment I get?"

A collective murmured "Aw" came from the Harriers as they awaited my next move. "Down-down, down-down!" they cheered, egging me on.

I swallowed half the beer until I feared I'd drown. I lowered the cup. *What to do with the rest of the amber liquid? I couldn't stomach another drop.* With a quick motion, I swung my arm over my head, attempting to pour most of what remained in the cup behind me while allowing a bit of it to splash on the top of my head and dampen a small section of the back of my T-shirt. The Harriers clapped in approval.

Relieved I had passed their test, I walked over to Wayne's tailgate to watch the rest of the celebration ritual. All the runners who didn't win had to partake in a down-down. Based on their enthusiasm, they'd all been waiting for this. Then the Brit who had won the race guzzled a cup. They continued calling out Harriers for down-downs: the two for their unauthorized shortcut, the one with the most outrageous outfit, the last person to arrive before the race began, the newest member of this Harrier group (thankfully, since I hadn't paid for membership, they exempted me from that toast), the last run of a group member moving to a new post. Any wacky idea out of the blue provided an excuse for another down-down. They sure loved their beer.

Before we left, Wayne pulled a towel from his gym bag in the back of the Jeep and offered it to me, along with a fresh bottle of water.

"Wet the towel and see if you can get the beer out of your hair. Then I'll try to rub it out of your shirt. You're a damn good sport to have put up with this. I'll make it up to you."

WE DROVE BACK TO HIS HOUSE, where he grilled hamburgers and toasted buns. He whipped up a batch of sauteed onions and mushrooms to smother the burgers, then topped them with slices of cheese which melted over the mound.

"I'd offer you a cold beer, but you'd probably throw it at me, so how about some iced tea or root beer?" He opened the fridge, ready to grab a drink for me. Although I loved root beer, just the word *beer* made me opt for the iced tea. When Wayne placed the gourmet burger in front of me, I inhaled the irresistible smokey aroma from the perfectly charred beef. The juicy medium-rare burger tasted heavenly, its flavors finally dispelling the lingering taste of hops from my mouth. Recalling memories of the day as we ate caused us to erupt in laughter over our haphazard trail and our punishment for screwing it up. Suddenly, jet lag hit me. My eyelids drooped despite my effort to keep them open.

"I think you need to take me back to the hotel if you expect me to show up for work tomorrow."

When Wayne dropped me off in front of the hotel, he said, "I'll have one of our drivers pick you up at quarter of nine. We can't wait to get started with your training."

RIGHT AWAY, upon arriving at the office, I noticed all my Sri Lankan colleagues had upbeat, playful personalities. Wayne enjoyed that they constantly exchanged jokes with him, creating a strong bond of mutual respect and camaraderie. They cleared a table for me in the open bullpen-style space where 10 finance, budget, and accounting staff worked. Namal, their IT expert, sat apart in the room housing the minicomputer that operated their information systems, but he spent a significant amount of time alongside us while I worked with Wayne's team.

The plan I'd drawn up included a group session at the beginning and end of each day, and one-on-one meetings with staff members sandwiched between to help them convert their projects into the new accounting software. Namal already had a firm grasp on how the software worked, but he learned a lot about the entries involved with governmental accounting during my training sessions. The rest of the staff, having expertise in the manual system, encouraged by Namal, swiftly learned how to use the software and eagerly started converting data into digital format. Wayne's staff didn't view their work as just a job; they functioned as a cohesive team, a trait as useful in business as in successfully navigating whitewater rivers or climbing through unfamiliar caves.

Their conversations amazed me as they effortlessly shifted between work-related queries, personal anecdotes about their families, discussions about local and global events, and even passionate debates about cricket matches. It gave me the impression of people chatting and enjoying themselves at a party.

Like background music, their nonstop chatter filled the air without a moment of work time being wasted. After spending a few days together, they became increasingly curious about my personal life, family, and viewpoints. They swamped me with a barrage of questions. I took it as a sign they'd accepted me as part of their team.

Like sibling rivals, they loved to play pranks on each other. Not a day passed when one of them didn't fall victim to a plot hatched by their coworkers. The pranks, always executed with good-natured intentions, never failed to elicit giggles from both the pranksters and those in on the mischief. One day, an accountant's favorite pen went missing. After an exhaustive search, Anaya located the pen in a most unlikely spot in Wayne's private office on his desk, where it had been cleverly hidden by one of her colleagues.

Another day, Rishaan, full of mischief, quickly snuck into the small enclosed kitchen space connected to the open bullpen, while his friend Nirved engaged in conversation with Wayne in his office. He grabbed Nirved's lunch from the refrigerator, hustling it to an accomplice who sat at a desk next to Nirved's. Upon discovering his food had disappeared, Nirved demanded, "Who took my lunch? Give it back right now!"

"No one stole your food. Maybe you left it at home," said the mastermind of the prank.

With Nirved out of sight in the side room, searching the refrigerator once more for his missing meal, the accomplice quickly transferred Nirved's lunch bag from her desk drawer, placing it into Nirved's desk drawer. It took him a while, but Nirved finally found his food. His colleagues all agreed the prank merited praise based on how long Nirved took to find his lunch. Of course, the mastermind couldn't resist taking credit for his success.

"Just wait. I swear I'll get you back, Rishaan!" Nirved waggled his finger at his friend.

Their good-hearted playfulness amused me until *I* fell victim to one of their tricks. The July temperature hovered at a muggy 80 degrees all day. Wayne had a small air conditioner in his office, but the Sri Lankan staff, comfortable with their warm climate, chose not to have their office cooled. I found it stifling and used a pleated paper fan for relief. I also kicked my sandals off under the table to keep my feet cool. Sometimes I even wandered about the office barefooted. This seemed to amuse the staff.

Generally, they left for home at exactly 5 p.m., but one day, one of the Sri Lankan staff remained behind with me. When I wrapped up my work, I felt with my toes for my sandals under my table. They weren't there. For the walk back to the hotel on the scorching asphalt, I needed shoes. I panicked at the thought of the soles of my bare feet sizzling as I stepped onto the overheated road. Desperate, I searched every inch of the floor space, hoping to find them.

"What are you doing?" asked Pranith with a mischievous glint in his eyes.

Damn. They had pranked me!

"Where are they?" I demanded.

"What do you mean?" He smiled coyly.

"You know what I mean. My sandals! Where did you hide them? I can't walk down the street without shoes."

He feigned ignorance. At the sound of my raised voice, Namal raced into the office to see if I had a problem. Pranith lowered his voice and spoke to Namal in their local Sinhala dialect. Namal nodded and smiled. As I grew more flustered, they pretended to join me in searching for my shoes, even searching Wayne's office. My sandals had simply disappeared.

I told Pranith, "I know opening everyone's desk drawers is an invasion of their privacy, but I *need* to find my shoes. Remember, just recently I watched Rishaan hide Nirved's lunch in a desk drawer."

As soon as I mentioned it, a look of alarm flashed across his face. "I can promise your shoes are not inside any drawers."

"Well, since you know where they are, just tell me." I couldn't hide my growing aggravation with their exasperating treasure hunt.

"You should look in a common space, maybe."

After witnessing their previous antics, I knew they'd hidden them in the most improbable place one would expect to find shoes. Where was that place? What common space had they used? I thought about the side room, which I'd already examined, *but* I hadn't looked *inside* the refrigerator. I dashed into the room and flung open the refrigerator door. Inside, a brown paper bag rested on a shelf. As I grabbed and opened it, I heard Namal and Pranith's hearty laughter behind me.

Pranith clapped his hands. "So, you found your sandals. I worried I might have to stay here until midnight waiting for you to make this discovery."

My angered quickly faded, as I realized they wouldn't have abandoned me. Pranith had obviously agreed to stay with me until I found my shoes or had a nervous breakdown!

THE NEXT MORNING, as the staff arrived, they eagerly inquired how their prank turned out. I willingly accepted and appreciated their cleverness, in line with their social norms.

"Well done. You had me frazzled. I hold no hard feelings—just don't do it again."

One of them wisecracked, "Then maybe you should keep your shoes on." Laughter filled the room.

It wasn't just pranking that the Sri Lankan staff excelled at; their work on the accounting system conversion stayed ahead of schedule. While I expected the team would need to work overtime to stay on track, the staff doggedly charged ahead, negating that necessity. Halfway through the project as a reward for our stellar efforts, Wayne invited his Chief Accountant, Namal, and me to have lunch with him on the outdoor veranda at the historic Galle Face Hotel, a remnant of Sri Lanka's colonial past. By the end of the 19th century, the hotel had gained a reputation as the most luxurious lodging east of the Suez Canal.

Wayne had reserved a table for us that offered a spectacular view of the Indian Ocean. A brochure I picked up in the hotel on our way out to the veranda mentioned that for more than a century, adventurers, authors, generals, and gentry had dined under the eaves of this veranda. Just being able to dine in such a revered setting made me feel incredibly privileged.

Comfortable wicker furniture and white linen-covered tables lined the double tiered 24-foot-wide polished wood floor. A dozen ceiling fans swirling overhead gently circulated the fresh brine-scented air. A server impeccably dressed in all white, including white gloves, led us to our table. Wayne highly recommended their famous crab curry, which he claimed was the best he had ever tasted. He didn't need to twist my arm. Namal insisted I try tea made with leaves from the island's tea plantations.

While we waited for our lunch to be served, the three of us gave Wayne an update on the progress of our conversion project, which left him delighted. Business talk finished just as the food arrived. The fragrant aroma of the crab curry seasoned with a blend of tropical spices served over rice paired with chunks of fresh tropical fruits created a heavenly flavor. This enchanting dining experience made me feel as though I'd truly landed in paradise. The intoxicating ambience of this veranda made me never want to leave.

As I sipped on my tea, Namal asked me, "Have you ever been to a tea plantation?"

"No. I haven't."

"Well then, I should take you. My brother, Rukmal, is a Senior Assistant Manager at the Opata tea and rubber tree plantation about three hours southeast of here. He can give us a great tour of the plantation, answer all your questions, and we can stay overnight in his bungalow."

"That's an offer you should take Namal up on, Brenda," said Wayne. "He's taken me there. The countryside is gorgeous and you'll learn so much."

This idea sounded more enticing than hiking through poisonous, snake-infested rice paddies. I enjoyed drinking tea, but I'd never given much thought to where it came from.

"Namal, that is a generous offer. I'd love to tour a tea and rubber plantation."

When I enthusiastically accepted, a smile lit up his face. "I'll call my brother tonight and tell him to expect us this weekend."

NAMAL PICKED ME UP AT 8 A.M. on Saturday morning, and we headed out of Colombo on a winding two-lane road. During our ride, Namal asked me what parts of the island I'd visited.

"A few days after I arrived, Wayne took me down the west coast to the south coast. We visited a batik factory and watched stilt fishermen at work. I couldn't believe how they could climb up to their perches and balance suspended five or six feet over the ocean for hours waiting for a nip at their bait."

Namal agreed. "That method of fishing is passed down from generation to generation. It takes skill and exceptional balance to catch fish that way."

"We also went out on the ocean in a glass-bottomed boat. I loved floating over the spectacular florescent sky-blue coral reefs. They're so different from anything I've seen."

"Did you and Wayne see any of the men harvesting coconuts?"

"Oh my God, yes! They walked across vines strung between the trees, 50 feet over the ground like skilled tightrope walkers. Those men scampered over those vines as carefree as they would stroll down the sandy beach. Talk about needing exceptional balance, and they had no safety net! I guess they don't harvest on windy days."

The stories I told of my adventures amused Namal. Whenever he spotted an item or place of interest, he'd go into full tour-guide mode, explaining the history, culture, fauna, and flora of the enchanting island of 17 million people, formerly known as Ceylon. He admitted he loved to get out to the natural areas of the island and claimed the city of Kandy, situated on a plateau surrounded by tea plantations and rain forest in the center of the country, held a special place in his heart.

The three-hour drive to reach the Opata Estate plantation passed quickly as we traded stories along the way. When we reached the entrance of the estate, we went into the headquarters building to register as guests and Namal to ask them to summon his brother by walkie talkie to meet us. Not long afterward, Rukmal strode into the headquarters. He greeted his brother with a friendly slap on the back, then turned to me and extended his hand.

"You must be Brenda."

I nodded and accepted his firm handshake.

"Good then. A friend of Namal's is a friend of mine. I understand you'd like to see how the plantation operates."

"Yes. I'm always curious to learn about new things. I've never been to a plantation."

Rukmal opted to show us the rubber tree forest first. We climbed into his Jeep and sped along the solid-packed dirt road leading into the heart of the Opata Estate. Along the way, we stopped at a hut where he spoke to a farmer who worked for the plantation. The older man had a weathered appearance from a life spent working outside. He wore soiled and threadbare clothes and cheap plastic sandals. Rukmal ushered him to the unoccupied back seat in his Jeep. From there, we followed a track deep into the woods rarely used by vehicles. When the farmer spoke, Rukmal stopped the car.

"From here, we walk," he said, pulling on a pair of knee-high rubber boots. "But first, we have to prepare you for walking through the forest." He pulled a bar of white soap from a backpack in his Jeep. "This forest is teeming with leeches."

"What! You mean bloodsucking leeches?" Just the thought of a slimy disgusting bloodsucker climbing up my leg filled me with panic. I had not expected to be fending off leeches.

"That's right, which is why each of you will rub your feet and lower legs thoroughly with this soap that repels leeches. They thrive in the feathery greenery on the floor of the forest. You can see there are narrow paths through the undergrowth. Stay on the paths. We'll be hurrying, but keep an eye out. If you feel one squirming on you, immediately pull it off before it can attach to your skin."

I rubbed so much soap on my legs that they almost turned white from the caked-on wax.

"Okay, let's go." Rukmal signaled the farmer to lead the way to his trees.

The plantation owners divided the property into sections that they leased to local farmers, who, in exchange for collecting the sap and caring for the trees, earned a share of the income from the latex they harvested. About 50 yards up the path, the farmer stopped. In front of us, one of his trees oozed a thick white sap from a diagonal slash in its bark. Gravity gently pulled the liquid downward toward half of a coconut shell fastened to the tree trunk to collect its precious liquid.

While we stopped, I kept marching in place, hoping to deter any nearby leeches from making their way onto my body.

The farmer removed a short knife with a curved blade tucked under his belt and skillfully shaved off a strip of the bark the thickness of a fingernail, barely enough to start the sap bleeding at a faster rate again.

Rukmal showed us the strip: eight inches long and half the width of a strand of uncooked angel-hair pasta. He explained, "The idea for the farmers is to remove the least amount of bark possible each day to prolong the productivity of their trees. Wasteful thicker cuts strip the bark sooner, shortening the tree's useful life. Every morning, the farmers visit each of their trees, delicately slicing the scabs of latex that dried on the surface of the previous day's cut with a tiny fresh cut to restart the flow of sap.

"Three hours later, the time it takes for the sap to nearly fill the coconut shells, their wives follow, pouring the sap into galvanized aluminum buckets. Because latex starts to dry within hours when exposed to air, the women hustle to the collection center, which is the next stop on our tour."

On our way back to the Jeep, bunches of dark brown leeches suddenly appeared on our pathway. Rukmal explained that the lighter color of our skin and human scent had attracted them. It astonished me how quickly they could propel their inch-and-a-half long, ugly bodies across the ground.

The leeches moved as an inch worm would, contracting the middle of its body into a hump, then stretching forward until flat on the ground. They could cover three feet in about nine seconds. I hopscotched along the path, trying to avoid stepping on them. Rukmal noticed two on the back of Namal's legs and swiped them off. Once we reached the Jeep, Rukmal inspected each of us thoroughly to be sure none had attached themselves to our skin before climbing into the vehicle. Namal insisted he'd never felt the two that had crawled up his legs.

Rukmal explained, "That's what makes them so dangerous. Most people can't feel them moving on their skin. But we are done with them now. There are no leeches where we are going next."

After dropping the farmer back at his hut, Rukmal drove us to the collection center. On the way, we passed several women walking there carrying buckets full of white sap. The collection center consisted of an outdoor weighing station, an indoor cement-block building with huge vats and presses where chemistry converted liquid sap into solid rubber, and a separate smokehouse.

We visited the weighing station first. Dressed in short sari tops that revealed their midriffs and cotton cloth skirts wrapped and roll-tucked at their waists, the women formed a line, eagerly waiting to hand over their buckets to the supervisor. They engaged in friendly conversation, their heads bobbing in agreement or disagreement. As they heard their name called, they promptly stepped forward, hoisting their heavy five-gallon bucket, carefully transferring their latex into an empty bucket owned by the plantation. The stream of viscous liquid pouring into the collection bucket looked like milk, but much thicker.

Rukmal explained, "Ever since a few entrepreneurial farmers figured they could make more money by diluting the pure sap with water to produce a greater volume of liquid, our supervisors test the purity of the latex in each bucket before the plantation accepts it. We pay the farmers by weight for the latex they collect, only if it is 100 percent pure."

We watched as a supervisor filled a small glass container to an exact mark with latex from one woman's bucket and placed it on a small scale.

"The testers know exactly how much the sample should weigh if it is pure. Since water weighs less than latex, any sample that weighs less than pure latex would expose the fraud, and the entire bucket would get rejected," Rukmal said.

Once the purity of the sample checked out, the tester added it back to the large bucket, which he placed on a heavy-duty scale to determine the earnings for the farmer. I watched as the factory workers dumped the incoming buckets into a couple of large rectangular cement collection tanks.

When the workers had nearly filled one tank with 100 buckets of latex, Rukmal continued, "Now they'll add acid and enzymes." We observed one worker dumping a bottle of liquid formic acid into the tank along with a smaller quantity of another liquid. Four workers walked around the vat with wide wooden paddles, continuously stirring the contents to promote controlled coagulation.

Rukmal continued with his lecture. "During this process, a substantial amount of water gets released from the latex as the particles of rubber clump together, a concept similar to making cheese. We end up with a massive hunk of pliable raw rubber which the workers coax into and through these large presses that flatten and squeeze out any remaining water."

One sheet of ribbed raw rubber emerged from the press as an inch-thick, three-foot-wide by 12-foot-long rectangular sheet.

"Come, follow me," said Rukmal.

Two of the workers carefully folded the heavy fresh sheet and carried it from the building. We followed close behind as they headed to the smokehouse. Instead of having floors, this building had a grid of long wooden logs crisscrossing on three levels, with a ladder-like stairway providing access to each. The sole window-like opening on the top level of the outer wood frame provided the only light source, yet the muslin cloth that covered it muted the brightness it let in. On the ground, a wood fire billowed smoke that drifted up, penetrating all three levels.

The two men carried the sheet up to the top level, where they unfolded and draped it evenly over a long pole. With the skill of a tightrope walker, one man balanced the pole above his head and stepped onto two of the logs that formed part of a grid on that level. Cautiously, while holding up the weight of the rubber sheet, he inched forward barefoot along the log until he reached the far side of the building. He locked the long pole into place between two logs spanning the length of the rafters.

As my eyes grew accustomed to the dim light, I saw many other sheets hung suspended in a row from wood racks like bedsheets drying on a clothesline.

"We use this acrid smoke to cloak the rubber sheets, purifying them from any embedded microbes. After a few days in the smoke-house, they remove the sheets and roll them into bales for export," said Rukmal. "Our rubber is used to manufacture everything from car tires to high-quality medical tubing."

I snapped a photo of the man's risky undertaking before climbing back down the stairs. I couldn't quite reconcile the sight of the smokey raw rubber with the thought of sterile tubing delivering life-saving chemicals into the body of a cancer patient.

"READY TO SEE TEA BUSHES?" asked Rukmal as we approached a different section of the estate. The landscape, like a magnificent open-air amphitheater, extended in tiers all around us. Interspersed among the tiers, women bent over the waist-high bushes pinching off the tender young leaves from the small branches.

"Come, let's watch them picking."

Rukmal led us toward the start of a row of the tea bushes. Before we ventured onto the hillside where the rows of densely packed tea plants would block our view of our lower limbs, I wanted to make sure I wasn't putting myself in danger.

I asked, "Do we have to watch out for leeches or snakes out here?"

He laughed. "These women are all barefooted. So no, the most dangerous thing out here is the sun. You see how the women dress in clothing that covers their upper bodies? And they all have scarves covering their heads to prevent them from getting scorched by the sun."

Before me, the valley stretched out, blanketed in lush green as far as the eye could see, devoid of any shade. The narrow path we followed required that we walk in single file, with a row of the shaggy bushes brushing against us on one side and a sheer drop-off to the tier below on the other. When we reached the first tea picker, Rukmal squeezed himself in between two plants, to make space for me to get close to the woman. He explained in a local dialect that I wanted to see how she picked tea leaves.

She nodded while continuing her work. It surprised me how fast her thumb and forefinger moved in a continuous snipping motion, deftly plucking only the top two green leaves from each stem, leaving the rest of the stem undamaged. Snip, snip, snip. The outermost foliage disappeared from the top of the bush as her hands raced from left to right, gathering the inch-long green leaves. After every few snips, she tossed her leaves into the woven wicker basket on her back, secured by a leather strap across her forehead. Rukmal said, "On a normal day, this woman will pluck 44 pounds of tea leaves."

She gestured for me to help. I resorted to using a one-handed approach, after discovering that only my right hand had enough dexterity to mimic my mentor's swift leaf-snatching technique. An amused grin spread across her face as she watched me fumbling to collect leaves. She could easily pick 10 leaves for every four I gathered. Obviously, I didn't possess the requisite skills to be a successful tea picker. But now, whenever I sipped a cup of tea, I'd have a greater appreciation for the work that went into allowing me that pleasure.

We continued further along that tier, reaching a section of unharvested bushes. There, Rukmal told us about a special type of tea leaf. "Here at the very tip of this stem, there is an unopened bud where the tiny leaves are still forming." He snipped off the end of the stem and passed it to us for a closer look. "See the color of the outer surface of the bud? We call this a silver tip. These immature buds are tender and lack the bitterness of mature leaves, so once they are dried, chewing them releases the delicate flavor of the tea."

"Silver tips are my favorites," said Namal, giving a thumbs up gesture. "I really enjoy their unique flavor."

Rukmal explained that the window for picking the buds lasted only a few days. In order to promote the future growth of the bush, the pickers selectively removed only a few buds from each one. With proper care, a tea plant could live and be productive for up to 50 years. The plantation assigned certain women to gather only silver tips, which commanded a much higher price than tea made from the mature leaves. Rukmal told us that wealthy Saudi Arabians frequently ordered silver tips from his estate.

"Now let's go to the factory so you can see how we process the leaves."

INSIDE THE PROCESSING FACTORY, rows of long rectangular tables made of a fine screen surface surrounded by a wood frame cradled leaves in various stages and colors of drying. Being a tea drinker, I paid close attention to Rukmal's description of how the leaves got converted into my favorite beverage.

He said, "When tea leaves arrive here, we weigh the raw leaves. Then the workers fluff up the leaves and spread them out on the screens to wither. That means the leaves will lie here for 18 to 24 hours, slowly losing moisture. Withering is complete when about two-thirds of the moisture present in the raw leaf has evaporated." We walked to another section of the factory, where Rukmal continued, "The worker here is using this device to roll or crush the leaves, releasing enzymes that react with air on the leaf tissue. When he's done, he'll again spread the broken leaves out on tables for just a few hours exposed to air, during which the leaves turn a coppery orange. The final step of drying takes place in chambers heated to 210 degrees Fahrenheit. This stops the oxidation and shrinks and darkens the leaves."

By the time we'd finished our tour of the plantation, it was late afternoon. Rukmal encouraged Namal and me to explore the factory store while he made sure no tasks demanded his immediate attention. I felt like a kid in a toy store. How could I decide on which types of tea to buy? I wanted to have them all—some to savor for myself and others to share as gifts. After all, Ceylon teas were renowned for being the epitome of tea excellence. Their loose tea came sealed in a foil-lined bag packed into small wooden boxes attractively stamped with the plantation's logo. I decided on six boxes of different varieties.

WE RETURNED TO RUKMAL'S modest but modern bungalow on a prominent ridge with a spectacular view over the valley below. He invited Namal and me to make ourselves comfortable in chairs out on the brick terrace, while he fired up his grill to cook us a simple dinner of chicken, rice, and vegetables.

"Would you like a beer?" Rukmal asked.

"Great! Thanks," said Namal.

Not beer again. At least here, I wouldn't be forced to drink it.

"No, thanks," I replied. "You wouldn't happen to have a cup of tea, would you?"

We all burst out laughing at the irony of the question.

"I think I might be able to scrounge up some tea for you. Black, green, or white?"

"Surprise me," I said. "Bring me your favorite one."

When he returned, he handed me a steaming cup with the rich aroma of a bold black tea.

"I hope you enjoy this. I also have a small gift for you." He handed me a packet the size of a deck of playing cards. "This is our finest silver tips tea."

His unexpected surprise caught me completely off guard, leaving me momentarily speechless. I couldn't believe it. Had he just given me a pouch filled with the same leaves treasured by the Saudi kings? I stammered out a thank-you, my voice trembling with a mix of gratitude and astonishment.

"Let me show you how to use them." Rukmal took back the pouch and carefully opened it. He pinched a couple of dried silver tips, tossed them in his mouth, and gently chewed without swallowing them.

"Try some," he said, offering the pouch to me, then to Namal. I took two of the tips and followed Rukmal's lead. Their texture felt velvety, not crunchy like regular tea leaves. As I bit down on them, they crumbled into delicate pieces, releasing a pleasantly delicate flavor of tea in my mouth. I took my time chewing, savoring the rare treat as Rukmal and Namal watched for my reaction.

"My God, this is so delicious. I could eat these like candy."

"No, you don't want to do that." Rukmal shook his head. "Those buds have more caffeine in them than tea leaves. Just take a small pinch when you feel like having tea."

Against the vivid backdrop of the sunset's deepening colors, we ate supper. Our discussion revolved around all I'd learned that day: the miraculous white latex dripping from the trees that could produce sterile medical tubing to save a life, the number and speed of the rubber forest leeches I'd managed to outrun, and that I'd never qualify to be a tea picker. Though my admiration had grown for the women who earned their livings working outside day after day gathering the leaves for the beverage millions of people around the world loved.

"This amazing island has it all. Everywhere I look, I see gorgeous landscapes, and the Sri Lankan people are so hospitable. I love it here. It's like a magical paradise." I opened my arms wide, taking it all in.

As the last vestiges of daylight slipped away, Rukmal leaped to his feet. "You want magic? *I* will show you magic." He waved at us to follow him. I glanced at Namal, trying to discern if he was aware of his brother's intentions. Namal looked perplexed. "Let's go," shouted Rukmal, waiting impatiently by his Jeep.

Absent the light from a moon not yet risen, the night suddenly turned pitch black. The road stretched out before us, carrying us on a journey that felt like a cosmic voyage into the heart of the Milky Way. After a mile, Rukmal stopped and turned off the Jeep's headlights. Once out of the Jeep, a trillion small twinkling lights encircled us. The glimmering lights appeared both right in front of us and infinitely far away. The flickers of light, one moment on, the next suddenly extinguished, gave me a euphoric feeling of floating in space among the stars. I could feel my feet, still flat against the ground, but darkness concealed any other point of reference. Being in this spot felt thrilling, mysterious, and mindboggling all at the same time.

"Where are we? What is this?" My voice quivered with uncertainty.

"We are in the firefly tree forest."

An astonishingly dense sparkle of fireflies, their tiny flickering bodies, surrounded us. The dazzling sight mesmerized me. As I twirled around and around with glee, an overwhelming sense of pure joy filled me. It revived a childhood memory I'd almost forgotten. On hot summer days, just at twilight, Mom would hand me an empty jar to catch fireflies in our backyard.

I remember frantically chasing after the elusive specks of light, clutching my jar tightly as I tried to scoop them out of the air. On a good night, I captured five or six of them before I capped the jar. I would bring the jar to bed and lie there entranced, watching them light up and turn off until I drifted off to sleep. The next morning, Mom made sure they regained their freedom.

"Guys, I can't even remember the last time I saw a firefly, let alone a billion of them all in one place." It thrilled me to know that these tiny magical creatures still thrived in some parts of the world, though they had disappeared long ago from my backyard.

Rukmal replied, "Everyone falls in love with the fireflies. How can you not?"

"Thank you so much for bringing me here. I'll remember this place forever."

Before I fell asleep that night, I couldn't help but reminisce about the new discoveries, close calls, good-hearted pranks, gorgeous tropical landscapes, and especially those fireflies that made my time in Sri Lanka unforgettable.

Women at latex collection center

UPDATE:

I never crossed paths with the Hash House Harriers again. For years, Wayne and I corresponded during the holidays. He spent many more years working for USAID on assignments around the world. When I told him I wanted to retire and had considered moving south, he tried to convince me to come to Naples, Florida, where he had a home. Sadly, Wayne passed away in 2020.

Namal continued to work for USAID for another 13 years. He visited me when he came to the US for training in Washington, DC. Since I couldn't show him rubber or tea plantations, I showed him witches in historic Salem, Massachusetts. He has since retired and spends his time perfecting his photography and traveling. His brother Rukmal immigrated to the US in 2002 and now works for USAID as a contracting officer.

Sri Lanka is the world's fourth-largest producer of tea, and one of the primary sources of foreign exchange for Sri Lanka, earning over 1.3 billion US dollars in 2021. Its tea industry employs, directly or indirectly, over 1 million people, providing livelihoods for tens of thousands of families.

When I visited the Opata Estate plantation, a governmental organization, the Sri Lanka State Plantations Corporation owned it. During the mid-nineties, the government divested the property to the private sector. It is now one of many plantations in Sri Lanka owned by Dilmah Ceylon Tea Company. Today, you can buy Dilmah silver tips tea on Amazon for $29.95 for 10 tea bags.

The world celebrates World Firefly Day on the first weekend of July. In 2024, researchers discovered two new species of fireflies in Sri Lanka, though their numbers have decreased due to the loss of suitable vegetation and increasing light pollution, which hinders the fireflies' ability to find mates.

On the day after Christmas in 2004, I woke up to the shocking news that a forceful tsunami, triggered by a massive 9.0 earthquake in the Indian Ocean, had ravaged the east and south coasts of Sri Lanka. A series of 30-foot high waves of water slammed into coastal villages, killing over 35,000 people and wreaking horrific devastation on everything in its path.

Tea picker

AUTHOR'S NOTE

SEPTEMBER 1, 2024

I will always be immensely grateful for the opportunities I had as a young woman to travel to 40 countries on five continents, to live abroad for eight years and become proficient in four languages. There are literally thousands of people who supported my travels and hundreds who shared my discoveries. I thank everyone who touched my life, inspiring me to see, learn, and understand more about people of other cultures and to seek out some of the special secret places in our diverse world.

The most important thing I learned from my travels and living abroad is that all human beings aspire to the same common ideals, whether from Ethiopia's isolated Omo River tribes, Sri Lankan tea pickers, or Tunisian underground-dwelling troglodytes. All humans strive for enough food and water to nourish their bodies, adequate shelter from nature's fury, and good health for themselves and their families. Ideally, they want to live in peace and create supportive communities where neighbor helps neighbor. All living beings share this planet, and we need to share its resources to survive.

I also discovered that human beings can be the most dangerous living creatures on the planet when their greed upsets the natural balance. I find it sad that wilderness areas, and their people and animals, are vanishing at alarming rates. When I debated about becoming a river guide 45 years ago, my soon-to-be-boss at OARS, Inc., George Wendt, shared his motivation for taking people rafting. He said, "**We save what we love and we love what we know**. Our job is to show people how truly special these rivers are, so they will engage with us to preserve them forever." His wisdom convinced me to give up a job in the business world, which over a lifetime could have made me wealthy. I left that job behind to begin a quest for a different type of wealth: knowledge of the world in its entirety. I've never regretted that decision.

My travels around the globe opened my eyes to amazing people, places, and things, but also to some horrific situations. I wish everyone could have followed in my footsteps to observe the world I witnessed during the 1980s. Maybe then they could comprehend the drastic impact of humans' actions on the lives of people, animals, and landscapes of this planet in just the last four decades.

I hope my stories have heightened your awareness of these ongoing irreversible changes. *If* we are to *save* the places where I found beauty and awe, humans have to be educated, either in person or through exposure by word of mouth from those who do know that they exist. My telling of these stories is merely my humble start in that direction.

While many people have shared their thoughts on certain chapters of this book, it is my intrepid writing partner, Ruth Heilgeist, and my dear friend, Monica Langley, who have meticulously read the entire book—some parts even twice or more—providing me with invaluable feedback. My deepest thanks go out to every one of you who had a hand in making this book a reality.

If it hadn't been for Richard Bangs, my boss at Sobek Expeditions, guiding and inspiring me to venture into the unknown beyond the safe borders of this country, I'd never have made the discoveries that shape these stories. Richard, I hope you are proud of how your sage advice and prodding empowered me.

The exceptional collaboration I experienced with the publishing experts at Paper Raven Books on my last book, *Becoming Fearless,* gave me complete confidence that once again *Becoming Amazed* would be in capable hands. Though I've learned so much about self-publishing, I still appreciate the specialized skills and guidance of their team and my fellow Paper Raven authors. You are all so appreciated!

Thank goodness my mother and grandmother, both career librarians, instilled in me the love of reading books and the importance of telling stories! Even after 60 years, there are still moments when I'm confronted with a challenging situation that I can't help but wonder—what would Pippi do?

Thank you for joining me on this journey through the pages of *Becoming Amazed*. Sharing these stories has been both a privilege and a reminder of our deep connections as global citizens. But the adventure doesn't end here. I continue to explore, write, and reflect on the world's wonders and challenges. If you'd like to join me for more reflections on my adventures and receive updates on new stories, thoughts, and insights, I invite you to sign up for my email list. By subscribing, you'll get exclusive access to my latest blog posts and updates on my next book. I'm already busy at work drafting a more recent and unusual adventure, discovering I am living with an extremely rare, progressive, and incurable disease called Stiff Persons Syndrome.

Head over to www.eyeopenerpress.com and be the first to receive the stories that continue to unfold. Let's keep discovering the world together, one story at a time.

www.ingramcontent.com/pod-product-compliance
Lightning Source LLC
Chambersburg PA
CBHW051144130726
47988CB00005B/1986